RETHINKING AFRICAN
CULTURAL PRODUCTION

RETHINKING AFRICAN CULTURAL PRODUCTION

Edited by Frieda Ekotto
and Kenneth W. Harrow

Indiana University Press

Bloomington & Indianapolis

This book is a publication of

Indiana University Press
Office of Scholarly Publishing
Herman B Wells Library 350
1320 East 10th Street
Bloomington, Indiana 47405 USA

iupress.indiana.edu

© 2015 by Indiana University Press

All rights reserved

No part of this book may be reproduced or utilized in any form or by any means, electronic or mechanical, including photocopying and recording, or by any information storage and retrieval system, without permission in writing from the publisher. The Association of American University Presses' Resolution on Permissions constitutes the only exception to this prohibition.

⊖ The paper used in this publication meets the minimum requirements of the American National Standard for Information Sciences—Permanence of Paper for Printed Library Materials, ANSI Z39.48–1992.

Manufactured in the United States of America

Cataloging information is available from the Library of Congress.

ISBN 978-0-253-01597-6 (cloth)
ISBN 978-0-253-01600-3 (paperback)
ISBN 978-0-253-01603-4 (ebook)

1 2 3 4 5   20 19 18 17 16 15

Contents

Acknowledgments   *vii*

Introduction: Rethinking African Cultural Production /
Frieda Ekotto and Kenneth W. Harrow   *1*

1. The Critical Present: Where Is "African Literature"? / Eileen Julien   *17*

2. African Writers Challenge Conventions of Postcolonial
Literary History / Olabode Ibironke   *29*

3. Provocations: African Societies and Theories of Creativity /
Moradewun Adejunmobi   *52*

4. In Praise of the Alphabet / Patrice Nganang   *78*

5. African Cultural Studies: Of Travels, Accents,
and Epistemologies / Tejumola Olaniyan   *94*

6. *Le* Freak, *C'est* Critical and *Chic:* North African Scholars
and the Conditions of Cultural Production
in Post-9/11 U.S. Academia / Lamia Benyoussef   *109*

7. Reading "Beur" Film Production Otherwise:
The Poetics of the Human and the Transcultural /
Safoi Babana-Hampton   *127*

8. Revealing the Past, Conceptualizing the Future On-Screen:
The Social, Political, and Economic Challenges of
Contemporary Filmmaking in Morocco / Valérie K. Orlando   *142*

9. Thresholds of New African Dramaturgies in France Today /
Mária Minich Brewer   *159*

10 Island Geography as Creole Biography:
    Shenaz Patel's Mauritian Literary Production / Magali Compan   177

    List of Contributors   197
    Index   199

Acknowledgments

THIS COLLECTION WOULD not have been possible without the assistance of many units and people at Michigan State University, whose collaboration in the initial symposium has resulted in this book. These include the College of Arts and Letters and James Pritchett of the African Studies Center, whose support for so many projects has been unstinting and whose leadership has been inspiring.

I (Frieda) would also like to thank the many units at the University of Michigan, in particular the Department of Comparative Literature. I am grateful to Yopie Prins for her generous support and encouragement. Finally, I would like to offer thanks to Patrick Tonks for his keen and astute attention to the many details of the symposium and to Emily Goedde for her ongoing support of my work. It is always a great pleasure to work closely with them and the many other graduate students whom I have the honor to teach.

RETHINKING AFRICAN
CULTURAL PRODUCTION

Introduction
Rethinking African Cultural Production

Frieda Ekotto and Kenneth W. Harrow

THE ORIGINS OF this collection lie in a joint conference held at Michigan State University and the University of Michigan in October 2010. At that conference we proposed to explore conditions of African cultural production, interrogating the extent to which African literature and cinema are being produced increasingly by writers and filmmakers who live abroad. Although the continent continues to be a site of robust creative forces, there are also considerable limitations that often lead to a marginalization of African artists' works on the global stage. Migration of cultural capital in an age of globalization tends to flow more in some directions than in others. Publishers whose titles reach global markets typically focus on the metropolitan centers of the global north. More and more frequently we have found that many of the African authors and filmmakers whose works we study and teach do not live in Africa: some live abroad, and some travel between Africa and elsewhere. Only a percentage of those whose works are widely diffused as "world literature" or "world cinema" live solely in Africa. This shift has created issues that earlier scholarship did not address.

As we see it, yesterday's struggles for national liberation have passed. Movements against neocolonialism have passed. Pan-Africanism, Negritude, and many other artistic, cultural, literary, and philosophical movements have passed. We are immersed in shifting paradigms that are subsumed under vague headings such as "postcolonialism" or "globalization." This collection considers this new phase of African cultural production and juxtaposes work produced outside of Africa with work from the continent. It also broadly addresses ways to present the notion of indigenous cultural production, like that of the alphabet created by the sultan of Bamum, and ways in which contemporary patterns of globalization can be read in new technologies and apparatuses.

In this volume, scholars engage with this new era of cultural production in various ways. Magali Compan asks, "How does a 'home' geography or place affect an author's writing and authorship? What are the relationships among location, a sense of place, and one's identity formation, not only as a writer but as an individual or a member of a community? What influence, if any, does place exert on one's identity? How do sites of production and histories together generate authorship and identity, francophone or otherwise?" In signaling the different conditions for those working on the continent from those who are abroad, and usually in the west, Tejumola Olaniyan comments, "Artists in all media, though many could do with more and better training to sharpen their native talents, are working prodigiously to shape form and meaning out of their demanding specific contexts and the intricate ways those contexts interact with the world." But when it comes to critical production, the situation seems less positive: "The conditions for the training of intellectuals and cultural critics are far less than adequate and . . . an overall healthy development of cultural creativity, the type that continually breaches accepted boundaries and invents new forms and suggests new meanings, depends on a robust interaction between talented artists and discerning critics, between the creative and the critical imagination." The notion of a divide has fostered a range of responses, some of which denigrate African cultural or critical production as secondary or as providing "raw materials" for the West to digest and explicate. At the limit, this replicates the capitalist structures of colonialism, now updated in global flows. Lamia Benyoussef argues that the view of Africans writing abroad with greater latitude to produce experimental or sexually explicit materials reflects patronizing European constructions that "infantilize . . . African writers as suppliers of raw materials (plays, films and novels) for Western metropolitan consumption, that is, literary criticism and theory. Such a position wrongly assumes that only the African author in Europe or North America has the freedom to be creative, avant-gardist, and inclusive of others, as if 'creativity' or 'morality' could crop up only on 'Western' soil."

The differences between metropolitan-based authors and critics and those located on the continent multiply when we consider the passages between north and south as well as between African urban centers. Nonetheless, conditions of production today represent a new configuration, and we need to understand their implications. Part of what the authors consider in the following essays is how conditions of movement have created a gulf between those who can travel and those who cannot, a gulf that has become both greater than ever before and yet also more permeable. This is due to both politics and economics. Western nations have largely created insurmountable physical and financial barriers to the poor and disenfranchised while permitting those who "qualify" to pass borders in both directions more easily. The latter now fly with great comfort and speed, reducing voyages that used to be enormous undertakings to quick hops from continent to continent, while the former often live in legal limbo, if not purgatory, with few rights and fewer resources.

In addition, the distance between those who travel abroad and those who do not is increasingly demonstrated both by differing perspectives on the world and in the genres and mediums of the works themselves. This leads us to our particular concern for this volume, which is to consider whether current critical approaches are adequate to the task of assessing work produced by authors who live in different geographic and cultural milieus. The new conditions of globalization have generated possibilities for subject positions that cannot be simply defined by terms such as "exile," "hybrid," "creole," or "diasporic." As such, we would like to suggest that earlier critical approaches do not take into account the diversity and differences of current cultural production. They do not, and perhaps cannot, take into account situational differences, which are tied to choices of style and subject matter and, ultimately, to ideologies. We need to interrogate what we now understand to be African literature and cinema, and, more importantly, we need to reevaluate and to rearticulate new epistemologies in contemporary critical approaches so as to keep apace with this change.

One might begin to consider the differences in works produced on and off the continent by looking at genre. For example, it is commonly held that there are proportionally more working poets and playwrights in Africa among creative writers than one finds in the diaspora. This is in contrast with the focus on fiction that has taken priority abroad.[1] The essays also address stylistic modes and subject matter. Is it true that writers living in Africa often stay within the mode of realism, while many of those who live outside the continent turn to postmodernism, magical realism, or some variant of avant-gardism? This might seem to be the case with African writers whose training as writers has been in Western university writing classes, but there are still many questions we might raise about the creative choices of African writers on the continent and in the diaspora. For Benyoussef, this can be explained by the differences in context faced by many authors: "Even if it is true that publications in North and sub-Saharan Africa have been largely realist, this realism translates less the absence of creativity than the integration of African writers within their social and academic environment."

In regard to social commentary, many African writers are conservative in their treatment of sexuality, especially homosexuality. Indeed, many of those who do address homosexuality in their works use it as a means to show aberrance and transgression. Lindsey Green-Simms and Unoma Azuah have shown in their work on contemporary Nollywood films that there is a tendency to "erase the homosexual character . . . pretending that the topic does not exist. Many of the films end with the death, arrest, conversion, or spiritual 'salvation' of the criminalized and degenerate homosexual character" (37). Works written by Africa writers on the continent that address diverse sexualities in a positive way could begin to mediate the legally and culturally sanctioned violence that LGBTQI individuals are subject to in many African countries and to dispel notions that homosexuality is a Western phenomenon and inherently un-African.[2] Questions of identity that mark sexual orientation and gender are central to the project of this volume as we consider not only how current models of cultural production have changed but also who is effecting that change.

Indeed, one of the questions implicit in several of the essays that follow is what it currently means to be African. These essays interrogate discourses of authenticity that are rampant in both the West and Africa, pointing to the harm this kind of classification can cause for those who do not fit neatly into predefined categories. They argue that attention needs to be given to writers who are redefining and problematizing such categories. A case in point is the new generation of African women writers, particularly those living abroad, who have redrawn the landscape of contemporary African literature. Living and writing globally, their works are often marked by the occupation of multiple spaces and a movement into gender politics. These perspectives have been translated into their writing styles, underscoring emotional landscapes and global settings. Authors Fatou Diome and Chimamanda Ngozi Adichie address gender issues in ways similar to those employed by Aminatta Forna, Doris Baingana, Helen Oyeyemi, and Sefi Atta; they articulate subject positions that speak directly to doubleness.

Fiction like Forna's *The Memory of Love* (2011), Adichie's *The Thing around My Neck* (2009), or Diome's *Belly of the Atlantic* and films like Abderrahmane Sissako's *La Vie sur terre* (1999), Dominique Loreau's *Les Noms n'habitent nulle part* (2002), and Kingsley Ogoro's *Osuofia in London* (2004) create epistemologies with dual standpoints, both in terms of the past and present and in terms of the global north and south. They have abolished old-school hybridity and incorporated cinematic techniques that suture the reader into emotional exchanges, renewing old soap-opera formulas in new worlds. In works like Forna's *The Memory of Love*, living in both worlds defines issues of crime and ethics for characters like Adrian and Mamakay, whose passion crosses from England to Sierra Leone and whose historical framing moves from Sierra Leone's independence to the recent period of conflict and violence.

Perhaps more frequently, however, it is through the evocation of family memories that the subjective locations of immigrants today are defined, both at home and abroad. This can be seen in Forna's *Ancestor Stones* (2006), Oyeyemi's *The Icarus Girl* (2005), and Diome's *Belly of the Atlantic*. In the latter, Diome creates a telling portrait of the dual locations and doubled subjectivities of the immigrant/emigrant. She writes of her homeland, in the dark of the night in Strasbourg, where her memory "chooses to project films shown elsewhere, under different skies," and brings forth stories buried deep "like ancient mosaics in a city's subterranean tunnels": "My pen, like an archeologist's pickax, unearths the dead and discovers remains, tracing on my heart the contours of the land that witnessed my birth and my departure. From incidents I once barely even registered, I now compose the sustenance of exile and, above all, the weaver's yarn supposed to mend the ties broken by distance" (159). Then she speaks of her homesickness, guilt, absence, and sadness, whose lacunae she attempts to bridge with her words, especially words connoting travel and distance—"suitcase words":

> Words too limited to convey the miseries of exile; words too fragile to break open the sarcophagus that absence has cast around me; words too narrow to serve as a bridge between here and elsewhere. Words, then, always used in place of absent words, definitively drowned at the font of the tears to which they lend their taste. And finally *suitcase words whose contents are contraband, whose meaning, despite the detours, leads to a double self: the me from here and the me from over there.* (159–60, our emphasis)

We can read this passage as that of a shot/reverse shot where the two figures in dialogue, confronting each other, here now, there before, suture the reader into the magical site that occludes the presence of the camera and the subject of the enunciation. The more we attend to the exile and its position vis-à-vis home, the more we lose sight of the subject of the enunciation who is ostensibly penning the words. Normally, shot/reverse shot involves two people talking to each other. It arranges the camera's angle so as to allow the spectator to identify with each character's point of view, even as it occludes the fact that the image is produced through a precise camera angle, with its distinct physical location.

But what if the two characters are, like the two sides of Fatou Diome, simultaneously occupying the different locations of the travelers' suitcases: the "suitcase words," the suitcase images, the suitcase lives? If in 1994 Homi Bhabha wanted (in *The Location of Culture*) to place subjectivity in an interstitial space grounded in *différance*, in the present world of globalized traveling, the time for hybridity, for mixing, for mixing in, is no longer available, and *doubling* has replaced the interplay of otherness and self. As in a fugue (Forna's central trope in *The Memory of Love*), where traveling is a flight from oneself, there is a crossing—the occupancy of a space that separates two worlds while belonging, paradoxically, in both and in neither. An emigrant/immigrant always occupies two subject locations, but the sense of belonging in one comes to be supplanted by the physical location of the other. *Traveling* shots (as tracking shots are called in French) carry us from one location to another in order that the vision of a traveling subjectivity can be normalized. It smoothes over the bumps in the road.

This occupation of two subject positions is what Fatou Diome seeks to escape by going abroad with a notion of exile that attempts to erase any recognition of the internal Other. But her history cannot accommodate her need. She reconstructs the passage abroad, redefining exile in globalized spaces: "Wanting to breathe without offending anyone, so the beating of my heart wouldn't be considered sacrilegious, I stepped onto my boat and turned my suitcases into vanishing cases. Exile is my geographical suicide" (161). She sees her new land as a place that enables her to "give birth to oneself," accepting the bitterness of separation and "the kilomètres of sorrow." But above all, as Hélène Cixous and Catherine Clément had written for their mothers' generations, Diome can turn to the freedom ensconced in the act of writing when she is abroad. She says that writing "smiles" at her; now that she feels "free, I write to say and do everything that my mother didn't dare say and do. Identity papers? All the folds of the earth. Date and place of birth? Here and now. Identity papers! My memory is my identity" (162).

Together with her sense of being a foreigner and a stranger, Diome's subject position returns and splits her into a double identity, the newly constructed subjectivity for the global frame: "An outsider everywhere, I carry an invisible theatre inside me, teeming with ghosts" (162). Her subject location, like that which Paul Gilroy defines in *Black Atlantic,* is marked by the spaces she traverses, where *im*migration and *e*migration cross with each voyage.

> To leave is to die of absence. You return, of course, but you return a different person. On going back, you seek but never find those you left behind. Tears in your eyes, you resign yourself to noticing that the masks you'd made for them no longer fit. Who are these people I call my brother, my sister etc.? Who am I to them? The intruder who carries inside her the woman they're waiting for, whom they despair of ever finding again? The stranger who turns up? The sister who leaves? *My dance between the two continents is fraught with these questions.* (162, our emphasis)

In her story "Imitation," Chimamanda Adichie similarly constructs a "dance between two continents," this time for a Nigerian expatriate wife living in New Jersey. In this version, Obiora leaves his wife, Nkem, in the United States while he makes frequent trips home to Lagos. Nkem's world becomes divided, split into two homes that she cannot *not* occupy. Nkem describes how her neighbors try to understand their situation as a divided couple, but their points of reference are not adequate. They would ask, "Where was her husband? Was something wrong? Nkem said everything was fine. He lived in Nigeria *and* America; they had two homes. She saw the doubt in their eyes, knew they were thinking of other couples with second homes in places like Florida and Montreal, couples who inhabited each home at the same time, together" (24). Nkem speaks to the wife of another "Big Man" about how she managed with a similar arrangement and whether she planned on returning home to Nigeria: "The woman turned, her eyes round, as though Nkem had just betrayed her. But how can I live in Nigeria again? she said." The woman then explains that this change was beyond her control: "When you've been here so long, you're not the same, you're not like the people there. How can my children blend in? And Nkem, although she disliked the woman's severely shaved eyebrows, had understood" (29).

However, even after the Americanized Nigerian wife has learned to settle in and to be at home in America, after she concludes she really belonged to this country now, "this country of curiosities and crudities, this country where you could drive at night and not fear armed robbers, where restaurants served one person enough food for three," still, she misses home. Home is conveyed through the familiar ties of family and friends, of language and the music of speech. But it is the immediacy of the physical environment that underlines how immigration has changed her. She describes the times when there was so much snow it covered the hydrants, "[and] she misses the Lagos sun that glares down even when it rains." She thinks about going home "but never seriously, never concretely." Wonderfully, Adichie captures the everyday contours of familiar spaces to demonstrate how a person from one place can also become someone from another place—and have two homes. Adichie's prose is "at home" here, in both worlds: "She goes to a Pilates class twice a week in Philadelphia with her neighbor; she bakes cookies for her children's classes and hers are always the favorites; she expects banks to have drive-ins. America has grown on her, snaked its roots under her skin" (37).

Adichie is sensitive to the registers of accent, culture, food, language, gender relations, taste, contemporary styles, and so on, all of which constitute the American presence. Indeed, Adichie's language records each of these in Nkem's double consciousness, at times in ironic tones but more frequently through her chic postures and idiomatic turnings of phrase. These details render the portrait so perfectly that they suture the native-born reader into its perspective—occluding the non-native position of the speaker's subjectivity.

This occluding is the ultimate goal of the suture, but it is also the result of its violence. In accomplishing the act of identification, of being American, Nigerian, Senegalese, French, the holder of the passport occludes the eye of the camera, keeping its presence away from the eye of the spectator and ear of the reader. The violence that springs from this assumption of Oneness—via the suture— consists of forgetting the violence involved in the act of constituting oneself as *One*. Each literary or cinematic move to include the reader or spectator in the place of the character commits this violence because it excludes the other angle, and, as it excludes the perspective of the camera and the subject of the enunciation in order to constitute itself, it turns otherness into the possibility for an act of revenge. This is how the subject is built. Or, in Jacques Derrida's summation: "L'Un se garde de l'autre pour se faire violence" (The One protects itself from the other *because* it makes itself violence and *so as* to make itself violence) (*Archive Fever* 78). If every formulation involving the One entails the other, if the One is always divided against itself, it is because the assumption of subjectivity is based on the act of division, of splitting—of recognizing both self and other. The violence turns on the fact that "the Other is the condition for the One" (79); the rule of the camera and the authority of the pen complete this revenge.

In considering the violence in the production of subjectivity, we should acknowledge that not all identities are the same and are not all formed through identical means. Because of this, disavowals cannot be identical. Even so, there is a pattern in identity formation that entails loss, disavowal, renunciation, and an acting out of the grief occasioned by loss (Butler). In the works of these African women writers, there is a strong undercurrent of loss that draws attention to double subjectivity. The pain this loss creates accounts for the work of the suture (Silverman) and the melodramatic effort to stitch over loss through the doubling of the subject's position.

Writers from the continent are considering loss and doubleness in ways that are different from but no less interesting than those of authors such as Adichie and Diome. Contemporary melodramatic films and novels, like Nollywood, have a style pointedly marked "for today," and require new critical sensibilities, which are attuned to the truth of the telenovela, to the all-embracing reach of the globalized economy, and especially to the subjectivities that correspond to the worlding of contemporary African literature. Not unlike such popular filmmakers, Diome and Adichie do not shy away from highly charged emotional scenes, with globe-trotting protagonists, "star-crossed lovers," despair, and death, but they are more apt than the filmmakers to present patterns of mixing, blending, combining, and then falling apart, which fit better into the figure of the off-grid rhizome than of the multicultural hybrid, which is often presented as simply a new iteration of earlier identities that have come together in new combinatory patterns.

Here again we find that the high cultural and political aspirations of yesterday are grounded in notions of unified subjectivities that no longer exist. Scholars such as Bhabha have deconstructed the colonial subjectivities that marked and wrote back against empire. Nollywood and jet travel have redefined commodity capitalist markers with a vengeance. We must be prepared to move in both worlds, to be simultaneously here and there. We are no longer figures caught "in between"; we are no longer creolized, much less hybridized. If ever the feminist claim of less than one and double applies, it is in this age where doubling is the condition for traveling subjectivities (Irigaray; Harrow).

Perhaps we might consider the new conditions of production from which African cultures and perspectives emerge in terms of "flows," as in "diaspora flows." We suggest Arjun Appadurai's term "flows" to draw attention to its change in original meaning. Previously, workers and students flowed back to their homes in Africa; now they flow across borders between poor and rich states, none of which are necessarily their countries of origin. In addition, the economics of the flows have changed: the two ends of the economic spectrum—the rich and the poor—are all part of these bi-directional flows. Currently, in addition to the labor force that travels, often painfully and illegally, between Africa and the West, the elite are shuttling between diverse geographic spaces. They carry with them the language to articulate the narratives of their home countries and cultures in their newly adopted spaces, and, as they transport entire cultures, religions, and epistemologies, they use this knowledge to transform the countries into which they enter. Not only do they move away from Africa, they also return home with values and cultures that have been created and nurtured abroad. In other words, these bi-directional flows often include wealthy, highly educated, and creative figures, who then become catalysts for cosmopolitanism and for combatting conventional forms of domination and patterns of difference, both in their adopted and their original homes.

Even with this in mind, we still cannot discount how those who stay in Africa are effecting their own changes, often in response to the power differentials that dictate that they emulate wealthy countries' standards—for example, for scholarly publishing (as with publishing standards for university, not local, presses), as well as for commercial publishing and filmmaking. The flows of people, ideas, and money also generate new critical orders in ways that do not entirely displace older ideologies of engagement and national struggles. They continue these ideologies even as they transform them into the new ideologies of geography, globalization discourses, and nation.

* * *

The essays that follow reflect the highly complicated nature of African cultural production in the contemporary world. Location, within its historical and temporal frame, gives definition to the local as well as to the global. It is the interplay of these factors that gives definition to culture and must be analyzed in its own right for the interplay of the new global configurations of culture to be understood. This is the burden of Eileen Julien's article, "The Critical Present: Where Is 'African Literature'?" For Julien, differences in "location" have their effects, but "new emphases and experimentation in the creative works of African artist-intellectuals are more a matter of 'time,' which is to say history, than 'place.'" In developing this argument she returns to the conditions under which modernism developed, following the lines formulated by Raymond Williams, who claimed that the migrations of metropolitan capitals facilitated the shift of creative writers out of "traditional, closed societies." Metropolitan modernism marked the formation of Negritude in Paris, where African and Caribbean writers lived abroad, and in some cases in exile. But what gave rise to these various modernisms analyzed along lines that followed certain "ideological" trends, such as those that interpreted African literatures of the 1960s and 1970s as being in the service of national liberation, occluding other dimensions of the literature that were already there.

As some writers, like James Baldwin, found their own growth in Paris, breaking internal "barriers" or limits, other writers like Gertrude Stein found it necessary to live abroad in order not to become stagnant, to find the "detachment" needed for creativity. Edward Said, especially, found in exile a path to cosmopolitanism, enriching his own subjectivity while not compromising his commitment to political struggles. On the other hand, such detachment, creativity, or breaking of boundaries might well be accomplished without having to leave one's native land, as we see in the examples of Boris Diop or Jo Ramaka, although the latter in fact has lived abroad as well as in Senegal for decades.

In assessing the complex understandings of "context" in relationship to authors' sensibility, Julien turns to the broad condition of globalization, "the ever-intensifying process of 'globalization,'" which she identifies with current "political, economic, and social realities." This she calls "the motor behind our sense of urgency with respect to thinking anew our theoretical assumptions and practices." African writers are undoubtedly affected by this new age of commodity capitalism and the neoliberal economic order, where Africans are living abroad more than ever. Yet, she argues that "'place' may not be . . . the *cause* of new sensibilities. Rather than a rupture or crisis in artistic production, necessitating a new critical paradigm, a change of place might be better seen as an *effect* of this new historical context." Ultimately, in considering the impact of Ramaka's *Karmen Geï* (2001) in Senegal, she sees anxieties about "religious, national, class, and sexual identities; levels of education; and wealth and power" as determining points of view and interpretation, both for those living at home and for those abroad. She concludes by noting that in a global age, where it is increasingly important that we put in dialogue the work of artists from around the world, the only meaningful way for that dialogue to be carried out is by recognizing the importance of the local knowledge of the multiple places that constitute the global—and in this case, the local—as identified with African culture, be it on the continent or abroad.

Following Julien, the next three essays in the collection—Olabode Ibironke's "African Writers Challenge Conventions of Postcolonial Literary History," Moradewun Adejunmobi's "Provocations: African Societies and Theories of Creativity," and Patrice Nganang's "In Praise of the Alphabet"—assess the ways in which literature from the continent has come to be read in the Western academy, particularly in postcolonial scholarship. They offer different methodologies and critiques, suggesting how we might reexamine our theoretical approaches to contemporary African cultural production.

According to Ibironke, the conventional perception of postcolonial literary history is that African literature was for the most part produced overseas, and this perception has shaped contemporary understandings of aesthetic modalities and functions of African literature. To challenge this, Ibironke offers a selection of texts to demonstrate African writers' active engagement with the politics of literary production and their transformational agenda for culture and local political situations in Africa. Reading these texts, Ibironke suggests, will give us another means with which to define African literature that does not depend on misleading theoretical constructs, which have their origins in perspectives of global production. For instance, in David Damrosch's notion of world literature, which depends upon the concept of origins, Ibironke finds that "the condition of the production of African literature ... stems from that unusual experience that does not fit into the established modes of thinking about notions of world literature. This is probably why of all the texts of world literature examined by Damrosch, not a single one of them is by an African author!" The category of postcolonial world literature complicates dominant global north theoretical frames, just as world literature as a dominant category occludes the formulation of the category of African literature. Postcolonial literature remains a stumbling block for thinking grounded in global "flows" and "scapes."

Adejunmobi also draws attention to lacunae in contemporary scholarship. She argues that greater attention should be given to critical approaches that engage with the problematic of creativity. In Adejunmobi's view, a shortcoming in current critical approaches is that they do not fully account for the expressive and representational practices within African societies or ask what use they have for contemporary societies—why they matter. Engaging with works of African cultural production will enable us to pose the crucial question of how this will make the case for the public relevance of humanities research. Posing this question in an African context allows for the visibility of the moral dilemmas attached to research to emerge. To do this, it is necessary to attend to the role that "technologies of mediation play in connecting individuals to networks of artists, critics, and publics with varying levels of toleration for different types of aesthetic, ideological, and instrumental departures from the norm." Formal theorizing that has enjoyed a dominant position in the Western academy has had its advantages but comes up short when deployed in significantly advancing our understanding of African cultural production or in "adequately justif[ying] the salience of its own subject matter." The values attending the studies of mediation in African cultures cannot be separated from the ethics that undergird choices of theoretical approaches. Adejunmobi forces us to ask what benefits accrue to society in our undertaking of literary analyses of the singular text.

Finally, Patrice Nganang suggests that in the study of African texts, scholars should avoid rushing to new materials and approaches—especially topics that might be typified as "sexy" in the Western academy. He argues that we normally organize the history of African literature into certain broad categories: a precolonial literature that is predominantly oral; an anticolonial moment, which is defined by its militancy; and a literature of displacement, which marks the beginning of contemporary postcolonial literature, only to the extent that we accept the global as our paradigm. He writes, "Disillusionment and emigration ... mark ... the beginning of contemporary postcolonial literature, *provided* we choose the global paradigm to be the condition of possibility of African literature. And the independence of African countries from Europe in 1960 becomes a turning point in the many-thousand-years-old intellectual history of the African continent *only because* of the global paradigm through the frame of which that history is read." We can remain open to the condition of possibility of an African literature by addressing its own framings, such as could be provided by turning not to the question of "African" or "language," that is, to identitarian formulations, but to the building blocks of literature itself, the alphabet—and in particular to the Bamum alphabet created by the sultan Njoya in the early twentieth century. Now more than ever, with diaspora and dispersal as marks of modernity, Nganang recasts the central question posed by V. Y. Mudimbe, "What is Africa?," by looking outside the strictures of the global paradigm, which imposes the conventional chronology measured by Western, even colonial periodizations, and finds in writing itself the key for a new paradigm. Nganang's conclusion is noteworthy, as he finds that Ibrahim Njoya could be overlooked in the national histories of African literature only because he asked the question of literature from the point of view of writing. "Thus, instead of providing an answer to the question '*What is African literature?*' that nagged our best critics since 1962, or rather since 1939, what inspired him throughout his life was the drive to discover *how* literature can be produced on the African continent in the first place." From there to ask how African literature can be produced in the diaspora is an equally fascinating question, especially as the form of the diaspora today has radically shifted since the times of Negritude, of Independence, and of the first generation of authors who followed.

The five essays that form the middle section of this collection continue the critique of contemporary scholarly practices by focusing primarily on African cultural production outside of the continent. Tejumola Olaniyan questions the poetics of exile and draws attention to the ways in which knowledge from Africa—and indeed Africans themselves—is interpreted and categorized in the West. The next two essays by Lamia Benyoussef and Safoi Babana-Hampton develop this critique through examinations of specific literary and cinematic texts from the Maghreb. Benyoussef highlights the precarious position the Muslim woman academic and intellectual occupies today, especially in the academy. The final essay by Valérie K. Orlando draws attention to post-1999 Moroccan films, arguing that they address parts of the country's past that are largely ignored in international conversations about Moroccan cinema.

In "African Cultural Studies: Of Travels, Accents, and Epistemologies," Tejumola Olaniyan examines the ways in which African voices are typically read in the West by highlighting the imprint of place on the accents of African cultural theorizing and criticism. More specifically, Olaniyan examines the different— and frequently opposed—ideological orientations of theory and criticism written by scholars in Africa and scholars in Europe and America. Olaniyan suggests that the process of migration from Africa to the West often "domesticates" African scholars and causes them to develop a "scholarly accent" in line with generally accepted Euro-American categories. Olaniyan then assesses the impact of this transformation on the diversity of voices speaking on African cultural production across geographical regions. He frames it as a broad historical evaluation: "My findings here constitute partly a cultural history of a scholarly method, partly an institutional history of cross-continental discourse formations, and partly an intellectual biography of a generation." He then contrasts the dominant critical trends in Africa, which he dubs "affirmative," with those in the West, defined as "interstitial." The latter is marked by postmodern terms and has enjoyed a dominant position in African literary circles, at times imposing its cultural capital on the African academy. He sounds a warning note, at the end, against an all-too-easy assumption of its predominance: "I will say that an increasing embrace of the interstitial accent by scholars in Africa is far from desirable, so long as the generative center of that discourse remains outside of Africa."

In "*Le* Freak, *C'est* Critical and *Chic*: North African Scholars and the Conditions of Cultural Production in Post-9/11 U.S. Academia," Lamia Benyoussef critiques scholarly reading practices by demonstrating how literature produced within the Maghreb is read differently from works written by those in the North American diaspora. In so doing, she continues the lines of argumentation from the essays above and suggests that Western scholars read African texts according to certain narrowly defined categories. More specifically, she argues against the commonly held thesis that African writers living abroad are more likely to be more experimental, explicit in their treatment of sexuality, and inclusive of marginal groups than are their colleagues at home. Benyoussef proposes instead that this dichotomy is a construct of Euro-American scholarship. Specifically, she claims that the atmosphere created since 9/11 has poisoned the atmosphere for North African scholars so that when expatriate Maghrebi writers focus on language and sexuality, "it is less an indication of their newly found liberty than a sign of their academic ghettoization after 9/11. Under the corporate (and imperial) notion of diversity as spectacle, the only place for a North African scholar/author in American academia, in particular, is that of the exhibitionist-voyeur who unveils ad nauseam the Muslim female body, the Arab mind, and Islamic patriarchy while remaining on the threshold of the American dream." She explores the themes of expatriate Maghrebi authors, which include the Holocaust, the Spanish Inquisition, and Mexican immigration. Her central argument is that these trends are "the direct outcome of ghettoization and identification with former/current marginalized groups rather than a sudden ennoblement by the Western values of tolerance, freedom, and diversity, which are endemic to their host countries."

Safoi Babana-Hampton's essay, "Reading 'Beur' Film Production Otherwise: The Poetics of the Human and the Transcultural," also addresses the limitations of contemporary Euro-American scholarship in its treatment of texts from the

Maghreb, specifically its films. She examines dominant approaches in Maghrebi cinema today and reveals both their limitations and their possibilities. In particular, she problematizes critical reception of films from the Maghreb that privilege them for their documentary and testimonial value, demonstrating how this approach often causes an eclipse of the Maghrebi filmmaker as artist. She quotes Gilles Deleuze to the effect that "truth" as a standard appropriate to documentary film, as opposed to fiction film, does not function as a basis for the documentary but rather as a product it imagines itself to be based upon: "The cinema can call itself *cinéma-vérité*, all the more so because it will have destroyed every model of the true so as to become *creator and producer of truth:* this will not be a cinema of truth but the truth of cinema" (151). She suggests that other approaches that stress both the sociocultural content of the films and their aesthetic and philosophical concerns would offer a more nuanced and accurate reading of Maghrebi cinema, Beur cinema, or what she prefers to call, following Hamid Naficy, "transnational cinema." Thus she intends to go beyond the conventional readings of such films as exhibiting the traits of sociorealist fiction and to respond to Karim Dridi's claim that "social cinema" does not exist; rather, "as an artist he never sets out to make social cinema through his films but to make films that question the social order."

In the final essay of this section, "Revealing the Past, Conceptualizing the Future On-Screen: The Social, Political, and Economic Challenges of Contemporary Filmmaking in Morocco," Valérie K. Orlando argues that post-1999 films from Morocco depict a country that is dynamic and connected to the global sociocultural economy of the twenty-first century. At the same time, they represent the closed, obscure past of the nation's history that has never before been told, drawing on themes such as human rights abuse, the former incarceration of thousands during the Lead Years (the years of dictatorship during the reign of the former king Hassan II), women's emancipation, poverty, and claims for social justice. Orlando found that many topics in the films involved restoring suppressed or obfuscated memories (with film functioning as a *lieu de mémoire*) and critiquing contemporary sociocultural challenges, including the need to heal the wounds of the past. Western scholarship could benefit from a closer reading of how Moroccan cinema weaves these two historical moments into complex stories of loss and doubleness and engages in what is now felt to be the "New Morocco." She concludes that Moroccan filmmakers, whether living abroad or at home, whether male or female, view their roles as "keepers of the collective consciousness of Morocco" and as such are "both generators and agents of change."

The final set of essays in this collection explores how movement between cultures and continents is both a resource and a risk for many African authors and artists. This movement can give artists access to both material and intellectual capital, but it also can open them to criticism, often regarding the degree to which we can continue to use the term "African" naively, as though there were no further qualification necessary to gloss its work as a broad signifier of identity. These essays continue the argument developed above that scholarship must change if it is to take into full account the range of possibilities these texts offer in the production of cultural knowledge.

In her essay "Thresholds of New African Dramaturgies in France Today," Mária Minich Brewer continues with the consideration of work by artists who move between Africa and Europe. In particular, she discusses the critical and dramaturgical significance of the generation of dramatists that includes Koffi Kwahulé, Marcel Zang, José Pliya, and Kossi Efoui. Brewer argues that their works, written in France and Africa and performed globally, demonstrate the creative and theatrical possibilities of being "in-between." Theater itself, she contends, engages its public in "critical considerations of and across borders." Indeed, these possibilities of in-between-ness are made visible in many of the plays through a recasting of social and symbolic dimensions. Brewer's readings are grounded in Jacques Rancière's approaches to politics and aesthetics, and in particular in what Rancière means by "making-sensible," as well as making visible. Its radical nature, its "newness," consists of approaches that redefine what had been taken as subversive in the past, as "it works to undo what might be called established syntaxes of the cultural imaginary." The new works challenge "entrenched regimes of the visible and the communicable," which are "displaced" and "deactivated." She considers theater itself as a "threshold," thus opening a space for "theorizing theater's specific potential for creating mobile passages between languages, the modern and the ancient, here and elsewhere, the other and the same." In an exciting twist to the notion of the threshold, she claims that the spectators themselves come to perceive their own role as being marked by the threshold position as well.

Similar to the essays above, Magali Compan's "Island Geography as Creole Biography: Shenaz Patel's Mauritian Literary Production" locates Patel's work in Mauritius, her home. In this essay, Compan examines the francophone author Shenaz Patel, who writes novels, plays, and short stories in both French and Creole. Compan discusses how unlike many of her Mauritius literary contemporaries, Patel has maintained residence and pursued her career on the island. As a local journalist, author, librarian, translator, and fiction writer, Patel's authorship is shaped by her lived commitments to Mauritius. Writing in both French and Creole, Patel lives the Mauritius voice she generates in her novels, thereby creating a poetics of the contemporary Indian Ocean. She poses key questions for our volume, considering how African cultural production is marked not only by diaspora or emigration but also by remaining at "home," where equally compelling issues about place are posed: "How does a 'home' geography or place affect an author's writing and authorship? What are the relationships among location, a sense of place, and one's identity formation, not only as a writer but as an individual or a member of a community? What influence, if any, does place exert on one's identity?" Patel poses the question of "home" through language as well as geography, where Mauritius remains the site of her novels' settings and languages.

In short, this diverse and exciting collection of essays addresses the worlding of contemporary African literature and this age, where doubling is the condition for traveling subjectivities, no matter whether the author has or has not left the African continent. These chapters demonstrate how we must be prepared to move intellectually between worlds, to be simultaneously here and there, to be aware of the ways in which texts both expose and occlude duality. We need to interrogate what we understand African literature and cinema to be, and, more important, we need to reevaluate and reshape our own critical approaches.

Notes

1. This is related to the fact that "transnational" or "global literature" awards confer fame on those whose best-selling works speak to an audience expecting texts and styles commensurate with their sense of a world culture and come in the genre most commonly read in the West: fiction.

2. See Karen Martin and Makhozazana Xaba, comps. and eds., *Queer Africa: New and Collected Fiction* (Cape Town, South Africa: Ma Thoko's Book, 2013). This collected volume of short stories offers stories on same-sex relationships written by a diverse body of African writers in the continent.

Works Cited

Adichie, Chimamanda N. "Imitation." In *The Thing Around Your Neck*. New York: Alfred A. Knopf, 2009.

Butler, Judith. *The Psychic Life of Power: Theories in Subjection*. Stanford: Stanford University Press, 1997.

Deleuze, Gilles. *Cinema2: The Time-Image*. London: Athlone, 1989.

Derrida, Jacques. *Archive Fever: A Freudian Impression*. Translated by Eric Prenowitz. Chicago: University of Chicago Press, 1996.

Diome, Fatou. *The Belly of the Atlantic*. Translated by Lulu Norman and Ros Schwartz. London: Serpent's Tail, 2006.

Gilroy, Paul. *The Black Atlantic: Modernity and Double Consciousness*. London: Verso, 1993.

Green-Simms, Lindsey, and Unoma Azuah. "The Video Closet." *Transition* 107 (2012): 32–49.

Harrow, Kenneth W. *Less Than One and Double: A Feminist Reading of African Women's Writing*. Portsmouth, N.H.: Heinemann, 2002.

Irigaray, Luce. *This Sex Which Is Not One*. Ithaca, N.Y.: Cornell University Press, 1985.

Silverman, Kaja. *The Subject of Semiotics*. New York: Oxford University Press, 1983.

1 The Critical Present
Where Is "African Literature"?

Eileen Julien

FOR BABA SY

For borrow we certainly must if we are to elude the constraints of our immediate intellectual environment.
    Edward Said, "Traveling Theory"

WE ARE ALL agreed that conditions for the production of literature, cinema, and visual arts by Africans continue to evolve rapidly in the era of intense globalization[1] and are today quite different from those of yesterday, the period of decolonizing nationalism. One symptom of the "unevenness" of the current context is that vast numbers of African artist-intellectuals live in metropolises outside of Africa where they typically have greater access to readers and spectators worldwide and to prestigious invitations, awards, and grants.

What happens, then, to "African" literature, film, and arts when African artist-intellectuals reside and produce their work abroad?

Is there a vast difference between the *texture* of texts produced by those living and working in Africa and that of texts produced by those living and working abroad? Does old-style realism remain the dominant literary mode on the continent? Are explicit depictions of sexual acts or queer sexualities, postmodernist and avant-gardist experiments, which are rife elsewhere, eschewed in Africa? These are the questions highlighted in Ken Harrow and Frieda Ekotto's call for papers that framed a lively discussion at the 2010 Michigan State University–University of Michigan workshop on critical theory and the production of African literature and cinema. There are important assumptions behind these questions: first, an artist's location would seem to be a critical determinant of his or her creative work, and second, scholars and readers in search of effective critical approaches should take their cues from thematic and formal shifts in literary and film texts that are a result of artists' new locations.

So, are our longstanding protocols of literary analysis—specifically postcolonial theory, which itself has morphed or expanded from its early heyday of fierce anticolonial paradigms (master-slave, resistance-accommodation, and Manichaean binaries) to more strategic essentialisms, hybridity, and "promiscuity"[2]—adequate to account for and shed light on new cultural products, born of disparate transnational parentage instead of in a local, fixed genealogy?

It would seem that while narratological protocols or analysis of tropes and rhetorical figures or other textual processes, for example, remain viable and still find work in a new era, they are less visible or have become ancillary to protocols based on the interplay of texts and contexts—which is to say forms of governance, modes of production, social organization, and hierarchies. The latter protocols that work more or less well in one temporality may be far from adequate in another.

The relationship of literary forms to material conditions is a complex issue, but establishing a correspondence between conditions and practice is often a fundamental gesture in theorizing cultural production.[3] The question of "place" with respect to the work of African artist-intellectuals falls within this dynamic. To be precise: What impact does residence abroad—or the continual shuttling between host country and homeland—have on literature and film by Africans? It is foolhardy to think we can establish definitive answers to all these questions. But we may be able to do a bit of space-clearing with respect to this debate so as to think more clearly about them.

To place this new cultural production in perspective, it is imperative to reconsider several truisms on the "old" production because they bear directly on the problem before us: first, the aesthetic or literary genealogies of these older texts, which are frequently (and debatably) called "first generation"[4]; and second, what we take to be these texts' single-minded postcoloniality.

"African" Was Never *Only* African

The aesthetic origins of the texts that for the last fifty years we have called "African" lie and have always lain both within and *beyond* Africa. Many of the graphic, literary, and filmic texts most profoundly engaged with African localities, histories, realities, and aesthetic traditions have never been purely "African." Our most classic or neo-traditional texts, dealing with race and imperialism in their innumerable guises—Chinua Achebe's early novels of the 1950s, *Things Fall Apart* and *Arrow of God*; Birago Diop's *Contes d'Amadou Koumba* (1947); Amos Tutuola's *Palm-Wine Drinkard* (1953); Thomas Mofolo's Sesuto-language *Chaka*, translated and published in English in 1931; Sol Plaatje's *Mhudi* (1930);

Shabaan Robert's Swahili-language novel *Kusadikika* (1951, Believable); Sembène Ousmane's *La noire de . . .* (1966, Black Girl)—are products of wide-ranging experiences in education, culture, work, written and oral modes of artistic expression, and African and indigenized languages. They straddle forms, languages, and national borders.

Such straddling is signaled by Simon Gikandi, who has written provocatively on the engagement of African autobiography and novels with Western social scientific theses and texts on Africa, and by Rhonda Cobham-Sander, who has demonstrated the inventive use of the dual anthropological personae—informant and narrator—in the early Achebe works and in Camara Laye's *L'enfant noir* (1954). I myself have read Ferdinand Oyono's character Toundi (*Une vie de boy,* 1954) as ethnographer and interlocutor with Andre Gide's 1902 *récit, L'immoraliste* ("Of Colonial").

A whole range of creators—certainly those who write in indigenized European languages and those whom we read most often in European, American, and African classrooms—have often stood astride diverse and multiple physical worlds, and perhaps they have always inhabited multiple subjective worlds. As Tayeb el Salih remarked at a conference at Brown University in the early 1990s, Africa has always been syncretic. Achebe, too, has argued that no one can pick a particular moment in the past and claim that it is *this* moment that is authentically African. Moreover, the decolonizing, nationalist, largely past-fixated movement of *négritude* was, after all, also born outside the continent, in Paris! One can plausibly argue in fact that Negritude's contradictions are due precisely to its hybrid origins.

One Train Can Hide Another

Second, we have come to think of this early production as stable, bound to the continent and associated with the seemingly timeless conventions of decolonizing nationalism. Yet, as many scholars point out, what we considered to be the heart, the raison d'être, of Euro-language "African" literature and film was tied to a particular temporality. It was the scripting of the fight against the colonizer; it was the reclaiming of (a typically male) subjectivity vis-à-vis a colonial archive. And as urgent as these thematics were, they nonetheless obscured twists of plot, contradictions of character, ambiguities in meaning, and other fundamental facets of African experience, the interplay of gender, religion, ethnicity, and sexuality, for example. Even the texts of this era, then, in Akin Adesokan's words, "say things behind their [authors'] backs; the works speak beyond their authors' declared or implied intentions" (3).

But readers and scholars of decolonizing African texts typically read in allegiance to a macro-political agenda and ignored or minimized the incoherence and contradiction that are woven into every text. Thus while scholars, if not the artists, writers, and filmmakers themselves, did not look beyond the macropolitics, many aspects of social experience that went beyond the decolonizing agenda were in fact perceptible even in the high texts of decolonization, had our *selective* ways of reading, oriented by metacritical discourses on the "authentic" and the "true," not prevented us from seeing them (Gikandi; Julien, "Towards New Readings"). My point here is simply that the "old" production was surely more complex than we were able to perceive and admit. In other words, even as current literary, film, and artistic production by Africans residing abroad can clearly be associated with new emphases and experimentation, we are not in the midst of a shift from a closed, stable literary arena to a brave new world. These visible changes, signs of intellectual and artistic vitality, are the continuation of processes that are immemorial and ongoing.

The Michigan call focused above all on the *displacement* of writers, filmmakers, and other creators, the shift in their home base from country of origin in Africa to the West—and, we might add, to the East or to yet another African nation. There may be an important reason for this: creative texts by Africans have generally been defined *spatially:* They "come from 'Africa,'" perceived as the closed arena with fixed genealogies and topoi, as observed above. These boundaries and specificities are closely linked to a deeply rooted belief in an intractable African "exceptionalism." Whatever its intellectual benefits—and there are many—Africanists trained under the "area studies model" may find it particularly difficult to conceptualize "Africa" in the new dispensation privileging transcontinental and comparative studies, where historical legacies seem to be discounted.

Thinking about "Location"

There is, then, a long history of nuanced, and sometimes conflicting, perspectives on the relationship between *location* and creative practice that may offer insight into this issue as part of contemporary processes.

Here, I start with *The Politics of Modernism*, Raymond Williams's critique of the scholarly "normalization" of a very selective European modernism. Williams asserts that the presence of so many immigrants in the metropolises, especially in early twentieth-century Paris, created a sense of "liberating diversity" (43) and helped establish the only community available to this diverse multitude of artists and writers: "a community of the medium; of their own [artistic] practices" (45).[5] For Williams, "small groups in any form of divergence or dissent could find some kind of foothold, in ways that would not have been possible if the artists and thinkers composing them had been scattered in more traditional, closed societies" (45). It would be hard to challenge this argument that the ruptures, fragmentation, and individual subjectivities that are characteristic of metropolitan modernism would not have found a receptive audience in small, tight-knit towns or rural communities. It is important not to lose sight of the fact that Williams's overall argument is that the parameters of modernism that hold sway in scholarship today are *ideological* rather than logical and that they have blinded us to *other modern practices of art* that do not fit the established paradigm of metropolitan modernism. Williams's view thus parallels the one I have just presented above, that while we see what is happening in the creative practice of Africans now living elsewhere and that takes center stage, which is to say the metropolises and international circuit, might we have overlooked the formal innovation or the representation of "marginal" behaviors in creative practice on the ground in Africa itself? Moreover, while we seek to understand creative practice "at the center," we should not take it to be "normative."

Writing some ten years later, Edward Said agrees with Williams's assessment of the "liberating diversity" of "exile" and the lesser freedom of "traditional, closed societies," but he assigns the coefficients differently. Said stresses, in an echo of Nietzsche, the problematic "naturalization" of "home": "Home and language . . . become nature, and their underlying assumptions recede into dogma and orthodoxy. . . . Borders and barriers, which enclose us within the safety of familiar territory, can also become prisons." If, for Said, those who stay at home are more likely to espouse dogma and orthodoxy, it is exiles who "cross borders, break barriers of thought and experience" (*Reflections* 185).[6] This commonsensical claim, which is the basis for the celebration of hybrid identities, is aligned with Ekotto and Harrow's assertion of important creative breaks beyond the confines of "home." Barrier-breaking in exile is nonetheless a complex phenomenon, and the celebration of its possibilities might be counterbalanced by other considerations. For example, Senegalese novelist Boubacar Boris Diop suggests the possibility of a creative, productive self-exile *in the context of home:* "I'm interested in the ways a person can be torn, the ways he can be separated from the group. And I think a writer is always separated from the group" (Sugnet 159). Diop's praise of separation is not an allusion to spatial dislocation but to the vantage point offered by a certain social marginality within one's community.

If on the other hand the borders and barriers to be crossed are of our own making rather than those imposed by our society, these still more powerful forms of imprisonment stay with us, regardless of where we find ourselves. Perhaps the most important caveat with respect to this view is that the exile of an artist-intellectual abroad, who is "playing to the market" rather than to the audience, carries its own risks of entrapment in the paradigms and stardust of the metropolis, which also have the capacity to reify, as Said himself warns.

In a foreshadowing of this romantic, if not elite, understanding of what we now call cosmopolitanism, Gertrude Stein, the grande dame of the "lost generation" of American writers who called Paris home from the turn of the century through much of the 1940s, claimed similarly that writers "needed two countries because the creative life depended upon that detachment or ungrounding *only available in a foreign place*" (Kennedy 26, my emphasis). While Boris Diop espouses "detachment" as a critical disposition, his remarks cited above challenge the view that this distancing can be had only in a foreign place. But foreign ground does offer a greater possibility of creative distance—especially if we consider that the artist-intellectuals to whom Said refers are not simply going in search of grist for aesthetic production: they are typically the targets of censorship or violence at the hands of religious fundamentalists, ethnic or racist partisans, rapacious states, or global corporations.

Gerald Kennedy writes on the transformation of "space" into "place," thanks to the emotional investment, memories, and meanings with which we associate our homes, villages, and cities. He offers rich insights, in a "humanist" vein, on the question of exile and expatriation for the Hemingway–Stein–Dos Passos cohort in early to mid-twentieth-century Paris. He asserts both that "narratives *of exile* (including novels, short stories, autobiographies, and diaries) seem more likely to incorporate reflections on the problem of place and the relation of place to writing" (25, my emphasis) and that displacement may be "an elective strategy of replenishment," in which case "exile is a quest for a more productive milieu" (26). Kennedy thus distinguishes between, on the one hand, artist-intellectuals whose creative work is set in the places they find themselves, places where subjectivities are transformed, and, on the other, those artist-intellectuals who retreat, pragmatically, to locations of greater possibility. For the African American artist-intellectuals who journeyed to Paris in the early to mid-twentieth century to flee the stifling atmosphere of racism and lack of opportunity in the United States, Paris was certainly a place of possibility, and in the case of James Baldwin, for example, it was also the stage of self-discovery and transformed subjectivity.[7] Of course, the fact that Paris represented "possibility" to African Americans in this period did not mean it was so for all its *immigrés*.[8] This seems to me a critical point: no place *in and of itself* is inherently or universally a place of possibility or opportunity. This will depend at the very least on identities and host country receptivity (Julien, "'Now You See It'").

With respect to narratives "of exile," an interesting shift has taken place in representations of Europe and America by African writers. In many literary texts of the 1930s, 1940s, 1950s, and 1960s, Europe was largely the symbolic space of profound cultural alienation. Once back on the continent, contact with this metonymically "white" world, or with European outposts in the colonies, could often spell madness or death. One thinks, of course, of Chinua Achebe's *Things Fall Apart* and *Arrow of God*, Ousmane Socé Diop's *Mirages de Paris* (1935), Birago Diop's "Sarzan" (1947), Ferdinand Oyono's *Une vie de boy*, David Diop's "Le Renégat" (1956), Cheikh Hamidou Kane's *L'aventure ambiguë* (1960), Sembène Ousmane's *La noire de...*, Tayeb Salih's *Season of Migration to the North* (published in Arabic in 1966), and, even as late as the 1980s, Ken Bugul's *Le baobab fou*.

Little by little, however, Africans, including a slew of writers, have chosen to live abroad or to go back and forth to the continent—because of unemployment and impossible dreams or often enough because living at home has proved dangerous. Europe and America have been transformed from purely negative symbolic markers in the struggles for decolonization and African nationalism to "sites of possibility" (see Mariama Bâ's *Une si longue lettre* [1979]) or complex, textured spaces where protagonists are challenged nonetheless by the racial and ideological histories and dynamics of the "host country": see Ama Ata Aidoo's *Our Sister Killjoy* (1977); Pap Khouma's Italian-language memoir, *I Was an Elephant Salesman* (1990); Calixthe Beyala's *Le petit prince de Belleville* (1992) and *Maman a un amant* (1993); Alain Mabanckou's *Bleu-blanc-rouge* (1998); Chimamanda Ngozi Adichie's *Purple Hibiscus* (2003); Fatou Diome's *Le ventre de l'Atlantique* (2003); Mohammed Ali's *The Prophet of Zongo Street* (2009); Dinesh Mengestu's *The Beautiful Things That Heaven Bears* (2007). Often, these new homes abroad enable a reimagining or new representations of the old places.

Similar to Kennedy, Akin Adesokan notes that in material terms, the metropolitan location may present today's African artist-intellectuals with "opportunities for funding, technical support, publishing ... in short for economic security" (179). And, one might add, for transnational co-productions of films, exhibition spaces, and intellectual debate. This pragmatic understanding of the metropolitan location or life abroad strikes me as the most productive—with the caveat that to reside abroad is not necessarily to abandon "home." With respect to the latter, Ayo Coly has written convincingly about a problematic pattern of celebratory insistence on disjunctures and rootlessness in postcolonial and postmodern theory and a concomitant denigration of "home," which, à la Said above, is associated with stasis, lack of questioning, and indifference to others across boundaries. Challenging the smugness of the cosmopolitan paradigm and the glorification of the postmodern turn in new writing by Africans residing in Europe and the United States, she asserts that "home" is still a loaded matter for postcolonial Africans residing beyond Africa.[9]

Thus while "location" can be critical in any number of ways, I would argue that new emphases and experimentation in the creative works of African artist-intellectuals are more a matter of "time," which is to say history, than "place." Current political, economic, and social realities, which we associate with the ever-intensifying process of globalization, surely drive our sense of urgency with respect to thinking anew our theoretical assumptions and practices, for artistic production worldwide is being reshaped ceaselessly under the now relentless global traffic of commodities, people, and ideas. And this is true of African artists *on the continent* as well as of those abroad. It is perhaps most prominent in the work of musicians and visual artists.

"Place" may not be, then, the *cause* of new sensibilities. Rather than a rupture or crisis in artistic production, necessitating a new critical paradigm, a change of place might be better seen as an *effect* of this new historical context, a yearning for a certain kind of artistic freedom and familiarity with worldwide currents in literature, film, and arts *that precedes departure.*

If the current age is "characterized by networks of connections that span multi-continental distances" for economist Joseph Nye, the positive face of this new context may be the sense of possibility held out by such connections that go beyond or bypass the state. For Fredric Jameson, this positive face has activated "new intellectual networks and ... exchanges and discussions across a variety of nations" (65): thus, collaborative intellectual projects across national boundaries, languages, and cultures and the enabling of new solidarities against innumerable forms of repression, such as homophobic violence, the life-threatening conditions of sweatshops, sex trafficking of young girls, and other contemporary forms of slavery. By virtue of new technologies, Africans on the continent and in diasporas abroad, with their ethno-cultural and geospatial identities in tow, participate in a global "commons" and create a "global Africa."

At the same time, globalism—whose forms Nye identifies as environmental, economic, military, and social—is neither the promise of "even" development nor necessarily an improvement in conditions for people worldwide. One of the most eloquent inquiries into the downside of the current context is Djibril Diop Mambety's *Hyènes* (1992), produced some twenty years ago, on the cusp of today's warp-speed in global processes. Adapted from *The Visit*, the 1956 play by Swiss writer Friedrich Dürrenmatt, *Hyènes* was directed and filmed in Senegal. This film, for all these reasons, challenges a bipolar reading of artistic production on and beyond the continent. While the Dakar suburb of Colobane is the setting of the film, the issues *Hyènes* explores cinematically are not limited to a specific place, for the whole world is implicated in this new dispensation—or rather, this new temporality. Ours—regardless of our country or city—is an environment characterized by savage political regimes; a dearth of educational, employment, and creative opportunities; failing infrastructure and systems in health and public welfare; lack of support for creative and cultural endeavors; and the ills of a rapacious capitalism, supported by neo-liberal governments, which in Africa, at least, are the latest avatar of colonialism on steroids.

Yet globalism has not rendered postcolonial perspectives obsolete. Despite global threats and challenges, the nation retains significant, if attenuated, power: Who can cross borders? Who has access to the protections, rights, and privileges of citizenship? Who can claim redress, when nations fail to live up to their ideals? States still possess the means to enforce their will. Former colonizers still intervene. So, postcolonial critique is valuable even if partial, and its limits are now visible in ways they were not decades ago.

At the same time, there are many formations and issues, some of which I have referred to above, that exceed locality and the state and are transforming our world: the environment and health; neo-liberalism, which has spawned "structural adjustment" (in Africa) and now "austerity" (in Europe); new technologies and media.

To what protocols, to which paradigms, then, do we turn? This does not seem to me to be a matter of throwing out one set of tools for another but rather of *expanding* the toolbox.

Following Jonathan Haynes, who argues that we should leave aside "classical interpretative strategies . . . located in the humanities" and increasingly take into account the *context of production* of Nollywood film, Harrow and Ekotto have suggested that we evaluate current or traditional critical approaches to literature and cinema so as to develop more relevant strategies for the study of "new" African production.

It has become clear that no text—literary, cinematic, or graphic—produced at the height of decolonization or in this moment of fierce globalization, whether on the continent or beyond it, can ever be adequately understood with reference to sheer formal qualities and "content" and to the neglect of contexts of *production and reception,* whether around the continent or around the world.

If we take the example of Joseph Gaï Ramaka's film *Karmen Geï* (2001), a transnational production screened at Cannes, Sundance, and the Los Angeles Pan African Film Festival, where it won Best Feature, reliance on both "humanistic" and contextual approaches leads us, in my view, to the fullest grasp of meaning-making: first, to representations of freedom, marginality, and women's power (or agency) that Ramaka himself evokes and that allow us to compare the film vis-à-vis the nineteenth-century novella by Prosper Mérimée (1845) and Georges Bizet's opera (1875), to situate these forms in their varied historical and social contexts, and to "understand the critical change—in time and place—that occurs between one writer and another" (Said, *World* 237). Yet a deep engagement with contextual factors, production processes, distribution, and reception, such as that offered by Mari Maasilta in her remarkable empirical study of Ramaka's film, deepens understanding of the *production of meaning* as a contemporary process in multiple localities. Maasilta treads lightly in many instances because of the innumerable uncertainties surrounding discussants and their points of view, but she concludes, for example, that among Senegalese in Senegal and abroad in online forum discussions in 2001–02, "there was very little interest in aesthetic and generic matters and the concern was mostly in the cultural content of the film" (315).

She asserts moreover that

> the importance of *Karmen* lies in the fact that it provided Senegalese people living in the country and abroad with a channel to negotiate the burning psychological, political and ideological issues related to the Senegalese identity and society of today. The . . . debate . . . could have [crystallized] through any other cultural product or event. . . . The debate about *Karmen* activated

especially Senegalese religious and nationalist groups to articulate their fears and hopes about the state and future of the Senegalese society and the nation-state. The adherents of several Muslim tendencies profited from the occasion to negotiate their identity with regard to each other and especially with regard to more secular Westernised intellectuals. (319)

One might dispute Maasilta's claim that any other cultural product or event would have crystallized this debate, but these multiple and diverging centers of interest for international and Senegalese audiences that she signals suggest not that the artist-intellectual's *location* is the singularly important or even one of the most critical factors in determining a work's content or meaning. Rather, reader-spectator anxieties about religious, national, class, and sexual identities; levels of education; and wealth and power shape points of view and interpretation, for those within state borders and beyond them.

It is futile to "prescribe," as Said has written, appropriate "theoretical paradigms for contemporary criticism" (*World* 230), because there is an explosion of critical discourses and just as many ways of reading. But it seems clear that since the whole world has indeed become a shared stage, we must take into account especially the critical role of readers and spectators worldwide and their readerly transformations of texts. Biodun Jeyifo exemplifies this approach in an analysis of productions of Wole Soyinka's *The Road* in the Caribbean, India, and London. We must also put literary, film, and visual arts by Africans in dialogue with the work of artists from Asia, Europe, and the Americas. Such comparative study will require more—not less—"local" knowledge of these multiple places and will recognize both African specificities and Africa's presence in the world.

Notes

1. For economist Joseph Nye, *globalism* refers to "a world characterized by networks of connections that span multi-continental distances," while *globalization*, in contrast, "refers to the increase or decline in the degree of globalism. It focuses on the forces, the dynamism or speed of these changes." See Nye, "Globalism vs. Globalization," http://www.theglobalist.com/storyid.aspx?StoryId=2392.

2. See Achille Mbembe, *De la postcolonie, essai sur l'imagination politique dans l'Afrique contemporaine* (Paris: Karthala, 2000).

3. I am thinking, for example, of the development of the sonnet and romance under the aristocracy and the court in medieval and renaissance Europe. Similarly, standard accounts of the nineteenth-century novel maintain that it is the narrative form that corresponds to the rise of the European bourgeoisie, the Protestant work ethic, and a philosophical turn toward individual subjectivities, as outlined by Georg Lukacs, Ian Watt, and Michael McKeon. So, too, is realism seen as the narrative mode, par excellence, of decolonizing nationalism in Africa, while hyperrealism, magical realism, or animist realism would seem to characterize fictions of failed states and dictatorship in the age of neocolonialism and structural adjustment. See Edna

Aizenberg, Richard Bjornson, Brenda Cooper, and Harry Garuba for a discussion of these concepts in the context of Africa.

4. See Eve Eisenberg's unpublished manuscript, "'Hallowed' Writing and 'Verandized' Reading: Chimamanda Adichie's Challenge to African Authorial Personae," 2012.

5. Pascale Casanova extends this view and ties it to the market and cultural capital.

6. An interesting instance of the rejection of orthodoxy by those "staying at home" can be found in young anti-establishment Senegalese rappers. In the early 1990s, groups such as Positive Black Soul began to disassociate themselves from the tradition of the Sahelian bard (*djeli* in Wolof, *griot* in French), whom they saw as the historical ally of the political class (Henry).

7. See, for example, Baldwin's essays "Equal in Paris" and "Stranger in the Village," collected in *Notes of a Native Son,* and his short story "This Morning, This Evening, So Soon," in *Going to Meet the Man.*

8. See Gondola as well as the Baldwin short story and essay "Equal in Paris."

9. In this regard, Senegalese filmmaker Joseph Gaï Ramaka, who has lived abroad for most of the last two decades—mostly in Paris, now in New Orleans—gives a noteworthy response on this question in a 2002 interview. Asked about his permanent domicile, he replied, "I believe that I carry my permanent home inside me" (Maasilta 156). This was precisely the situation and mindset of African American artist-intellectuals who became expatriates in Paris in the early to mid-twentieth century.

Works Cited

Adesokan, Akin. *Postcolonial Artists and Global Aesthetics*. Bloomington: Indiana University Press, 2011.

Aizenberg, Edna. "*The Famished Road*: Magical Realism and the Search for Social Equity." *Yearbook of Comparative Literature* 43 (1995): 25–30.

Baldwin, James. *Going to Meet the Man*. New York: Dial Press, 1965.

———. *Notes of a Native Son*. Boston: Beacon Press, 1955.

Bjornson, Richard. Personal correspondence. Spring 1989.

Cassanova, Pascale. *The World Republic of Letters*. 1999. Translated by M. B. DeBevoise. Cambridge: Harvard University Press, 2004.

Cobham-Sander, Rhonda. "Forewords and Foreskins: The Author as Ethnographer in African Literature." In *The Locations and Dislocations of African Literature: A Dialogue between Humanities and Social Science Scholars,* edited by Eileen Julien and Biodun Jeyifo. Trenton: Africa World Press, forthcoming 2014.

Coly, Ayo. *The Pull of Postcolonial Nationhood: Gender and Migration in Francophone African Literatures*. Lanham, Md.: Lexington Books, 2010.

Cooper, Brenda. *Magical Realism in West African Fiction: Seeing with a Third Eye*. London: Routledge, 1998.

Garuba, Harry. "Explorations in Animist Materialism: Notes on Reading/Writing African Literature, Culture, and Society." *Public Culture* 15, no. 2 (2003): 261–85.

Gikandi, Simon. "African Literature and the Social Science Paradigm." In *The Locations and Dislocations of African Literature: A Dialogue between Humanities and Social Science Scholars,* edited by Eileen Julien and Biodun Jeyifo. Trenton: Africa World Press, forthcoming 2014.

Gondola, Didier. "'But I Ain't African, I'm American!'" In *Blackening Europe: The African American Presence,* edited by Heike Raphael-Hernandez, 201–15. New York: Routledge, 2004.

Henry, Jean-Christophe. "Senegal: The Hip-Hop Generation: 1988–2010." Master's thesis, Indiana University, 2012.

Jameson, Fredric. "Notes on Globalization as a Philosophical Issue." In *The Cultures of Globalization,* edited by Fredric Jameson and Masao Miyoshi, 54–77. Durham: Duke University Press, 1998.

Jeyifo, Biodun. "Whose Theatre? Whose Africa? Wole Soyinka's *The Road* on the Road." In *The Locations and Dislocations of African Literature: A Dialogue between Humanities and Social Science Scholars,* edited by Eileen Julien and Biodun Jeyifo. Trenton: Africa World Press, forthcoming 2014.

Julien, Eileen. "'Now You See It, Now You Don't': Josephine Baker's Films of the 1930s and the Question of Color." In *Black Europe and the African Diaspora,* edited by Darlene Clark Hine, Trica Danielle Keaton, and Stephen Small, 48–62. Champaign: University of Illinois Press, 2009.

———. "Of Colonial and Canonical Encounters: A Reciprocal Reading of *L'Immoraliste* and *Une vie de boy.*" In *Literary Theory and African Literature,* edited by J. Gugler, H.-J. Lusebrink, and J. Martini, 75–88. Hamburg: LIT Verlag, 1993.

———. "Towards New Readings of Neo-traditional Tales: Birago Diop through the Prism of the Local." In *The Locations and Dislocations of African Literature: A Dialogue between Humanities and Social Science Scholars,* edited by Eileen Julien and Biodun Jeyifo. Trenton: Africa World Press, forthcoming 2014.

Kennedy, Gerald. *Imagining Paris: Exile, Writing, and American Identity.* New Haven: Yale University Press, 1993.

Lukacs, Georg. *Theory of the Novel.* 1920. Translated by Anna Bostock. Cambridge: MIT Press, 1971.

Maasilta, Mari. *African Carmen: Transnational Cinema as an Arena for Cultural Contradictions.* Tampere, Finland: Tampere University Press, 2007.

McKeon, Michael. *Origins of the English Novel.* Baltimore: Johns Hopkins Press, 1987.

Said, Edward W. *Reflections on Exile and Other Essays.* Cambridge, Mass.: Harvard University Press, 2000.

———. *The World, the Text, and the Critic.* Cambridge, Mass.: Harvard University Press, 1983.

Sugnet, Charles J. "Dances with Wolofs." *Transition* 87 (2001): 138–59.

Watt, Ian. *The Rise of the Novel.* Berkeley: University of California Press, 1957.

Williams, Raymond. *The Politics of Modernism: Against the Conformists.* London: Verso, 1989.

2 African Writers Challenge Conventions of Postcolonial Literary History

Olabode Ibironke

> I refuse to be put in a Negro file for sociologists to come and examine me....
> I refuse to be put in a dossier.
>   Ezekiel Mphahlele, "On Negritude in Literature"

> Every great and original writer, in proportion as he is great and original, must himself create the taste by which he is to be relished.
>   William Wordsworth, "Letter to Lady Beaumont"

> [Nigerian] novels published in Britain are far more likely to use village settings than novels published in Nigeria, and this preference is holding steady....
> In fact, however, Nigerian novels are far more likely to feature traffic jams in Lagos, a boss's assaults on his secretary's virtue, or how urban youth confront temptations to easy money through crime. Political novels, on the other hand, are disproportionately more likely to be published in Nigeria than in Britain.
>   Wendy Griswold, "Nigeria, 1950–2000"

DAVID DAMROSCH ARGUES in *What Is World Literature?* that the term "world literature," coined by Goethe, was one that "crystallized both a literary perspective and a new cultural awareness, a sense of an arising global modernity" (1). It could be construed that Damrosch attempts to establish the criteria by which works enter into world literature. This essay addresses how in African postcolonial literary criticism, the vexed question of the thresholds of world literature takes off precisely from where the question of the thresholds of African literature ends: from the moment when African texts become, as Franco Moretti has argued with regard to Chinua Achebe's *Things Fall Apart,* "world texts." The chapter also examines the consequences of "world" and/or "global" as pedagogical and theoretical categories for grouping and orienting African and postcolonial literatures.

The concept of world literature developed by Damrosch encompasses "all literary works that circulate beyond their culture of origin, either in translation or in their original language. . . . In its most expansive sense, world literature could include any work that has ever reached beyond its home base. . . . [A] work only has an effective life as world literature whenever, and wherever, it is actively present within a literary system beyond that of its original culture" (4). In giving world literature a general theoretical orientation, Damrosch reproduces or replaces the first world–third world binary with an original–foreign culture binary. Some of the important questions that arise from this include: What is the notion of an original culture? Would original culture refer to the culture portrayed in the text, or to the cultural perspective from which texts look at the world? Would the original culture be the culture of the novel as a genre or that of the author? What would be the original culture of a multicultural text? The notion of "original culture" appears to be a back door to reaffirming the origin of literature in national culture so that the reading of world literature becomes the analysis not only of destinations but also of origins.

Damrosch's further attempt to clarify this concept does fall short and in fact complicates the cultural marker already laid down by introducing yet another marker, the linguistic: "a work enters into world literature by a double process: first by being read as literature; second, by circulating out into a broader world beyond its linguistic and cultural *point of origin.* A given work can enter into world literature and then fall out of it again if it shifts beyond a threshold point along either axis, the literary and the worldly" (6, my emphasis). This theory assumes a given threshold above or below which a text might be considered world literature. It also assumes that the boundaries of language and culture are coextensive and coterminous—that literatures could not cross linguistics boundaries without also crossing cultural boundaries and vice versa. The condition of the production of African literature, as would be discussed here, stems from that unusual experience that does not fit into the established modes of thinking about notions of world literature. This is probably why of all the texts of world literature examined by Damrosch, not a single one of them is by an African author! In fact, the chapter "English in the World," which could have opened up the whole question of postcolonial literature, focuses instead exclusively on Anglo-American and immigrant writers in England and the United States. Postcolonial and African literatures today, constituted by texts that are written in international languages and from a sense of a shared transnational, if not global, cultural experience, are given a passing glance in only one paragraph: "Intimately linked to translation as it is, world literature can also be found when a work circulates across cultural divides separating speakers of a single widespread language like Arabic, Spanish, or French. A Senegalese novel written in French can enter world literature in an effective sense when it is read in Paris, Quebec, and Martinique; translation is only a further stage in its worldly circulation" (212).

There is a preference, evidenced in the focus (or lack thereof) on it, for world literature in translation over postcolonial world literature. The former species of world literature, as Emily Apter's *Translation Zone* very transparently presents it, is the old comparative literature with a focus beyond European languages and literatures and with less of an emphasis on studying literature in its original language. One of the consequences of this recalibration is the tendency to compare and to cluster "minority literatures" and "third world" literatures together, especially along the lines of diaspora literatures. This territory has been effectively conceded by theorists of world literature despite the obvious fact that "the age of colonialism was characterized in large part by a process of linguistic and cultural unification" (Casanova 116), a fact that automatically eliminates the specificity of boundaries of linguistic and cultural distinctions that Damrosch seems to put down as marking the threshold of world literature. Indeed, it is the elimination of the mirror of the Other and of old boundaries in postcolonial literature that makes it difficult for conventional concepts of world literature to accommodate it and why theorists like Damrosch are not able to expand their theoretical base to include African literatures in English. The critique of this threshold or entry point by Rey Chow is succinct and summative in this regard: "The grid of intelligibility here is that of literature as understood in Europe, and historical variations are often conceived of in terms of other cultures' welcome entries into or becoming synthesized with the European tradition" (76).

To elaborate, Goethe's view of world literature could be argued to be a form of "imperial self-projection," to see itself reflected in the mirror of the vast landscape beyond, one in which a global perspective of imperium ascertains the constitution of literature from place to place and ascribes values as to what is a useful contribution and "of great value to us" (Damrosch 9). In Goethe's actual formulation, however, a less critical conclusion could be reached that defines world literature as literary texts that serve as "windows to foreign worlds." In this case, the literariness and value of these texts would still be based on the needs of the receiving culture, which would then require texts from abroad to be authentic representations of foreign cultural processes. The origin of world literature or global literature, as we also refer to it today, could be traced to these formulations that derive from Goethe. Among several early attempts in the last three decades to reconceptualize world literature has been Kristin Ross's essay "The World Literature and Cultural Studies Program." Ross argues that it is important to establish "a global comparative field" in order to "present both dominant and emergent cultures as dynamically related" (667). From this perspective, the "world" in world literature would mean "merely a relational way of thinking about global literature and culture" that does not isolate Europe and the United States. This in a sense would allow for comparison not based on a first or third world oppositionality but on a realization that "the conditions that prevail for the vast majority of people in the so-called underdeveloped world are now those of, becoming the lived experience of, the people inhabiting the world centers of capitalism" (675). Ross's attempt is to contravene the hierarchy and peripheral position of the non-Western implicit in the configurations of world literature courses in the West. However, her intervention relates to world literature within a pedagogical framework peculiar to the U.S. academy.

The time has come to salvage the Marxian concept of world literature from other dominant forms of world literature by emphasizing its basis in international languages and markets. This is to effectively enter a moment of African and postcolonial literature that moves away from a culture-based to a market-based theory of literature. The view of Karl Marx and Friedrich Engels in *The Communist Manifesto* that serves as a reference point for Damrosch presents a different perspective from Goethe's, which Damrosch surprisingly does not fully engage: "The bourgeoisie has through its exploitation of the world market given a cosmopolitan character to production and consumption in every country. . . . National one-sidedness and narrow-mindedness become more and more impossible, and from the numerous national and local literatures there arises a world literature" (qtd. in Damrosch 4). For Marx, world literature is coextensive with a world market precisely as a consequence of the cosmopolitan character of production and exchanges that world market engenders. The sense of a rising global modernity is perhaps what the notion of extroversion in African literary experience advanced by Eileen Julien attempts to capture. What Damrosch defines via Goethe as world literature as we know it is what I hereby challenge through an understanding of literary production derived from the connection of literature to global exchange/marketing systems. This process has, according to Marx, a universal application not peculiar to the African novel. Part of Marx's teleology was that at some point the global processes of production and consumption would override the protective barriers of nation-states so that literary sensibilities and forms would become more open and mutually permeable. Given that, unlike other aspects of Marxist theories, the weakness in this case lies not in the inevitability of the teleology. It is in the inability of his prognosis to anticipate the unequal spread of the effects of global market forces that a space for critique and further exploration presents itself.

Here, Jean-Luc Nancy's thoughts on globalization or the "world" are very useful in understanding the reciprocity between "world" and "art" and how literature can provide a template for sensing the world. According to Nancy, "It can be noted, provisionally, that it is no accident that art provides the most telling examples: a world perhaps always, at least potentially, shares the unity proper to the work of art" (42). He nonetheless further highlights Marx's world of production as a world outside of the world of representation, even if it retains features of representation. Julien's argument similarly conflates this "sense," which is not just ambience, of global modernity with a literary "sense" that foregrounds or stages an apparatus of perception in the African novel, that is, how the modern African writer through his or her fictional characters "takes the measure of his world" (694.) Julien's notion of world literature deploys the language of Marx but is ironically more in tune with Goethe's; it is a theory of literature anchored in the conflated sense of the world and of the literary that requires the sense of sense, the metasense, which is not a sense of one's self but a sense of one's world and a sense of one's place in that world as reflected in the sense of one's relations to all others, in the intersections of beings, becomings, and meanings. Nancy concludes in the chapter "Urbi et Orbi" that "the creation of meaning . . . requires its forms, its inventions of forms and the forms of its exchange. Worldhood, in this regard, is the form of forms that itself demands to be created, that is not only produced in the absence of any given, but held infinitely beyond any possible given: in a sense, then, it is never inscribed in a representation, and nonetheless always at work and in circulation in the forms that are being invented" (52). Thus, world literature as the metaform, the form of forms, is the literature of literatures that is "always at work and in circulation in the forms that are being invented." The worldhood of world literature is from the foregoing indissociable from exchange value amplified by the constellation of the modern epoch within metropolitan and postcolonial cities that attest to the essential global relation of material production and literary cultures. Indeed, it appears impossible to speak of literary culture outside of the political economy of modes of existence and production that are increasingly interlocking and intermediated. Taken to its conclusion, this logic implies that whenever one speaks of "world literature," one is necessarily speaking about cultural and aesthetic forms and effects of globalization.

As we shall see, this view differs from Goethe's conception of worldhood, world consciousness, and world literature. A postcolonial reappropriation of the Marxian appropriation of the term "world literature" challenges what Rey Chow describes as "the signature aspiration of 'more than one,' of going beyond restrictive national boundaries, that has been used to define 'world literature'" (71). The rationale and necessity for this challenge has been well interrogated by Chow: "Why is it such a good thing to transcend national boundaries? Is not such a transcending, which signifies a certain privilege of mobility, always part of a power dynamic, with those who can apparently transcend the boundaries . . . setting the criteria for evaluation?" (80). Instead, "world" in the postcolonial Marxian sense designates a field of practice similar to what Jean-François Lyotard in

The Postmodern Condition terms "the narrative 'posts'" (21) around which are organized the relations of different multinodal networks of production, circulation, review, and consumption of texts.

Eileen Julien replicates the threshold theory in an article titled "The Extroverted African Novel," published in Franco Moretti's 2006 edited volume on the novel, in which she could be taken to suggest that "the African novel" enters world literature through its extroversion. From this moment forward, I want to examine aspects of the material and transnational conditions of the production of African literature and how they ostensibly shape artistic forms in Africa in ways that cross the thresholds of world literatures. Julien states that "written by novelists who often enough are living beyond their countries' borders, they [African novels] all speak outward and represent locality to nonlocal others, be they expatriate communities abroad, other African nationals on the continent, Japanese, European, Brazilians or U.S. students" (684). The phrase "they all speak outward" is so strikingly familiar, and is similar to Fredric Jameson's claim that all third world literatures are necessarily national allegories, that it justifiably invites significant curiosity. However, Julien attempts to preempt such alignment of her proposition with that of Jameson by suggesting that "extroversion" in this instance is at least one step removed from the claim of "national allegory." She argues that "it is easy to see how on the basis of standard extroverted novels taken to represent the whole, Fredric Jameson could claim that the third-world text is always a national allegory" (696). The questions that I examine within the broader concerns and stakes of world literature today are how and when such attempts to "foreground this interactive, dialogic dimensions of African novels" (684) constellate into dominant modes of reading and a theoretical accent that force to the background the self-understanding and reflexivity that some argue are crucial to the internal properties of the novels—in other words, how extroversion constitutes, to use Derrida's concept, a form of formal fatality.

Julien sets out with a fascinating and attractive premise that the practice of novel writing in Africa rewrites the history of the novel in ways that question the Eurocentricity ingrained within accounts of the origin and rise of the novel as an exogenous form imported to Africa, which, like modernity, needs to be locally adopted and adapted. Julien pronounces: "The novel is world historical in its inception, not in its spread. The modern novel is creole, a literary 'forma franca' born from the contact of peoples and cultures. It may well be the first global cultural product" (675). In this instance, however, I side with Gayatri Chakravorty Spivak, who in her recent book *An Aesthetic Education in the Era of Globalization* cautions that "the claims made by the 'great non-western' civilizations, of historically having had words that could have, or did, serve the same, similar, or better functions than 'literature' [read novel] in the European context . . . are also not yet useful" (457). The immediate and more useful task for Spivak, here and now, would be to unpack the stakes and space of a world literature and consider why in the first instance the inquiry is necessary concerning the contradictory demands on the African novel, as Julien frames it, to be "'universal' but to display its 'difference'" (676), or why it has been the trend more recently in African literary criticism to explore the defining feature of the African novel "based neither on narrative mood, mode, nor authorial intention but on practices of production and reception governing African novels" (681). This trend, within which my own work has also been hitherto situated, requires some deconstruction for the simple reason that it has the reverse danger of grounding our understanding of the literature, and the writers, too, on the vagaries of remote conditions and publics.

There is no way around the necessity for an understanding of the immanence of the unique and dynamic and the synchronic and diachronic histories of the novel or the worldliness of the novel as a genre of world literature. Whether works circulate within closed or open, local or international, circuits or whether they possess facilities for circuit crossings ought to be an important aspect of theoretical determinations of generic developments and artistic forms. However, a binary emerges in this form of analysis that seeks to delineate and compare local and global forms. The question for Julien is no longer "What makes the novel African?" (676). Instead, in an attempt to specify the "defining [or primary] feature of what we have come to call 'the African novel'" (669), Julien asserts, "That division, I submit, between the works deemed to be 'novels' [and other "novelistic" narrative traditions in Africa] has been primarily a matter of which narratives have traveled or of what can be called their *extroversion*" (681). Compellingly, therefore, she tackles the Eurocentrism implicit in the narrative of the rise and spread of the novel, claiming for it a universal status at the same time that she gives us the basis for its distinctive orientation in Africa.

A brief genealogy of the concept of extroversion reveals its roots in theories of the socialization of form, as with the example of Biodun Jeyifo in his book on the Yoruba traveling theater, and in psychoanalysis, as with the example of Eric Neumann's *The Origin and History of Consciousness*. Extroversion becomes a way of theorizing globalization in ways that align spatial transitions with transformation in conditions and publics that impact modalities of writing and reading. Julien's extroverted novel is nothing other, it would seem, than the transference and translation of Jeyifo's logic and language of the traveling theater as an itinerant form onto the genre of the novel, making it into the traveling novel. Highlighting extroversion within Jeyifo's conception of the Yoruba traveling theater as a contextual frame for understanding its broad implications when applied to the African novel brings into focus significant issues implicated in the claims of the extroverted novel that we shall return to presently:

> As against, or indeed because of these conventions, the acting styles are generally improvisational, broad, extraverted: utterance, gesture and movement are generally magnified to the third or fourth power of the natural scale, and there is considerable latitude for the repetition of the routines and expres-

sions which delight the audience.... For the magnifications repetitions and heightening of word, action and gesture are scaled, not to some pre-existent, regulative norm of internal structural and stylistic consistency in "art," but to the mood and pitch of the characteristically liberal interventions of the audience. (Jeyifo 19–20)

In striving to rescue the African novel from its label of "ornamental detail" within the world historical genre as megaphone for locality, Julien's political economy of globalization, her "complex cultural ecology" (696), presents an unintended ironic view of the novel in Africa that is "scaled, not to some pre-existent, regulative norm of internal structural and stylistic consistency in 'art,' but to the mood and pitch of the characteristically liberal interventions of the [Western] audience." As we will soon discover, this is an echo of a persistent charge or "allegation" and dilemma that has dogged the debate on the African novel from its inception.

The second important issue generated as an effect of the notion of an extroverted novel is the implications, from the psychoanalytical point of view, concerning the development of personality. The extroverted novel not only resurrects the shadowy anthropological questions of the half-formed person or the drab overlay of reactive, social consciousness in African aesthetics; if indeed personality in psychoanalysis is the equivalent of characterization in literature, extroversion also implies a basic response mechanism as the ontological frame of the character in African fiction and of the African imagination. According to Neumann, among several twentieth-century theorists of the Jungian school of the evolution of consciousness, "the development of personality proceeds in three dimensions. The first is outward adaptation, to the world and things, otherwise known as extraversion; the second is inward adaptation, to the objective psyche and the archetypes, otherwise known as introversion. The third is centroversion, the self-formative or individuating tendency which proceeds within the psyche itself, independent of the other two attitudes and their development" (219). Thus, either the African novel is remotely conditioned such that it is primarily "scaled" to external modulation from the outside, or it fits within a broader developmental stage already part of the hierarchy of modernism and the standard discourse of the rise of the novel that Julien critiques. Because of the far-reaching surreptitious implications of these kinds of approaches to the study of African literature, it becomes pertinent to examine African writers' positions on these matters as a way of coming to a view that is informed about the depth and scope of the contestations.

It is worth noting that Julien's position is consistent with trends in the global production relations of twentieth-century literature described by Pascale Casanova in *The World Republic of Letters*: the conventional perception of postcolonial literary history is that African literature, much like literatures from ex-colonial territories, was produced for the most part overseas. Added to this is the view that the literature primarily addresses a Western audience precisely as a consequence of its being produced and canonized abroad. Theories of the African novel by other critics such as Wendy Griswold are examples of how this perception of the imperatives of production and canonization abroad has shaped understandings of aesthetic form and function in African literature.

African writers actively engaged the geopolitics of literary production in the light of their transformational agenda for culture and local politics in Africa, thereby (re)defining African literature in ways contrary to the theoretical thrusts of global production. In order to underscore this tension between the two determinative conditions of postcolonial cultural production, I will explore little-known but radical essays and interviews that demonstrate the commitment, however constrained, by these writers to "moving the center" of cultural production. The writers included in this study are Femi Osofisan, Wole Soyinka, Ngũgĩ wa Thiong'o, and Chinua Achebe.

"The condition of being turned outward" has also been described by other critics so that it has since become one of the myths of the African novel. Wendy Griswold formulates a form of double bind in her study of Nigerian literature: "Foreign readers of this Nigerian literature exhibit a preference for serious literature and for novels set in villages and in the past. Meanwhile, Nigerian authors are determined to write about contemporary social and political problems at home—to 'bear witness' to corruption, military arrogance, ethnic conflict, and the dislocations of urban life—but they have difficulty getting their books published and distributed within Nigeria" (529–30). One can rightly understand Griswold as attempting to describe the process of the invention of what some now refer to as global literature. I have chosen here the term "invention" long after it has become passé because it allows us to highlight an ironic and critical stance toward understandings of the production of African world literature that are presently in circulation. The historical center of colonial global production maintains and advances its centrality, and the margins are being pushed further off-limits, not only in the area of political economy but also in exigencies of the production of taste. A grand narrative is reinscribed through contemporary research and discourses of comparative literature that measure reflections of anthropological differences in creative and critical concerns as induced or inflected by geocultural structures and political economies. Julien, too, underscores the split between local and global circulatory determinants of literary form as a pervasive and overriding distinction when she states:

> This split between "the novel" and novels for local consumption is reproduced in the area of film and video as well. Birgit Meyer's recent research on Ghanaian videos indicates a comparable difference in focus between films that travel in international circuits and more cheaply produced and easily obtained

videos that, against the same setting of urban migration and abuses of power found in films on the international circuit, address daily preoccupations of local consumers. (688)

We have now entered unannounced, it would seem, an era of literary geodeterminism, similar to the geodeterminism of nineteenth-century cultural relativism; we are to believe that the writer is constrained overwhelmingly by forces from one direction: outside. The dilemma that Julien and Griswold present derives from realities of contemporary African experience but may not have taken adequately into full account writers' abilities to navigate through and around the horns of the false dilemma; after all, in the scene of writing, the waves of creativity are eternally washing against the levees of constraints. In the article "An Experience of Publishing in Africa," found in *The African Writer's Handbook*, Femi Osofisan, a foremost Nigerian playwright and the most published author within Nigeria after Cyprian Ekwensi, writes,

> I believe it is common knowledge now that I began as a member of a small group of aspirant writers who met in Ibadan in 1973, and decided for a number of reasons to publish and promote our works uniquely in Nigeria. We took this decision because first, we believed that writing had, or ought to have, a direct political purpose, and therefore that publishing outside the country would divert us from this noble purpose. The foreign publisher, we reasoned, would be obliged to ask the author to tame his or her work for foreign readers, whose concerns, naturally, would not be the same as those of our people. Already we felt that this kind of pressure was responsible for the orientation in African books of the time toward exoticism, for the preponderance of the theme of cultural alienation, rather than the more urgent problems of our society's political and economic development. We saw that our nation was under the threat of disintegration into a bloody civil war, through military coups d'etat, corrupt leadership, economic clientilism, and such woes; whereas our authors were writing about ethnographic customs and rituals, and being celebrated for these in the western presses. (32–33)

Although Osofisan confirms the dichotomy between Western preferences and the concerns or needs of his local Nigerian audience that Griswold elaborates, he nevertheless projects an acute sense of this problem and a well-developed means of engagement with it. It is the sense of how each writer in his or her own unique and self-conscious ways responds creatively to the multiple loci of material production and the multiplicity of pressures that he or she encounters in the course of writing and publishing within the network of transnational institutions that is missing in most of the current theories of cultural production in Africa.

In any case, both Osofisan and Griswold are treading very tenuous ground by suggesting that writers who eventually publish their works outside their countries of origin, abroad, may somehow have contorted themselves to suit the tastes, and prejudices, of a foreign audience or compromised something in their work that is so fundamental. In a consolatory afterword, Julien remarks, "What should be clear, however, is that extroverted African novels are not to be blamed for a supposed inauthenticity . . . ; this is their niche as a literary form" (696). This claim mirrors Damrosch and is a more progressive view than his; "as it moves into the sphere of world literature, far from inevitably suffering a loss of authenticity or essence, a work can gain in many ways" (Damrosch 6). Achebe and Soyinka write about traditional rituals but have also written about the same urgent sociopolitical and existential problems that Osofisan identifies as local concerns. Indeed, their so-called ritual works set in the past that were supposed to be ethnographies written solely as explanations or testimonials to a Western audience have been rightly interpreted as illuminating a single problematic: the present interruption of community in Africa due to British, and European, uninformed interferences and impositions. This line of thinking argues that Achebe was very much expressing his anxiety about the destabilizing effects of electoral manipulations orchestrated by the British that tilted the balance of power among the nationalities constituting Nigeria when he wrote about disintegration in *Things Fall Apart*. It is evident in this sense therefore that both concepts of "bearing witness" or "speaking outward" are problematic for the simple reason that they presuppose that the writer's function is to present the truth before the absent party whose judgment and ultimate intervention is required, despite not having been a part of a situation or an observer thereof.

There are differences in the politics of "bearing witness" and of being "turned outward." The politics of indictment, "that the world somewhere may know" enunciated by Dennis Brutus, served as a vehicle for generating awareness, galvanizing consensus and action against crimes against humanity and abuse of human rights. Extroversion, however, takes on a slightly different import, as Julien describes it: "The burden of extroversion in this novel [Boubacar Boris Diop's *The Knight and His Shadow*] derives from Khadidja's liminality and a sense of futility, the obligation to speak and to remain unheard, perhaps even uncertain of the value of the message. Whether writers the world over in the age of globalization recognize themselves as Khadidja before the door is debatable, but it is certain that Diop sees Khadidja and Latsoukabe as emblems of modern African Writers." The story of Khadidja is that of a woman "hired to go daily to a bourgeois home and speak to a figure behind the door, whom she never sees and who never responds to her . . . until she suspects that there is no one behind the door" (692). Julien's formulation suggests a choice of, and privileging of, apostrophe rather than soliloquy, monologue, or dialogue. A critique of the choice of apostrophe is fundamental to the overall question of extroversion. The monologue with the shadow here repeats the gestures of the monologue with the ghost of Freud that Derrida deconstructs in *Archive Fever*. The specter of the monologue marks—indeed, castrates or threatens to castrate—"writers world over in the age of globalization," for as Derrida aptly demonstrates, contrary to Julien's assumption, the shadow or "the phantom continues to speak. Perhaps he does not respond, but he speaks. A phantom speaks" (62). By addressing the phantom, therefore, one admits that there is the phantom "at the price of some still-inconceivable complication that may yet prove the other one, that is, the phantom, to be correct." Derrida suggests further that this monologue with the phantom can have only one consequence: the phantom would always have the last word: "And perhaps always the paternal phantom, that is, who is in a position to be correct, to be proven correct—and to have the last word" (39). A reorientation of African literary criticism that seeks to know the meaning and effect of the silence through which the absent "figure" behind the door responds to Khadidja inscribes her in what Derrida calls the "all powerful vulnerability" (39). Such an approach would be a criticism in which the specter of the West haunts African texts. It is in this sense that extroversion or the monologue with the phantom constitutes a "formal fatality" that sustains the perpetual erection of the rules of the phantom. Derrida concludes, "The phantom thus makes the law—even, and more than ever, when one contests him" (61).

The claim of a somewhat apostrophic character of the novel haunted by the specter of "what is assumed" to be European and global audiences and discourses clearly echoes the views of some of the writers themselves; while "bearing witness" appeals at once to the passive distance and objectivity of an observer, "speaking outward" is grounded in the intertextual references in African literary texts and the transnational conditions of their production and consumption. Within the postcolonial condition, where a writer chooses to publish—that is, if such a clear choice presents itself—or to whom he or she directs his or her work is always already structured by the tensions between transnational production and a transformational agenda that is always local and immediate. Our view of the publisher is that of an organizer of intellectual labor who enlists the expert opinion of academics/critics and writers to build up a list of publications through which, conceivably, his or her promotional activities have consequences for simultaneous capacity building in reading publics, the cultivation of social and aesthetic taste, and the requirements and expectations of literary culture as a whole. In other words, we might ask, are the attention-grabbing promotional devices deployed by international publishers instrumental to the creation of what Michael Warner calls publics and counterpublics on a global scale? Publicity creates added value that transforms signs and meanings so that it is possible in this context to speak of the instability of texts as they transition through systems of use and exchange, rather than of any inherent openness of African novels.

The tensions identified above in works of African writers require new paradigms not currently available in theories of world literature. The effects of extended and globalized channels of production and distribution are perceived a priori as impacting textuality and form without thorough explorations of the nature of such impact. A theory based on production and circulation must in essence be an economic theory or at least be informed by the political economy in which texts become objects of, and objects through, a multiple relay system of exchange. Transnationalism and world literature without a full consideration of the operations of the overall exchange system that enables and engenders circulation leave us with reductive formulations such as "turned outward" or "bearing witness."

Stephen Owen has described in contemporary European literature the effects of globalization similar to those Griswold and Julien observe in African literature: the globalization of knowledge production and the transformation of knowledge production in a globalized world market. This leads to us to a second significant proposition linked to extroversion that Julien makes: "I am arguing that what passes for the African novel is created by publishing, pedagogical and critical practices" (685). Although Julien here addresses the object of literature, what she and others may have failed to consider is how writers resisted, sometimes with a measure of success, the pressures brought on by these very transnational institutions and even manipulated them for their own purposes. This is why James Ngugi's case, as we shall come to see, is highly instructive because, more than any other African writer, with the possible exception of Ayi Kwei Armah, the whole notion of "moving the center" of cultural production has been his abiding obsession. But this obsession reinforces impressions of a deep crisis within the creative process prompted by the difficult challenges that African writers confront and goes to support that aspect of Julien's assertion that a number of factors (publishing house, place of publication, and so on) could indeed leave their marks on the very nature of writing itself. It is this possibility, as Achebe put it, of an "allegation" of being marked by those material and external factors that Soyinka perceived and challenged at the earliest beginnings of modern African literature but without prognosticating the ways in which the nature of African and indeed other literatures would be impacted by the global institutions of commerce and travel, cultural production, and intellectual exchanges.

Thus, the texts are not necessarily turned outward but are dispersed like echoes of words in the wind, like seeds, scattered abroad in the diasporic sense, in a world of diaspora, and growing in different ambiences and climates into significantly different phenomena. The inexorable global distribution of these texts arguably constitutes a textual traffic analogous to the patterns of twentieth-century colonial migrations of people from the Southern Hemisphere to the Northern. The organic theory of art that Chinua Achebe articulated and Nuruddin Farah's notion of art as an instrument of reconquest highlight a unique function that African writers, at least at the beginning of the modern period, placed on literary texts. Books travel farther than their authors without those authors having control over when, where, why, and how. Authors dissipate into books that occupy several places at the same time. As Brutus wrote in *Letters to Martha*, "No therapy, analyses deter my person's fission" (1). This illustrates an idea of a material link between text and author, between textuality and subjectivity, permitting us to insert the novel idea of textual diaspora, of texts as metonyms or fragments of symbolically dispersed subjectivities. The legitimacy of the adoption of the term "textual diaspora" in this instance is informed by James Clifford's argument that "the discourse of diaspora will necessarily be modified as it is translated and adopted.... [Thus] a polythetic field would seem most conducive to tracking (rather than policing) the contemporary range of diasporic forms" (250).

Although the theme of the fragmentation of the godhead, the splintering and coming to being of the pantheon of gods, was already one that Soyinka sounded in *Idanre*, and although disintegration served as Achebe's metaphor for the advent of modernity, the organic principle of art had remained integral to the dialectical tension in Achebe's works, and in the works of most other African writers, with a dialectical tension between centrifugal and centripetal forces, between organic unity and internal disintegration and anarchy. In some of his earliest statements on African literature, which seem to have been completely ignored in contemporary theories of African literary production, especially those that proceed with the premise of, or affirm, international readership as the primary readership of African literature, Achebe takes on the claims of extroversion in an attempt to establish what he considers to be the raison d'être of modern African literature.

In his first major collection of essays, *Morning Yet on Creation Day*, Achebe laments that "we have all got into the bad habit of regarding that slice of the globe [Europe and the West] as the whole thing" (32). The effect of this habit is the uncritical exportation of categories of discourses from the West, which he calls "norms of colonialist criticism," as universally valid categories. His case in point ironically includes the writer Ayi Kwei Armah, whom Achebe accuses of importing existentialism and modern despair to Ghana, where these are more reflective of the writer's alienation than of the "human condition," as if Achebe's own works had not signaled despair. "Ayi Kwei Armah imposes so much foreign metaphor on the sickness of Ghana that it ceases to be true" (34). Achebe describes this as "the predicament of the African writer in search of universality" (36) who ignores the "inescapable grammar of values" that problematizes universal language. Claiming an artistic vision that is "necessarily local and particular" (69), Achebe is thoroughly disturbed by the penchant to read universality into African texts or to eulogize African writers "for not writing for a local but a universal audience" (70), which he says causes him "great discomfort." He asks: "Am I being told for Christ's sake that before I write about any problem I must first verify whether they have it too in New York and London and Paris?" (69). Achebe's critique of universalism is important as it represents a precursor to the critique of globalism, which is, in fact, also a form of universalism. He repeats this criticism as late as in *Home and Exile,* where the focus is not on Armah but on Salman Rushdie. Rushdie's statement "literature has little or nothing to do with a writer's home address" (qtd. in Achebe, *Home* 105) draws the dividing line between his postal correspondence metaphor of the process of decolonization, which Achebe approves of, and Achebe's relentless sense of a special imperative, which he articulated very early on in his career: "This deadly obligation—deadly, that is, to universalistic pretentions—[is] to use his considerable talents in the service of a particular people and a particular place" (*Morning* 34).

Achebe also directly addressed the question of readership very early on; as already noted, this question was one of the very first raised in African literary criticism: for whom does the African novelist write? This is the problematic of Achebe's famous essay "The Novelist as Teacher," in *Morning Yet on Creation Day,* which to many announced Achebe's ideology and philosophy of art:

> I am assuming, of course, that our writer and his society live in the same place. I realize that a lot has been made of the allegation that African writers have to write for European and American readers because African readers, where they exist at all, are only interested in reading textbooks. I don't know if African writers always have a foreign audience in mind. What I do know is that they don't have to. At least I know I don't have to. Last year the pattern of sales of *Things Fall Apart* in the cheap paper back edition was as follows: about 800 copies in Britain; 20,000 in Nigeria; about 2,500 in all other places. The same pattern was true also of *No Longer at Ease.* (55–56)

Achebe presumed that it was sufficient and self-evident to simply display the sales records of his works in the 1965 article as a way of effectively countering what he deliberately characterizes as "the allegation." The persistence of "the allegation" from that time on and in recent scholarship either ignores the relevance of the statistical element that sales records introduce to the debate on readership or takes for granted that the place of publication—where the head offices of the publishing firms of African literature are physically located—is synonymous with the location of the primary reading public for the texts, just as Achebe took for granted at the time that the writer and his society occupy one and the same place, an assumption that would inform his organic theory of literary production expressly stated in the chapter "Publishing in Africa," found only in the U.S. edition of *Morning Yet on Creation Day.* Indeed, the call he makes to publishers to relocate to Africa if they are serious about publishing African literature is based on the philosophy that writing is a communion, an inaugural and spiritual force of community. He defines community in these terms: "What is this sense of community, then, this thing that breaks the laws of logic and is able to remain alive when every pointer is toward its death? I believe it is two things—the sense of a shared history and, even more important, of an assumed destiny. We are still backward enough to think we can go forward; old-fashioned enough to think we have a future" (88).

The word "sense" is crucial in this formulation if already-referenced thoughts of Nancy were to be any guide. Written decades before and almost in anticipation of postmodernism's challenge to progressivism and before the poststructuralist accent of dissolution we see in Nancy's *The Inoperative Community*, Achebe's view is that community, a writer's community, even in a global colonial context, cannot be formed exogenously without undergoing first the process of integration within the commune as perpetually reborn spirit and with the dynamics of the commune as a living organism. This conversion or centroversion, the integration of external and internal forces within the commanding frame of the history and destiny of the commune, could be argued as the opposite principle of extroversion. In order to crystallize this point, it would be necessary to cite Achebe's full articulation of how his theory of community must actively alter production relations and the practice and theory of African literature:

> If I am not entirely deluded in my vision of the writer and his community moved together by a common destiny, of the artist and his people in a dynamic, evolving relationship, then the go-between, the publisher, must operate in the same historic and social continuum. It stands to reason that he cannot play this role from London or Paris or New York.... But we have got to the point where out [sic] literature must grow out of the social dynamics of Africa. The role of the publisher as catalyst is no longer adequate—that of initiating and watching over a chemical reaction from a position of inviolability and emerging at the end of it all totally unchanged. What we need is an organic interaction of all three elements—writer, publisher and reader—in a continuing state of creative energy in which all three respond to the possibility and risks of change. (*Morning* 88–90)

The argument enunciated here by Achebe represents an aspect of African writers' challenge to conventions of global literature production that Stephen Owen claims has formed the basis of our current configuration and understanding of world literature. Research into the processes of publishing African literature, while it visibly demonstrates the global dimensions of production and distribution, does not support the assumptions of a primary audience located in the West, at least not for the major part of the twentieth century. James Currey, the African publisher at Heinemann, corroborates Achebe's claim:

> In the 1970s the spending on education was increasing in countries in Africa. The oil price crisis after the Arab-Israeli war hit many countries but the commodity price hike temporarily helped Nigeria with its oil, Zambia with its copper and Kenya with its coffee—"black gold," much of it smuggled across from Amin's Uganda. Telexes of orders yards long came in for container-loads

of books for Nigeria. The [African Writers] Series was riding on a high. There were piles of the orange books in university booksellers. Something like 80 percent of the books were sold in Africa, about 10 percent in Britain and 10 percent in North America. (581)

The work of Bernth Lindfors also attests to the overwhelming nature of the statistics, as does the work of other researchers. As I will argue later in this piece, even after the book famine in Africa in the 1980s, the so-called shift in readership to the West was not emphatic enough to warrant claims of centroversion. Aijaz Ahmad's criticism of Jameson and of the hypercanonization of Western literary criticism is central, a critique that dates back to G. N. Devi in what he calls the "artificial respiration" of global reputation that metropolitan criticism, through an assumption "about the universality of critical values" (60) and a post/neo-imperial authority, lends to Indian literature in English, which is less representative of Indian society, literature, or critical production as a whole.

The desire by writers for fame, perhaps, or simply to be heard beyond their immediate locality for any personal, cultural, political, or aesthetic reason by a wider world sometimes goes with the territory of writing and publishing; to make it into a special feature of African writing is to overstate the peculiarity of the phenomenon. If there are special contexts for the globalization of African writing, which arguably must have changed in their essential dynamics since the inception of modern African literature, the leitmotif of the South African poet Dennis Brutus, as earlier noted in his collection of poems *Letters to Martha*, spells out what should indeed become a point of reference for the world outreach dimension of African literature, which truly could be misrecognized as extroversion:

> These are not images to cheer you
> [. . .] rather I send you bits [. . .]
> partly to wrench some ease for my own mind.
> And partly that some world sometime may know. (20)

The desire to be heard internationally speaks to the dimension of activism in that moment of African history when struggle defined the writer, when to be a writer meant an engagement in the struggle of the people against human rights abuses and calling for universal outrage and action under what is clearly an appeal to the universal ideals of justice and the imperative of humanitarian intervention in conditions of state violence. What we refer to as protest literature may well be a tradition of writing that is thoroughly grounded in the universal notions of mutually dependent and validating rights and the moral obligation for the protection of those rights on a global scale.

Travel or the exigencies of translation, rather than turn the writer or the text outward, haunt both with a reverse separation anxiety, a "talented tenth" guilt that drives them inward even as they move into the "world" rooted in their devoted attention to the struggles of particular peoples and particular places. This deep consciousness of particularity could be found in Achebe's reminiscence in *Home and Exile* about his first trip to London: "Perhaps I could make a living here merchandizing my inchoate perceptions of the city fabricated in the smithy of a gigantic unfamiliarity. But could I see myself taking that as my life's work? I would rather be where I could see my work cut out for me, where I could tell what I was looking at. In other words my hometown. And from there I would visit again when I could, happily without the trepidation I had had when I had imagined London to be all-powerful" (103). Achebe is describing the same feelings that empowered the Negritude poets in Paris at the beginning of the twentieth century, feelings that African and African American returnees who fought in World War II no doubt had, a consciousness of a particular place transformed by travel in the world. This mode of being-in-the-world is not simply self-constellation or distillation but an acute sense of "worldliness," a worldly orientation of a particular sense that Carole Boyce Davies argues in her book *Black Women, Writing, and Identity* is a unique consequence of the "migrations of the subject." The worldly oriented selfhood, a selfhood based upon worldhood, the worldhood of African World literature as a product of dispersion and dissemination through international travel and marketing, is obviously quite different from extroversion or the notion of world literature that Goethe espoused.

There are several bases on which one could classify and theorize world/global literature. The criterion that is being spotlighted here is the market: the totality of that mechanism constituted by "the literary chit-chat which makes the reputations of poets boom and crash in an imaginary stock exchange" (qtd. in Berube 96). There is no telling the impact that marketing has on the contingencies of the reception of literature, but there is no doubt that that category of what we hereby call global literature is arguably more dependent on the "market" and susceptible to market conditions and manipulations. Texts could appeal to readers based on cultural and national affinities and intellectual and entertainment values, but faced with an inward-looking detached audience, an additional layer of challenge presents itself to the impresario of global literature to highlight or create yet some other value for the texts. This is not because the texts lack an intrinsic value in themselves but because the conditions of production and distribution invest them with their fair share of "the crisis of evaluation" in literary and cultural studies. As Michael Berube has noted on the subject of the crisis of evaluation, "Because we are uncertain . . . about what counts as good literary, critical, and theoretical work, it sometimes appears that the only criteria of evaluation we have are mercantile criteria: what's hot, what's selling, what's the newest latest" (97). Nowhere is the evaluation of literary texts based on "currency" and "market value" more than in the editorial practice of (international) publishers. The relationship between market value and literary value is a complex one that matters to different actors, but it has a very lasting effect on the destiny of a text and, indeed, on the definition of a whole culture and its literary enterprise. Berube's description is correct about the workings of the culture and knowledge industries, in their totality, and even with regard to the promotion of literary texts: this is reflected in the publisher's letter to Ngugi on the publication of his very first novel, *Weep Not Child* (1964): "It always happens with a novel that sales come within the first few months of publication, though with a novel like yours one expects a small but steady hard-cover sale to libraries, etc., for some time. We want the person who cannot afford the hard-cover, however, to be able to buy the paperback whilst the novel is still news."[1]

The reason to emphasize this point is to finally introduce the notion of division of labor into the discussion about audiences and markets. Creative writers expend themselves in their work, creating the taste by which they are to be relished, as Wordsworth's epigraph to this chapter argues. This is where their labor naturally ends or should end. They may choose to market themselves as a number of other writers do, but they do not have to do this or be as concerned about their audience as extroversion suggests. They may choose to move on after turning over their work to a publisher whose professional expertise is in marketing the work by finding a matching audience or even by creating a new one. Publishers clearly have a more important role than "tinkering." This is their role as entrepreneurs. Their genius, like that of a sailor, must manifest in their aptitude for a presumptive calculus of the currents and the tides of the marketplace and of cultural attitudes that could be activated or created or that could either propel or turn against a particular publication. This is the moment of decision that the publisher is always to encounter. It is the moment that determines the career of a publisher. The idea that audiences are not always preexistent but could be generated and manipulated by the genius of advertisement, promotion, and the like is at the heart of the publishing enterprise as such. Every writer could be advanced by the availability of a platform for the dissemination of his or her work, but to claim that writing is primarily a search for a platform is to misunderstand the workings of the mythical muse. We might remind ourselves at this point, therefore, that the reader, though equally indispensable as consummation and support, is secondary in the writing process, and attempts to make that which is intuitively secondary primary will always require more justification of what would be rightly judged as a basically ideological or theoretical postulation.

It is in the light of the foregoing that the role of the institutions of literature could be more usefully engaged. Let us recapitulate at the risk of sounding trivial: an increasing awareness of the inextricable connection between literature and the marketplace permeates contemporary understanding of African and postcolonial literatures. The reality that the publication of literature is often tied to the book's potential market and to economic conditions is amply illustrated in correspondences between publishers and writers. The example of the Nigeria writer

Obinkaram T. Echewa is particularly explicit, as we see in his response to Vicky Unwin, the publisher who replaced James Currey in 1985 at Heinemann: "I would like to know when exactly they plan to publish the book. If its publication is tied to an index of economic conditions in Nigeria, the book may not be published till end of this decade."[2] At this point, the aftershock of the collapse of the Nigerian stock exchange in 1982 was already being felt throughout the continent. Unwin was no longer looking for sales for new titles in Africa but in the trade market in the West: "I think it will help us a great deal to have the US rights as the USA is one of the key markets these days. The Nigerian market is only important to us in general backlist terms as it is the initial printruns that we are worried about. The main market for the first printing of any AWS [African Writers Series] now lies in the west."[3] Were Griswold and Julien addressing this post-1982 moment of African publishing, then? Perhaps! But even then, what remains a puzzle for most observers of the development of African literature is why, despite the rise of the black studies programs and the establishment of African studies centers in the United States, a viable market could not be found to sustain publications like the African Writers Series. The prospects of a Western audience interested in African writing that could match or surpass interest and sales in Africa, despite all the problems of illiteracy and economics, may have been overstated. Yet, these continue to inform theories of African literary production.

The question for the African writer then was how to "move the center," how to produce "national" literatures in a global world and yet retain their "ontological sovereignty" in the midst of the multiplicity of imperatives and complex apparatuses that mediate, transform, subvert, invert, and pre-situate the reception of those texts. The whole notion of "moving the center" of cultural production has been an obsession of Ngugi. But this obsession belies a crisis, which has been with him throughout his writing career, a crisis that also finds expression in his transformation from James Ngugi to Ngũgĩ wa Thiong'o:

> ALAN MARCUSON: Do you have plans for any other books?
>
> JAMES NGUGI: No plans at present ... You see, I have reached a point of crisis—I don't know whether it is worth any longer writing in the English language.
>
> MIKE GONZALEZ: Would this not be playing up to the narrow nationalism of which you said earlier you do not approve—would you not be limiting your audience?
>
> JAMES NGUGI: It is very difficult to say. I am very suspicious about writing about universal values. If there are universal values, they are always contained in the framework of social realities. And one important social reality in Africa is that 90 per cent of the people cannot read or speak English ... the problem is this—I know whom I write about, but whom do I write for?[4]

Marketability forms part of the consideration in the making of aesthetic choices, but it would be a non sequitur to claim that it primarily defines writing anywhere. The African writer like Ngugi is no longer concerned about writing for that generic generous and free spirit for whom Sartre says a writer writes. Ngugi is increasingly uncomfortable separating the object of his writing from the subject. He is like Achebe, guilt-driven in a sense of being obligated to be the writer of a particular people and a particular place. The challenge to conventions of world literature is thus the attempt to retain particularity even as they embrace global institutions and platforms. Ultimately, about a decade after the above interview, when Ngugi decided to write in Kikuyu, he was deliberately attempting to sidestep the whole debate about the invention of the African writer by Western production, audiences, and institutions. Regardless of whether they live at home or in exile abroad, these writers have always insisted that their dialogue, their deepest and bitter quarrel, is primarily with Africa and for an African audience. It is not the work of a critic to advocate that we take African writers simply at their words but that the orientation of critical thought that is based entirely on the controlling force of foreign preferences requires further considerations. It is also not to say that such analysis cannot find its validity elsewhere in the works of that group of cosmopolitan writers who equally insist that they address themselves primarily to anyone in the world, who are returning to the idea of writing for that generic, generous, and free spirit for whom Sartre says a writer writes.

Sartre's "For whom does one write?" is a complicated question that will continue to generate contradictory responses. Even when writers claim commitment to a transformational agenda, it is entirely possible that insights such as those offered by the prominent fiction publisher John St. John of Heinemann will perpetuate what Achebe calls the "allegation": "The prosperity of the firm depended as always very largely on books which, judged by strict literary canons, might with justification be classed as 'popular' or even 'second rate.' A high percentage of the reading and particularly borrowing public craved entertainment above all, even though the literary levels of such entertainment might vary. It is not to disparage them to say that many authors went out of their way to satisfy this demand" (355).

A new generation of writers is floating in the currents of globalization, which was already underway at the very inception of modern African literature. There is a sense in which Griswold and Julien can be said to be engaging the question of how we could assess the role and impact of the transnational institutions of literary production on the creation of literature and in setting the general direction of literary writing. This is perhaps a problem that is unique in intensity to the entire range of literature that has been described as transnational literature and that is inextricably linked to the processes of globalization and market economy.

It is clear that while Ngugi shares in the general crisis of consciousness that the expansion and globalization of the field of African literature caused when community and collectivities could no longer be determined a priori, or when community lost its particularity, he would altogether reject the argument for inclusion in comparative or world literature that Spivak advocates. As Rey Chow has observed, the very notion of comparative or world literature, while it might engender "the notion of parity—in the possibility of peer-like equality and mutuality . . . a degree of commonality and equivalence [equally engenders a] hierarchical formulation of comparison. . . . These other histories, cultures, and languages remain, by default, undifferentiated—and thus never genuinely on a par with Europe—within an ostensibly comparative framework" (72–73, 77).

Notes

1. See letter dated April 27, 1964, Heinemann Archive, University of Reading.
2. See "The Crippled Dancer" file in ibid.
3. Ibid., Vicky Unwin to Echewa, 1985, 54.
4. James Ngugi interview by Alan Marcuson, Mike Gonzalez, Sue Drake, and Dave Williams in *Union News*, Friday, November 18, 1966.

Works Cited

Achebe, Chinua. *Home and Exile*. New York: Anchor Books, 2001.
———. *Morning Yet on Creation Day: Essays*. New York: Anchor Books, 1976.
Apter, Emily S. *The Translation Zone: A New Comparative Literature*. Princeton: Princeton University Press, 2005.
Berube, Michael. "Peer Pressure: Literary and Cultural Studies in the Bear Market." In *The Institution of Literature*, edited by Jeffrey Williams, 95–110. New York: SUNY Press, 2002.
Brutus, Dennis. *Letters to Martha: And Other Poems from a South African Prison*. London: Heinemann Educational, 1968.
Casanova, Pascale. *The World Republic of Letters*. Translated by M. B. Debevoise. Cambridge, Mass.: Harvard University Press, 2007.
Chow, Rey. *The Age of the World Target: Self-Referentiality in War, Theory, and Comparative Work*. Durham: Duke University Press, 2006.
Clifford, James. *Routes: Travel and Translation in the Late Twentieth Century*. Cambridge, Mass.: Harvard University Press, 1997.
Currey, James. "Chinua Achebe, the African Writers Series and the Establishment of African Literature." *African Affairs* 102, no. 409 (October 2003): 575–85.
Damrosch, David. *What Is World Literature?* Princeton: Princeton University Press, 2003.
Davies, Carole Boyce. *Black Women, Writing, and Identity: Migrations of the Subject*. London: Routledge, 1994.
Derrida, Jacques. *Archive Fever: A Freudian Impression*. Chicago: University of Chicago Press, 1998.
Devi, G. N. "Commonwealth/New Literatures in a Small Corner of Asia." In *A Shaping of Connections: Commonwealth Literature Studies, Then and Now: Essays in Honour of A. N. Jeffares*,

edited by Hena Maes-Jelinek, Kirsten Holst Petersen, and Anna Rutherford, 63–68. Sydney, N.S.W.: Dangaroo Press, 1989.

Griswold, Wendy. *Bearing Witness: Readers, Writers, and the Novel in Nigeria*. Princeton: Princeton University Press, 2000.

———. "Nigeria, 1950–2000." In *The Novel: History, Geography, and Culture*, edited by Franco Moretti, 521–30. Princeton: Princeton University Press, 2007.

Heinemann Archive. University of Reading, Reading, UK.

Jeyifo, Biodun. *The Yoruba Popular Travelling Theatre of Nigeria*. Lagos: Department of Culture, Federal Ministry of Social Development, Youth, Sports and Culture, 1984.

Julien, Eileen. "The Extroverted African Novel." In *The Novel: History, Geography, and Culture*, edited by Franco Moretti, 667–700. Princeton: Princeton University Press, 2006.

Lyotard, Jean-François. *The Postmodern Condition: A Report on Knowledge*. Minneapolis: University of Minnesota Press, 1984.

Nancy, Jean-Luc. *The Sense of the World*. Minneapolis: University of Minnesota Press, 2008.

Neumann, Erich. *The Origins and History of Consciousness*. Princeton: Princeton University Press, 1995.

Osofisan, Femi. *The African Writer's Handbook*. Edited by James Gibbs and Jack Mapanje, with Flora Rees. Oxford: African Books Collective in Association with the Dag Hammarskjöld Foundation, 1999.

Owen, Stephen. "National Literatures in a Global World? Sometimes Maybe." In *Field Work Sites in Literary and Cultural Studies*, edited by Marjorie Garber, Paul B. Franklin, and Rebecca L. Walkowitz, 120–24. New York: Routledge, 1996.

Ross, Kristin. "The World Literature and Cultural Studies Program." *Critical Inquiry* 19 (1993): 666–76.

Spivak, Gayatri Chakravorty. *An Aesthetic Education in the Era of Globalization*. Cambridge, Mass.: Harvard University Press, 2012.

St. John, John. *William Heinemann: A Century of Publishing 1890–1990*. London: Heinemann, 1990.

Warner, Michael. "Publics and Counterpublics." *Public Culture* 141 (2002): 49–90.

3 Provocations
African Societies and Theories of Creativity
Moradewun Adejunmobi

My objective in this essay is to argue that cultural studies scholars who focus on Africa should give at least some of their attention to producing scholarship that also provides a wide-ranging justification for humanities research as occasion demands, and that deciders and the society at large must understand that the value of humanities scholarship can never be taken for granted anywhere in the world. What is more, the need to address why humanities scholarship matters becomes all the more urgent in times of economic and political uncertainty when the temptation is highest to curtail, underfund, and if possible eliminate institutions dedicated to humanities scholarship. I shall make the argument for attending to such justifications by way of a commentary on current trends in studies of African cultural production.[1]

In 2012, the Kenyan writer Binyavanga Wainaina took advantage of an address to the African Studies Association of the United Kingdom to counter Taiye Selasi's celebration of the "Afropolitan."[2] As far as reactions to Selasi's declaration go, Wainaina's riposte did not represent an isolated incident. Selasi's 2005 manifesto "went viral" in its initial instantiation in an online magazine and generated considerable commentary in blogs dedicated to discussion of African culture and identity. Similar controversies trail the multiple national affiliations attributed to authors like Teju Cole and Dinaw Mengestu, among others, and the claims to African identity made for Tope Folarin, winner of the 2013 Caine Prize for African Writing.[3] Discussions of this question in print and online indicate a return to prominence of a certain kind of debate among both writers and critics about the identity and location of the African writer. While such debates about identity will always be topical for African literature, given the current and historical location of many "African" writers outside Africa, I will argue that the main shortcoming of the critical approaches often used today for analyzing African cultural production is not a failure to ask what exactly constitutes "African" as opposed to, say, "Asian" or "Western" cultural production. More important, the critical approaches that we have embraced do not fully account for the relevance of our scholarship on expressive and representational practices to broader trends within African societies at this point in time. They fail to ask *what else* and *what more* artistic activity signifies when it occurs under the particular conditions that typify contemporary Africa, and *why* imaginative activity matters for societies facing apparently more pressing challenges, other than as a form of social commentary that we as scholars are called upon to elucidate.

My essay therefore seeks to address what I see as an important oversight in the current scholarship on African cultural production by considering in particular how critical approaches that engage with the problematic of creativity might contribute to making a case for the public relevance of humanities research. It will also suggest that a full accounting of the diverse ways in which both individual artists and societies in contemporary Africa currently respond to the challenge of creativity is not possible without paying greater attention to the role that technologies of mediation play in connecting individuals to networks of artists, critics, and publics with varying levels of toleration for different types of aesthetic, ideological, and instrumental departures from the norm.

Trends in Studies of African Cultural Production

In the early twenty-first century, two trends appear prominent in scholarly criticism and analysis of African cultural production: the highly theoretical, on the one hand, and the case study, on the other. I describe as "highly theoretical" the studies that focus on discussions of abstract principles pertaining to the production, circulation, and consumption of cultural artifacts, while the case studies provide an interpretation of singular works, singular artists, or singular cultural patterns. There are valid reasons for pursuing these familiar lines of inquiry. In their more extreme and increasingly widespread formulations, however, neither approach, as currently deployed in the study of African societies, sufficiently advances our understanding of African cultural production or adequately justifies the salience of its own subject matter. The problem is not so much with the practice of theory, or with embracing the case study, as it is with the absence of regularly updated reflection on the rationale for carrying out cultural studies work about any kind of society at this point in time.

The sophistication of many theoretically focused discussions of African cultural production is not in doubt. Increasingly, though, a growing number of such studies appear trapped in an endlessly self-reflexive exploration of theory for its own sake, frequently disconnected from a sustained engagement with the forms of cultural production that supposedly fall under their purview. Such studies do well at enlightening readers about the theories in question without necessarily helping readers make sense of the significance of either established trends or new developments in African cultural production for the society at large. Furthermore, Africanists who work in this area often tend to distinguish themselves more so as appliers of their preferred theories than as initiators of bold new directions that are as likely to be adopted by scholars working on cultural production in Africa as by scholars working on cultural production in other locations around the world.

Among humanists and social scientists in North American universities, the continuing preoccupation with theory, understood as a highly valued intellectual undertaking privileging decontextualization and abstraction over empirical and applied work, owes its history to a particular concatenation of political factors. Several scholars in David Szanton's edited volume *The Politics of Knowledge* retrace this history with respect to the tensions that emerged between area studies and the disciplines, between applied work and theory, following the end of the Cold War. In addition, the corporatization of universities and the decline in public funding for humanistic research have served only to further intensify these orientations in North American research universities, leading to a growing detachment of the most celebrated forms of literary and cultural scholarship from major or minor developments on the ground. Relatively few Africa-based scholars in the humanities are in a position to keep up with the theory-driven direction of research produced outside Africa, resulting in a further detachment of a different order between Africa-based scholarship and "African" cultural production. At the same time, the space and opportunities for a locally initiated and publicly minded practice of theorizing have narrowed considerably in many African universities since the end of the twentieth century.

At the other end of the research spectrum lie case studies or close readings of singular works, cultural patterns, and the activities of singular artists. Ironically enough and for entirely different reasons, decontextualization can also be a problem in many of these close readings of singular works and cultural patterns. By decontextualization here, I mean a failure to consider the extent to which specific structures of production, distribution, and reception inform our reception and perception of specific works of art, and art in general. While providing detailed characterizations of the chosen subject matter or constructing elaborate taxonomies based on the particular texts, studies that focus on close readings appear to take at face value the self-evident significance of the particular work, artist, or cultural pattern selected for study. Why these particular artists, works, or cultural patterns matter more than other artists, works, or cultural patterns is a question that is seldom addressed in great detail. The functions of singularity are taken for granted rather than interrogated. And the ramifications of the individual work for the larger context in which it circulates are not examined any more than the conceptions and functions of singularity in a particular time and place are explored in depth.

One may thus legitimately inquire what to make of instances of singularity where singularity is associated with an object, namely the literature book, which in some parts of Africa is gradually disappearing from view.[4] In the past few years, I have taken to traveling through different countries in West Africa and visiting as many bookstores as I can find in capital or major cities. Even in somewhat more prosperous countries like Ghana, where bookstores can be found, literature books represent only a small fraction of the volumes sold. To the extent that fiction is sold in these bookstores, popular fiction by Western authors usually outnumbers either popular or high literature by African authors. One of my more startling experiences a few years ago was in Porto Novo, the small city in Bénin that gave us Olympe Bhely-Quénum, the creative writer, and the famous philosopher Paulin Hountondji. A drive around town turned up two or three bookstores, really stationery stores with a few textbooks for sale. Only one of those stores had a copy each of two works by one of the famous native sons, but it did not carry any works by contemporary Béninois authors.[5] Bookstores in the larger city of Cotonou were only marginally better in their supply of works by older and contemporary Béninois authors.

By contrast, sheds and stores filled with racks of Nigerian films in Yoruba were relatively plentiful in Porto Novo. In short, imaginative narrative circulated in that community mainly in video film format rather than in print. The point here is not that commercial films were more popular than literature books, which is undoubtedly true almost everywhere in the world. Rather, what I seek to emphasize is the scarcity of the literature book in these contexts and how we as critics engage earlier and contemporary literary texts that are materially absent from the societies with which they are identified. A close reading of the two literary works available for sale would undoubtedly shed light on the author's concerns, which may in turn have differed from the concerns of other creative authors from the same country, without however enlightening us about the current sphere of influence and status of the kind of text that we call literature in the community with which the author is identified as an "African writer." We can applaud close readings of this sort while also deploring the absence of contextualization that enables us to measure the significance of the author's intervention and why that intervention might be perceived as original, novel, and provocative in a particular time and place.

There are probably more "bookstores" in Africa at the present time than there were fifty years ago, and there are undoubtedly more books in circulation.[6] But literature accounts for a shrinking proportion of those books, even when we factor in literature texts assigned for school. In the typical "bookstore" that does not specialize in stationery and textbooks in many African cities, one is more likely to come across motivational books, self-help books, religious texts, autobiographies, and a wide variety of magazines than to encounter literature books or even popular fiction. By contrast, works from the "African" literary canon are more prominent in bookstores located in international airports, five-star hotels, and bookstores catering to a very upscale clientele.[7] These literature books are no less African for being scarce, but their scarcity does endow them with a particular kind of value locally that does not extend to objects that are more widely represented in local markets. The singularity of the material object that is rare even within its own genus undoubtedly represents a peculiar type of singularity, as does the capital (cultural and financial) that accrues to such rare objects and their positioning within a fluid and capricious habitat open to both toleration and repudiation of different types of expressive practices.

Even as literature books have become scarce, a new generation of poets has emerged across the African continent since the beginning of the twenty-first century whose works represent another kind of material singularity. Many of these poets identify themselves as spoken-word artists or slam poets who have consciously elected to bypass print without necessarily claiming affiliation with "traditional" forms of orality. In other words, these poets are not "published" in the usual sense, though they publicize their work through live and digitally mediated performances, which they themselves post on You Tube. In some respects, they enjoy more connection to selected local audiences through their live performances in their country of residence than do published writers. In other respects, though, limited access to the Internet in their respective locations makes their work relatively inaccessible, even to those who might be interested, while generating its own form of singularity. A short and incomplete list of such poets might include names like Outspoken (Zimbabwe), Maya Wegerif (South Africa), Willpoète (Togo), Ceptik (Senegal), Aziz Siten'K (Mali), and Mbépongo Dédy Bilamba (DRC), among many others.[8] Yet other poets continue to disseminate their poetry mainly in print, while a few like Ghana's Kofi Anyidoho are experimenting with a combination of print and audio dissemination.[9] I must also add here that an alternative wave of literary activity is growing and circulating, sometimes through print periodicals but more frequently through online journals instead of books. But there are also instances of online fiction, like Mike Maphoto's *Diary of a Zulu Girl* in South Africa, which aspire to become books.[10] The work of characterizing the cultural politics of literary activity connected with these new portals and of assessing the production of and responses to singularity in these formats has barely begun.[11]

To be clear, then, what interests me here is not so much the proliferation of authors on the continent as the growing variety of technologies of mediation to which these authors now have recourse and the different types of singularity that attach to works "published" using an expanded range of technologies. The shrinking amount of space allocated to literature books in "bookstores" across many African countries is merely a symptom of the trend toward a diversification of the media of publication for a broad range of verbal arts and a gradual shift in the material conditions that enable different forms of creativity.[12] In these instances, do we presume singularity based on the rarity of the material object itself or based on additional elements that are not expressly identified? Does the relative rarity of the work of literature in print or of poetry on You Tube increase local perception of its purported singularity? How do local responses toward these relatively rare objects differ from responses to other practices and objects characterized as unusual and innovative? In short, what does recourse to an expanded range of media and technologies of mediation suggest about the ways in which African societies currently process opportunities for creativity and innovation?

Creativity

Beyond minor criticisms of trends in scholarship about African cultural production, there are to my mind more substantive issues to be dealt with in adjudging the relevance of our work as cultural studies scholars. Whether we hew to the more theoretical orientations or privilege the case study in discussions of African cultural production, there are fundamental questions that we have left unanswered. Beyond enabling the work of scholarship to survive and allowing us to extend a kind of intellectual practice that may have existed for centuries, of what benefit is our work to society at large? Especially in a time of economic crisis and social unease, why should anyone be employed to do the kind of work that we do? Those of us who work in public universities in and outside Africa have greater reason than most to ponder these questions. The questions pertain, not so much to the study of African rather than, say, of Western cultural production as to the mission of cultural studies work itself in the postindustrial, industrializing, and nonindustrializing societies of the world.

It is not enough at this time to make the shopworn claim that the humanities humanize us. News of the elimination of departments in allied disciplines such as foreign language study in some public and private colleges in the United States should alert us to the fact that university administrators—and worse still, the public at large in wealthier societies—are no longer persuaded by such arguments, nor do they believe in the intrinsic value of many kinds of humanistic teaching and research.[13] And even in those public universities where foreign language departments are not being culled, the elevation of academic units that generate multimillion-dollar research grants above departments whose briefs do not apparently extend beyond providing service courses for the undergraduate population speaks to the progressive devaluation of humanistic work in general, and in particular of literary and cultural studies.

As university scholars and often as publicly funded scholars, we have an obligation to the public and cannot simply disregard the public's disenchantment with advanced humanities education, even if we think this disenchantment is often misguided and misdirected. Saving our profession and our jobs at individual institutions cannot be the only or even the main reason why we must make a more credible case for the work that we do and the questions that we research. We cannot be satisfied only with doing well the work that we do. We will also and frequently need to explain why it is important to do the work that we do. It is in this light that I propose, for the contemporary time, a vigorous defense of the practice of, and therefore the study of, creativity, which might serve as one of several productive points of departure for public debate and dialogue about subjects of professional interest to scholars in cultural studies and the humanities broadly. We need to make the case that studying the arts, and the problematic of creativity writ large, matters for the future of any society. Societies that become more or less accommodating to different types of creativity can experience either ameliorating or debilitating consequences over the long term. When societies fail to understand and foster creativity, this failure has enduring repercussions. Education that does not acquaint students with varied instances of creativity, with the functions of creativity, and, perhaps more important, with the effects of different social, economic, and political arrangements on creativity in different spheres of human activity has not equipped its graduates to adequately plan for and invest in a society's future, whatever they may accomplish for themselves as individuals.

I do not mean to imply here that the study of expressive and representational practices is always fully congruent and coterminous with the study of creativity. Nor do I intend to offer an intangible something called "creativity" as a panacea for all the challenges facing any society. I would like to suggest that the study of creativity offers one of the more obvious avenues for justifying advanced scholarship about expressive and representational practices. I do make the claim that when societies respond to the possibility of creativity in different ways, they have different outcomes whose values we need not prejudge, since different forms of creativity can be beneficial, just as they can be destructive. I do suggest that some of the questions animating the research by cultural studies scholars qualify them to engage in an examination of the ramifications of different responses to the challenge of creativity for individual societies, given the fact that expressive and representational practices occupy an important stretch along the broad continuum of what all societies acknowledge as examples of creativity. It is as a particular type of expert on the subject of creativity and on the consequences of an openness toward or constraints on creativity in different spheres for individual societies that we should be making our stand as cultural studies scholars, especially in a time of economic crisis and social malaise. What good does it serve for us to study the arts and varied spheres of imaginative representation if we will not and cannot comment on the place and value of creativity for the societies whose cultures we study? The work we do matters, especially to the extent that it equips fellow citizens to better measure and weigh the significance of a broad spectrum of creativity for their own future.

It is in this respect that I use the word "provocations" in my essay title. If we think not only of art but also of the products of creativity more broadly as provocations to a society, then an assessment of the settings, forms, and purposes of such provocations within given societies should constitute a central concern in the critical approaches proposed by scholars whose research focuses on the arts and varied spheres of imaginative representation. The arts manifested in a wide range of expressive and representational practices constitute one of the few areas where a limited or expansive degree of provocation is tolerated in all societies. The arts represent the area of activity where children might first encounter an appreciation of and opportunity for provocation within the norms admitted in a given society. Art itself is not always provocative, and when that is the case, questions may arise about the creativity of the artist, about the opportunities available for provocation within the artist's society, and about whether the work in question deserves to be described as "art." Furthermore, while varied expressions of creativity always exist outside the arts as one of many spheres of human activity, it is almost always through contact with expressive and representational practices that we first acquire our sense of what creativity is and the range of provocations permitted within the settings where we happen to find ourselves.

We already know that there is no society bereft of creative individuals, but degrees of societal openness toward creativity vary with respect to time, place, and context. I use the term "provocation" here, therefore, in relation to a society's ability to tolerate and accommodate original thinking and original activity from its members. This is a subject that goes to the heart of the questions we examine and on which cultural studies scholars can and ought to speak with authority. We should make it our goal not only to characterize the forms of creativity that we associate with the arts but also to track the degrees of openness, or lack thereof, toward diverse provocations and the variables that inform these degrees of openness at different times and in different settings. As cultural studies scholars, we should dare to weigh the philosophical, cultural, and social implications of the experience of singularity in the particular settings that our research focuses on.

We will not always find a correlation between responses to the provocations that might be described as artistic and other kinds of provocations within the same society. Nor can we assume that openness to artistic provocations necessarily makes a society more prosperous, more egalitarian, or more democratic. Under certain conditions, some societies are tolerant of aesthetic provocations but not of ideological provocations, with particular consequences for other spheres of individual and social activity. Under a different set of conditions, some societies are tolerant of both aesthetic and ideological provocations with different consequences for many spheres of individual and social activity. Yet other societies place severe restrictions on both aesthetic and ideological provocations. Nonetheless, even those societies that restrict the opportunities for aesthetic and ideological provocation may require citizens to display ingenuity and creativity in strictly circumscribed spheres of professional activity, expressly classified as work rather than play. Such restraints on opportunities for play will in turn have adverse consequences for opportunities for creativity. It is a matter for cultural studies scholars to evaluate the manner in which and how far creativity can be deployed under conditions that limit opportunities for what might be described as fundamental expressions of creativity in varying degrees. Michael Keane deals with precisely this question in chronicling recent changes in China in his article "From Made in China to Created in China" and in his 2007 book on the same subject.

Creativity studies already exist, but mainly as a branch of disciplines in the social sciences, in particular management studies and psychology. Collections of articles on creativity have already been published but are often dominated by contributions from professors in psychology and management studies. With the exception of work being done on what is now described as the "creative industries," however, cultural studies scholars are largely absent from this emerging field of study. Like many literary and cultural critics, psychologists in this area are mostly interested in characterizing individual genius, since in popular thinking creativity tends to be associated with the individual rather than with the group, with special attention given to the psychology of the exceptionally gifted individual. Scholars in management studies, on the other hand, tend to concentrate on the qualities and practices that make for successful business undertakings and entrepreneurship. Publications by scholars in this field are much more likely to frequently invoke terms like "innovation," "novelty," and "invention." John Kao's *Innovation Nation* is a famous example of this kind of orientation, woven into a book designed to be highly accessible to readers outside an academic setting.[14]

Andy Pratt finds the term "innovation" broader than "creativity" for his investigations of cultural production and the contexts of cultural production in particular locations (120). To my mind, the word "innovation" is somewhat restrictive because it often implies an applied dimension that is not always germane to the kinds of activities and subjects examined in cultural studies. I therefore tend to agree with Keane, who considers "creativity" a more flexible concept than innovation (*Created* 12). And despite my reservations about advertising our work under the rubric of "innovation," I am, like Jing Wang, committed to scholarship in an area that we might think of as the "applied" and, one would hope, publicly minded humanities (10). The particular provocations we study will not always have an applied dimension to them, but our analysis of these provocations should weigh the implications of such provocations for the public at large. The point, in any case, is that a discussion is already underway about the very appropriateness of creativity as a subject of discussion and about what the term means when it comes to research agendas, specifically in cultural studies. Given these developments, one would hope for a consideration of the principles, ethics, and conditions of creativity to occupy a more prominent place in both the theorizing and case studies elaborated by cultural studies scholars, and especially those working on African cultural production. In my opinion, "creativity" and other related terms would appear to provide a framework large enough to encompass the variety of questions and materials that cultural studies scholars are called upon to address in their research. Furthermore, debates around the problematic of creativity have the advantage of offering a platform for dialogue with a skeptical public that is often called upon to subsidize if not support the work done by cultural studies and other humanities scholars.

The distinctions and overlaps between provocation, expressiveness, and creativity require more clarification than I can provide here. Creativity involves originality, and originality is always provocative. But one can be expressive without being provocative, and one can be provocative without being expressive. The violence visited upon women in the war unfolding in the eastern Democratic Republic of the Congo in the early twenty-first century is provocative without being expressive. The surge of kidnappings unleashed on civilians in parts of southeastern Nigeria in the first decade of the twenty-first century is provocative without being expressive. Often decried, such provocations call for a wider discussion about the nature of provocation itself and when provocation is destructive rather than regenerative. Then there are provocations that contribute to our appreciation of the very idea of creativity and that are highly valued precisely as expressions of creativity. Other provocations have an applied dimension and are potentially regenerative in that they offer solutions to challenging problems or challenge the solutions already in place. Some provocations challenge established norms without yet having an applied dimension. Still other provocations are entirely self-serving, nihilistic, and regressive. The seemingly endless violence that we see in the eastern DRC and in parts of Nigeria fall into this category. Societies clearly experience different kinds of provocations, and cultural studies scholars should be at the forefront of differentiating between these varieties of provocations and what they signify for individual societies. Even more important, we should lead the charge in studying how societies respond to these varied provocations, whether they are expressive, regenerative, or regressive.

Assessing how African societies respond to varied provocations associated with literature and the verbal arts broadly in the twenty-first century will require us to extend greater attention to the specific technologies of mediation embraced by individual author-performer-composers[15] as well as to the particular critical and artistic networks through which their works circulate. In many African settings in the early twenty-first century, new media are redefining what creativity itself is. It comes as no surprise then that there are some instances now where it is the very fact of using new media rather than the content conveyed that counts as provocative.[16] The expanded or diminished access that individuals have to changing media and changing portals likewise affects local and diasporic perceptions of what constitutes imaginativeness, creativity, and provocation.

The fact that as many self-identified African author-performer-composers currently reside outside Africa as on the continent itself[17] further complicates the challenge of determining the extent to which their work will be considered provocative by diverse constituencies located around the world that may or may not claim to share a common identity with the artist.[18] Some critical and artistic networks are highly localized, whether they emanate from within or outside Africa. Others straddle entire regions within Africa and cut across continents. Growing access to digital media and the Internet means that author-composers whose works have not yet appeared in print can now seek validation through networks that are not completely localized to their country of residence. The performance poets resident in Africa and who post their performances on You Tube have made considerable use of these new opportunities. Short story writers and authors of serialized narratives who "publish" their stories exclusively in Internet-based literary magazines represent another group of verbal artists seeking validation in and beyond local artistic and critical networks.[19]

And even when we think of print-based publication, the range of publishers that has now replaced the once-dominant African Writers Series from Heinemann Books or Présence Africaine both on the continent and beyond connects authors to a variety of artistic and critical networks that sometimes intersect with each other and at other times advance along parallel pathways. Clearly, publishers like Ayebia Clarke (based in the United Kingdom), Cassava Republic (based in Nigeria), and Nouvelles éditions Ivoiriennes (based in Côte d'Ivoire), among others, circulate books published with them to a variety of artistic and critical networks that do not always overlap.[20] Thus, the artistic and critical networks through which the print texts of authors like Teju Cole, Abdourahman Waberi, Aminatta Forna, and Alain Mabanckou circulate may differ somewhat from those in which the print texts of authors like Lola Shoneyin, Binyavanga Wainaina, Kofi Anyidoho, and Regina Yaou circulate.[21] This isn't simply a question of location of the author, however: Kofi Anyidoho resides in Ghana but has been published most recently by Ayebia Clarke in the United Kingdom. Likewise, we are seeing Nigerian writers who are partly or mainly resident outside Africa arrange for works previously published in Europe or North America to be sold within Nigeria under the imprint of such local publishers as Farafina or Cassava Republic.[22]

If the location of the African author and artist does not necessarily preclude print publication and performance, inside or outside Africa, that of the network of readers and critics does matter for an appreciation of the work of art, especially to the extent that particular debates about art, culture, and politics in such locations inform reception and assessment of the artistic work. The relative disjuncture between particular networks of readers and critics in one location and debates about art, culture, and politics as well as the range of representational and expressive activity in other locations will make itself felt in the configuration and ideological tilt of responses to the work of art. Given the fact that the most prestigious forms of validation for works of African high culture often emanate from networks of readers and critics localized outside Africa,[23] artists themselves may be tempted to foreground aesthetic and ideological provocations that are more meaningful for readers and critics outside the continent than for those within the continent.[24] However, the frequently extraverted orientation of African high culture can and does also yield the opposite result, providing cover for an artist to embrace views considered ideologically contrarian and provocative by the general public within Africa but unexceptional for networks of critics and artists localized outside Africa.[25] To the extent that such works of art provide provocations that boldly challenge local norms, they represent in my mind the best of what art can offer in any society. But even when the work of art does not elaborate an oppositional stance with respect to local norms, scholarly interpretation of the work can evaluate prevailing provocations and initiate further conversation about the advantages and disadvantages of accommodating different types of provocations. It can also present an occasion for debating the wider social consequences of limiting or expanding the scope for provocation in that location—not just on the arts but on society at large.

Creative Industries and the African Setting

It is in this respect that an examination of the interfaces between the arts, various culture industries, and other forms of creativity becomes especially relevant. For this reason, the work being done on the creative industries comes closest to providing a framework for addressing the particular questions about creativity that interest me, without fully subsuming the entire range of research possible in that field. The term "creative industries" itself, and especially its relationship to an older term, "cultural industries," continues to be subject to debate (Wang 11; Keane, *Created*). In the meantime, the cognomen has been embraced with enthusiasm by at least a handful of institutions, as in the case of the Queensland University of Technology in Australia, which reportedly renamed its School of Arts and Humanities the School of Creative Industries, and by some government sectors in the United Kingdom and more recently in China that have made development of "creative industries" a part of their policy objectives for the near and short term (Keane, *Created* 154).

Some scholars question the degree to which the creative industries paradigm is even applicable to developments in Africa. Ramon Lobato has recently argued, for example, that the phenomenon of Nollywood should inspire further debate on the relevance of the creative industries paradigm for developing countries, given the fact that the Nigerian film industry is not an outgrowth of the kinds of elements that are usually associated with the creative industries. In postindustrial and newly industrializing societies, the expansion of creative industries has often been linked to a deliberate orientation on the part of local authorities toward building a knowledge-based economy with clear rules governing intellectual property rights.[26] With Nollywood, however, we see the emergence of a thriving commercial enterprise based in part on the creative talents of scriptwriters, directors, actors, and many others in a setting (Nigeria) where the local authorities appear substantially disengaged from the very notion of a knowledge-based economy,[27] even if it so happens that highly educated professionals occupy prominent positions in the local bureaucracy.[28]

Rather than simply dismiss the creative industries agenda for its own shortcomings, I would argue instead that we—meaning here cultural studies scholars who do research on Africa—should work to expand the scope of subjects to be investigated under the caption of creativity studies while addressing the criticisms made thus far of this area of study. Thus, for example, the kind of commercialized activity that we find in Nollywood and many of the other culture-themed businesses relying on new media in urban African settings provide useful pointers on what is possible under the conditions that we currently observe in many locations in Africa. Nollywood is particularly interesting as an example of a culture-themed business that has given a boost to other culture-themed, media-dependent businesses across Africa. Similar and smaller commercial film industries have since emerged in several other African countries, including Kenya, Tanzania, the DRC, Liberia, Sierra Leone, Bénin, and Mali, to name just a few. African developers of mobile phone "apps" who develop apps for entertainment also frequently turn to culture and distinctive African experiences for content. For example, a Nigerian company, Fans Connect Online Limited, has developed an app for Android-based phones called "Afrinolly" that enables Nollywood fans to watch movie trailers, music videos, and comedy from Nigeria on their phones.[29] At the time of writing, another Nigerian company, Maliyo, was developing video games for cell phones and drawing its material from distinctive and sometimes socially disruptive experiences in Nigeria.[30]

Furthermore, once we acknowledge the burgeoning size of Nollywood as one example both culturally and financially, we might conclude that these kinds of culture-themed businesses[31] represent the most hopeful revenue opportunity for a part of the world where Fordist production has not generally flourished, given conditions that are far from favorable to economies of scale. These culture-themed businesses already represent one of the few areas where value-added production is even locally sustainable. Culture might just be the one thing that Africa has to sell when extractive resources run out and industrialization fails to materialize. The increasing commercialization of culture for sale on local and global markets will have an impact on local responses to expressive and representational practices that deliberately eschew commercial priorities. But what we also have in commercialized African culture of the kind represented by Nollywood is a type of productivity that owes its emergence to a context characterized by uneven connections with the global economy, limited infrastructure, weak institutions of governance, and widespread disregard for intellectual property rights.

The prospects for commercialization of expressions of creativity under these circumstances impinge powerfully on the contexts for production of other art forms and the extent to which and ways in which they can be perceived as provocative.[32] And just as important, the growing prospects for the commercialization of culture raise questions about the emerging intersection between the arts, entertainment, social action, and policy making for a range of issues. As is already becoming evident elsewhere in the world and is confirmed by Jeremy Rifkin and Arjo Klammer, societies begin to organize and function very differently when creativity is increasingly and entirely subsumed under the weight of commercial considerations and when the majority of human interactions entail either vaguely or clearly defined commercial obligations.

Wherever creativity can be commercialized in contemporary African settings, it already has high social (and financial) value. Commercialized creativity is not, however, the only form of creativity that currently has social value around Africa. Beyond the sphere of commercial enterprise, aesthetic provocations are widely celebrated and encouraged, provided the practice of provocation is not deployed with the aim of challenging the diverse poles of authority within the society. The many provocations unleashed by men and women occupying high political office are a case in point. Popular expressions of creativity, too, are often provocative without being polemical, especially since the authorities may themselves legitimate certain forms of display and excess. Nollywood films illustrate this trend perfectly with story lines designed to be shocking and provocative without being polemical or calling into question the socially prevalent hierarchies. No matter how egregious the provocation that drives the story forward, narrative resolution almost always involves a reinstatement of the prevailing social norms.

The sphere of expressive activity largely tends to be so expansive and prominent that it almost seems to crowd out the possibilities for provocation in other spheres of activity, where tolerance for provocation, on the one hand, and social support for provocation, on the other, are strictly limited. There might in fact be an inverse correlation between the degree to which these societies encourage aesthetic provocation and the degree to which they approve and provide support for other kinds of provocations. Or to put it another way, there are settings where aesthetic provocations substitute for instrumental provocations and where aesthetic excess is as much a property of the collective as it is an attribute of the individual. The obverse would likewise appear to be true. In other words, there might be other settings where instrumental provocations largely substitute for aesthetic provocations.[33]

In Africa, aesthetic provocations that are explicitly noncommercial in orientation tend to draw support from major institutions more often located abroad than at home.[34] Socially conscious performance poets and musicians increasingly use the Internet to attract endorsement from and tap into such sympathetic networks of critics and audiences located outside Africa while burnishing their credentials with the very same audiences for whom Africa-based artists perform.[35] Within Africa itself, however, older and/or wealthier individuals continue to serve as patrons for some popular aesthetic provocations. Such patrons are less likely to provide sustained funding for instrumental innovation than they are to support aesthetic innovation.[36] Meanwhile, online literary journals founded by individuals resident in Africa are fostering an intellectual and artistic community that is already proving hospitable to other types of debate and experimentation and that might in due course become a source of validation for an expanded arena of provocations. But, as indicated earlier, these technologies are just as amenable to the production of narratives of conformity. Both Nollywood and Mike Maphoto's online narratives referenced earlier attest to this.

The deliberate intervention of politically oriented rap artists and musicians in the political campaign during Senegalese presidential elections since the late 1990s, however, were experienced as provocative, especially given a well-established practice of artistic support for so-called big men by more traditional praise singers and recently by pop music performers.[37] Across the continent, a number of socially and politically conscious musicians have chosen to be provocative in this way rather than to pursue the types of expressiveness associated with popular music where content and style are overwhelmingly shaped by commercial considerations.[38] It is our task as cultural studies scholars to document these forms of creativity, to explain the conditions under which they emerge and thrive, and to weigh the extent to which they might constitute socially significant provocations in a given time and place.

But, as mentioned earlier, nihilistic provocations are also proliferating, usually perpetuated by male youth with minimal opportunities for social advancement. Where and when it is available, formal education is about submission to appropriate forms of regimentation and not about learning to foster, formulate, and respond to provocative questions. Perhaps more so than in other places in the world, creativity as such is envisioned here mainly as an individual accomplishment that thrives without the support of institutions and infrastructure. In these contexts, creativity is something to be unleashed by the individual on behalf of the individual. The notion that expressiveness should be specifically fostered and supported for the common good has very little purchase here. Innovation is much less appreciated than novelty, especially in those instances where innovation unambiguously threatens established hierarchies. Nonetheless, particular forms of creativity and occasionally provocation emerge under these potentially unfavorable conditions. The significant growth in the development of mobile phone apps by individuals based especially in Kenya, South Africa, and Nigeria points to a form of creativity that is appreciated but not always experienced as provocative.[39]

Theory and Practice

There is a sense in which we cannot claim to have full understanding of a phenomenon in any discipline as long as we are unable to identify and distill or theorize the general principles responsible for the patterns we encounter in the subject of study. Thus, the most comprehensive insights into African cultural production can be derived only from a rigorous practice of theorizing. We likewise stand to benefit from case study–oriented work that sheds light on what Akhil Gupta describes as "structures of feeling that bind space, time, and memory in the production of location" (197). Here too, though, attention to the structures that produce location should ideally be accompanied by discussion of local responses to a variety of provocations present in diverse locations, as well as to the very notion of provocation itself under these changing conditions and circumstances.

By changing conditions and circumstances, I do not mean only such wide-ranging political and economic arrangements as we might associate with, for instance, colonialism or neo-liberalism; I refer here in addition to the political and material conditions in which particular expressions of creativity subsist. In the study of contemporary African cultural production, a partial list of such important conditions would identify, among others, the degrees of censorship afforded by assorted political dispositions, the potential impact of and opportunities for commercialization of creativity, and the operations of technologies of mediation and distribution. Given recent developments in African cultural production mentioned earlier, I recommend special attention to the role of technologies of mediation in any study of the current state of provocation within the arts on and from the African continent.

For some African constituencies today, politically themed blogs and websites are considerably more provocative and outrageous in an ideological sense than many literature texts associated with the same constituencies. To take one example, the continued existence of Nigeria as a single country is a settled question in the literary works by Nigerian authors, even when they come from the region that led the move toward secession, resulting in the civil war that lasted from 1968 to 1972. Chimamanda Ngozi Adichie's *Half of a Yellow Sun* is a famous and recent example. Blogs by Nigerians, however, dare to go where Nigerian politicians and even creative writers decline to venture in calling for secession and a breakup of the country.[40] Though the networks of audiences and critics for literature texts localized in different African countries tend to be more sympathetic to nationalist and nativist causes than networks of audiences and critics located outside Africa, these Africa-based networks are sufficiently diverse to make the expression of certain kinds of views unlikely in literature texts, especially when those texts are published by well-established local publishers seeking to sell books to a politically heterogeneous audience within a nation or region. By contrast, website managers and owners of blogs who do not share the same overhead costs or need for profit can afford to broadcast their more controversial opinions on a wide range of subjects. It is in this respect that we should pay attention to what various technologies of mediation enable or discourage when it comes to a variety of provocations.

The degree to which certain expressions of creativity can be appropriated for political purposes or commercialized for individual or corporate benefit often depends on the relative cost of access to different kinds of media. The cost of access will in turn inform the extent to which such expressions of creativity can be apprehended as provocations. The tension between commercialization and a commitment to socially conscious art is perhaps most obvious in the case of musicians who rarely have access to the kinds of grants and fellowships that are sometimes available to more famous writers and visual artists.[41] In this connection, Tyler Cowen's observation that falling costs tend to move art away from more popular taste and thus commercial considerations is especially relevant (20).[42] There are undoubtedly many considerations at work when the would-be provocateur employs distributive models accessible to relatively poor individuals rather than to media owned by corporate entities[43] and when the would-be provocateur turns to "art" rather than to some other channel of expression for his or her own construction of provocation. As cultural studies scholars, we might dare to speculate on what these considerations mean for a community's ability to generate and withstand provocations in other areas of activity.

In that vein, and speculating therefore on the significance of recent developments in African literature and the verbal arts broadly, I would suggest that thus far, the gravitation toward digitally mediated performance by some African creative authors has yet to shake the prevailing inclination within many African societies to alternatively celebrate or tolerate aesthetic provocations. At the same time, local authorities in these societies often provide minimal support for instrumental provocation and remain fairly intolerant of political and social provocations that challenge established hierarchies, especially when such provocations are mediated by locally important cultural brokers.[44] Aesthetic provocations associated with commercialized or politically significant expressions of creativity are acceptable to the extent that ideological conflicts within the work are frequently resolved in favor of the prevailing social order. As a rule, the ideological provocations offered by art and other noncommodifed forms of creativity tend to have relatively limited reach locally, even in countries with some semblance of freedom of speech, given difficulties of access—as manifested, for example, in the scarcity of print literature mentioned earlier. Ideological provocations in art are thus more likely to be recognized and experienced as provocative abroad rather than in the polity with which the artist is identified. The continuing tendency among some critics (mainly local and sometimes transnational) to place assessment of the artist's conformity to the particulars of circumscribed identities above other considerations further deflects attention from an engagement with the character of provocation revealed in the work, as well as from the social value and ramifications of entertaining such provocations in a particular time and place.

Artists subscribing to an agenda of opposition find themselves carefully negotiating the balance between radical politics for the benefit of artistic networks outside Africa and radical politics for local consumption. The most celebrated print texts now capture the ideological caution and agnosticism of a professional class of critics sometimes locally and especially outside Africa. In African high culture, a willingness either to challenge gender and sexual norms or to conflate the sexual and the political continues to be a form of provocation with resonance for artistic and intellectual networks located both within and outside Africa, but which also often triggers popular responses beyond those networks within Africa itself. Local responses to paintings and cartoons of President Jacob Zuma of South Africa in 2012 represent a well-publicized case in point.[45] Even and especially when the work of art does not lend itself to such popular reaction, there is room for a broader discussion regarding the place of and opportunities for provocation in society. Situating the work of art within wide-ranging deliberations involving evaluation of varied provocations in themselves and of the accommodations for different types of provocations is as good a place as any to start making a case for the public relevance of humanities scholarship.

To recapitulate, then, I am not proposing that our theorizing only be related to case studies and that our case studies pay attention to theorizing, which would be the hallmark of all great scholarship. Nor am I asking for all our scholarship to be immediately accessible to nonspecialists. What I am requesting is for cultural studies scholars to consistently make addressing questions of potential value to the public at least one of the many strands of their research agenda and to approach both theory and case study from this perspective as often as opportunity allows. It is in this spirit that I propose a research agenda that can feed public discourse on creativity understood as provocation. In making this proposal, I do not wish to stifle debate or foreclose arguments about acceptable subjects of discussion for cultural studies work. Rather, I wish to open up a space for questioning what, if anything, cultural studies scholars owe the public. I would contend that from time to time, cultural studies scholarship ought to intersect with public concerns and thus retain public relevance. And whenever it does, the problematic of creativity understood as provocation ought to be one of the subjects of discussion. What is at stake in cultural studies work is not just our understanding of the forms and contexts for the production, circulation, and consumption of expressive and representational activity but also our ability to contribute to both scholarly and public debate around creativity understood as provocation. If what we seek to provide is a justification for humanities scholarship in a given time and place, then surely we ought to be considering this question among others: What are the forms, settings, functions, and likely consequences of provocation in the contemporary world? It is at least in part by addressing this problematic that we can begin to defend our scholarship while also rethinking the preoccupations and orientations that currently dominate it.

Notes

1. Although the examples I will provide will be drawn primarily from literature, commercial film, and popular music, the argument I am making applies equally to the study of all forms of representational and expressive practices in Africa.

2. Selasi first elaborated her defense of the Afropolitan or an African version of the cosmopolitan in an article titled "Bye-Bye Barbar," initially published in 2005 in an online journal, *The Lip*, under the name Taiye Tuakli-Wosomu. It was subsequently republished in *Callaloo* (2013).

3. A writer like Cole has been alternatively described as "Nigerian," "American," and "Nigerian-American." Dinaw Mengestu's work is featured both in studies dedicated to American literature and in reviews of African literature. The selection of Tope Folarin as winner of the Caine Prize for African Writing prompted a flurry of handwringing about the identity of a writer born in Utah to Nigerian parents and raised in the United States. Some reports of the award described him as a U.S.-based Nigerian, while others asked "How African do you have to be?" See in particular Allison.

4. With the possible exception of South Africa, this observation applies as much, if not more, to literature books in African languages as it does to literature books in European languages, notwithstanding the hopes expressed by Ngũgĩ wa Thiong'o. The problem is not one of language alone but also of the costs of mediation and distribution and of genres of cultural production. Producers and distributors of audiovisual materials in Africa are better able to ensure profits at all stages of the value chain than are publishers of literature books, whether the literature books are in European or indigenous African languages. Literature books in an African language are most widespread in countries where the language of literature is also the language of official state business. But even in those settings, there are likely to be more video and audio CDs using the language in question available for sale than there are literature books. Indeed, the larger point that I am making is that Africans in the twenty-first century more frequently encounter imaginative narrative and the verbal arts broadly in audiovisual media (on radio, television, digitally mediated VCDs [video compact disks], and mobile telephones) than through print materials. See Adejunmobi (*Vernacular* 203–5) for further discussion of

the African language literature question. Kuria too provides an updated assessment of the challenges facing Ngũgĩ's vernacular-language literature initiatives in Kenya. Though Kuria examines only the specific case of Kenya, the problems he documents are to be expected in several other African countries.

5. The bookstore did carry one copy of a collection of short stories by the Ivorian author of popular literature Isaïe Biton Koulibaly.

6. My observations about bookstores derive mostly from travels in West Africa, though I have observed similar trends elsewhere in Africa. I have been particularly interested in bookstores in Nigeria, Ghana, Mali, Côte d'Ivoire, and Bénin, among other places.

7. For security reasons following a wave of bomb attacks in Nigeria starting in 2009, such bookstores have been removed from international airports in Lagos and Abuja. And in Accra, Ghana, the biggest upscale bookstore in the country, located at the Accra Mall, had shut its doors by 2011, presumably for lack of clientele, giving way to a smaller bookstore, located next to the Silverbird cinema, where audiovisual material and popular magazines dominated shelf space. The point here is that the literature book as material object remains relatively inaccessible, even in well-to-do African contexts, compared to other kinds of texts in print. Upscale bookstores in Abuja had only one title each of works by newer Nigerian authors like Helon Habila and Chimamanda Ngozi Adichie. Literature works by Nigerian authors of earlier generations were largely absent from many bookstores if they were not texts assigned for school curricula. So were the works of somewhat more iconoclastic writers like Chris Abani who appear to be much better known outside Nigeria than within Nigeria.

8. I provide here links to some of the performances by these poets.

- Outspoken in "Freedom Train": http://www.youtube.com/watch?v=zEGshiNX4Jk
- Maya Wegerif in "Why You Talk So White?": http://www.youtube.com/watch?v=onT-u_OXSHo
- Willpoète in "Lettre au mal du siècle": http://www.youtube.com/watch?v=4Bq1DEvmqT8
- Ceptik in "J'aurais aimé": http://www.youtube.com/watch?v=n-KPb_ZkA3E&NR=1&feature=endscreen
- Aziz Siten'K in "L'univers rouge": http://www.youtube.com/watch?v=bh8iP9EHQ-Y&feature=related
- Mbépongo Dédy Bilamba in "Le Congolais": http://www.youtube.com/watch?v=AEMuxgkZyf4

9. Anyidoho's two most recent collections of poetry (*The Place We Call Home and Other Poems* and *PraiseSong for the Land*) are sold in a book and audio CD combination. By contrast, the Nigerian poet Ogaga Ifowodo continues to disseminate his poetry exclusively in print. Ifowodo has published three books of poetry to date.

10. The South African Mike Maphoto's *Diary of Zulu Girl* (http://diaryofazulugirl.co.za/) started off as a blog and then became its own stand-alone site for the serialized story. In December 2013, it was announced that the story would be made into a television drama and subsequently published in print.

11. A partial list of such online literary journals would include *Kwani?* (Kenya), http://kwani.org/publications/kwani-journal.htm; *African Writing Online*, http://www.african-writing.com/eleven/; *NaijaStories* (Nigeria), http://www.naijastories.com/; and *Africanwriter.com* (mostly, though not exclusively, Nigerians), http://www.africanwriter.com/. Websites would include Nigerians Talk Litmag, http://nigerianstalk.org/category/litmag/editorial-litmag/; and the Yahoo group Krazitivity (Nigeria), among many others. With the possible

exception of South Africa, the challenges of publication and distribution continue to make the survival of literary journals in print rather tenuous in many African countries. Online literary journals appear to be less commonplace in French-speaking Africa, though several authors who write in French have their own websites and/or blogs. One of the possibilities that scholars of literature might find interesting is the development of "apps" for African literature. Thus far, this remains rare, but there is no reason to believe that apps could not become more widespread with the growth of the app-developing business in Africa's media hubs. One example that I am aware of: an audio app for iPad and iPhone has been developed for the first written imaginative narrative in the Yoruba language, which was serialized in a Lagos newspaper from 1920 to 1930. One can now listen to the "novel" on an iPad or iPhone. Written by an author called I. B. Thomas, it is titled *Itan Igbese Aiye Emi Ṣegilọla, Ẹlẹyinju Ẹgẹ, Ẹlẹgbẹrun Ọkọ L'Aiye* (The Story of Segilola, I of the Dazzling Eyes).

12. In August 2012, for example, I found that in the appropriately named Lifestyle Bookstore at the Accra Mall in Ghana, the ratio of locally authored literature books to local films was about one to five. The latest collection of poetry by the Ghanaian poet Kofi Anyidoho titled *The Place We Call Home and Other Poems* was on sale at this bookstore but was not available in most bookstores in Accra, including the bookstore at the University of Ghana, where Anyidoho is a professor of literature. Some locally authored autobiographies and history books were being sold at the Lifestyle Bookstore, but in this and many other bookstores, works of literature by Ghanaian and other African authors were a rarity. The lone exception to this trend was the University Bookstore at the University of Ghana, which presumably carried literature works assigned for various classes taught on campus. While the Lifestyle Bookstore in Abuja, Nigeria, carried more locally authored literature books than its sister bookstore in Accra, there too locally produced films outnumbered locally authored and published literature books. And in all other bookstores that I visited in Abuja and Lagos, locally authored literature accounted for very little shelf space.

13. The smaller private universities that have emerged in West Africa since the beginning of the new millennium also tend to avoid offering a wide selection of degree programs in the humanities (with the exception of degrees in theology for church-owned universities). Instead, many more prefer to offer degrees in business administration and finance. Courses in the basic humanities and sciences are more likely to be offered as an adjunct to degrees in education in these universities.

14. Lehrer's *Imagine: How Creativity Works* represents an analysis that is similarly designed to be highly accessible to readers outside an academic setting but is focused on individual creativity rather than on societal innovation. It is noteworthy that cultural studies scholars have largely and thus far not responded to growing popular interest in this subject. While it is true that Lehrer's book was subsequently pulled from circulation by the publisher after the author was discovered to have fabricated some of the citations in the book, the popularity it generated in a short space of time points to considerable public interest in matters pertaining to creativity.

15. I have chosen this formulation in recognition of the fact that we now have some verbal artists who do not seek publication and thus might not be described as authors, though they do write their poetry. The shift away from publication is a direct consequence of the new opportunities opened up by digital media. For a fuller discussion of how digital media is redefining the relationship between authorship, composition, writing, and performance in some African settings, see Adejunmobi, "Revenge."

16. Some of the new performance poets I identified earlier do not appear especially provocative either in the aesthetics of the poetry or in their treatment of a particular subject matter. However, the decision to perform their poetry rather than have it published in book form

already amounts to a form of provocation. In the case of Aziz Siten'K, for example, digitally mediated performance represents both a rejection of the style of poetry associated with the still powerful Malian *jelis* (or griots) and a rejection of the professional trajectories offered by print publication. See Adejunmobi, "Revenge," for a fuller discussion of the significance of the turn toward digitally mediated performance by many young Malian poets. For yet other performance-poets, the entirety of their performance (in terms of performance style, use of media, treatment of subject matter, and aesthetics) will be experienced as provocative in the location where they currently reside.

17. One could argue, though, that this has always been the case for African literature, at least since the twentieth century. The early Negritude writers, for example, produced much of their writing while living in France.

18. Thus, for example, some Nollywood producers are now choosing to deliberately cultivate and privilege diasporic audiences outside Africa rather than audiences within Africa for their films, even though audiences for Nollywood films within Africa are substantial and growing. The strategy of such film producers offers an interesting contrast to that of African noncommercial filmmakers seeking audiences in Africa but whose films end up in circulation mostly among audiences outside Africa.

19. Here again I think of Mike Maphoto, though he uses a stand-alone site to disseminate his work.

20. To consider one example: Mohammed Naseehu Ali is surely a Ghanaian author, though he is a resident of New York. The fact that his collection of short stories, *The Prophet of Zongo Street*, was published by a division of HarperCollins Publishers in New York might be the reason that I came across no copies of his work in bookstores in Ghana.

21. The former authors reside mainly outside Africa, while the latter group reside mainly in Africa. I mention print texts in particular since some authors are present on multiple media, while others work almost exclusively with print.

22. To consider a few examples, Helon Habila, resident outside Nigeria, and Chimamanda Ngozi Adichie, resident mainly but not exclusively in Nigeria, have made use of such options.

23. Indeed, we might provocatively describe the canon of African high culture as representing works characterized by a high degree of material singularity (or simply scarcity) in the societies with which they are identified and which are more frequently validated by networks outside Africa. Sylvester Ogbechie's recent book *Making History: African Collectors and the Canon of African Art* indirectly underscores this very point with respect to the visual arts when he argues for greater recognition (and power) for African collectors of art.

24. Increasingly, notable figures in these networks of readers and critics localized outside Africa are themselves self-identified Africans and members of a growing diaspora of African professionals.

25. Thus works that deal with controversial questions like homosexuality or female genital cutting are in many instances more likely to be acknowledged and celebrated by critical and artistic networks outside Africa than within Africa or in networks localized in Africa that are directly connected to networks localized outside Africa in some way.

26. See Cunningham (106) and Keane (*Created* 118–19) for more on this.

27. Scholars who do work in the creative industries often link the considerable growth of these entertainment-oriented industries in the Western world to the development of a knowledge-based economy producing individuals with skills in designing and operating digital technology, computer software, and other kinds of engineering systems. Hartley (5), Cunningham (106), and Keane (*Created* 118–19) elaborate on this presumed link. The absence of major investment in areas that are presumed necessary for the growth of media-dependent entertainment industries is what sets Nigeria and many other African countries apart when

it comes to the explosion of media-related film and music businesses in the early twenty-first century.

28. Goodluck Jonathan, the president of Nigeria at the time of writing, was a one-time university teacher with a PhD in zoology.

29. Several business and tech-oriented blogs about Africa reported that by August 2012, Afrinolly had achieved one million downloads, mainly from Nigeria, Ghana, South Africa, Brazil, and India.

30. One new game, for example, is titled "Kidnapped," while another popular one is called "Mosquito Squasher." For further information on this video gaming business, go to http://www.youtube.com/watch?v=Mi78LO7F_Og&feature=plcp.

31. Some sectors of the music industry in countries like Ghana and Nigeria provide another example of a culture-themed business that has flourished locally and internationally alongside the film industry. Local Ghanaian and Nigerian pop music stars like Sakordie and D'Banj now feature in African American music award shows (like the BET Music Awards), and some have produced collaborative music videos with famous African American musicians. Kanye West makes a cameo appearance in D'Banj's music video "Oliver" (2012), and the exceedingly popular "Chop My Money" music video by the Nigerian duo P-Square also features the Senegalese-American rapper Akon.

32. The refusal to situate one's creative work entirely within a commercial framework is itself experienced as provocative in settings where legal opportunities for earning considerable amounts of money are rare. Some examples are discussed below.

33. One thinks here of the kind of highly regimented societies that have thus far not emerged in Africa.

34. Literary prizes awarded by institutions in the Western world to writers from the developing world come to mind. Virtually all celebrated African writers have been beneficiaries of such international awards.

35. The Nigerian hip-hop artist Nneka, for example, has spoken in interviews of the importance of having relocated to Africa after her early music career in Europe. Nonetheless, she continues to embark on extensive tours in Europe and North America, appearing at various sites for alternative and socially conscious music outside Africa. These tours give her music some visibility in the Western world and undoubtedly help to raise her profile back in Africa, thereby generating a local following for her brand of socially conscious music.

36. As the laws governing the establishment of private universities have changed across Africa, wealthy individuals in countries like Nigeria have set aside funds to establish private universities. However, such individuals often treat the university itself as a money-making venture: capital-intensive courses are avoided, and for the most part few resources are allocated to research in such individually owned private universities.

37. Where politicians face competitive elections across Africa, they increasingly turn to popular music hits, especially in instances where the lyrics are aspirational without being explicitly political. See, for example, Nyairo and Ogude describing how the Kenyan duo Gidi gidi maji maji's hit song "Unbwogable" became an anthem for the opposition during the 2002 elections in Kenya with its popular refrain "Who can bwoge me? I am unbwogable, I am unbeatable, I am un-sueable." A number of Nigerian pop stars, notably D'Banj, campaigned for President Goodluck Jonathan during his presidential campaign in 2011. Praise singers in many West African countries have always provided support for big men through their music. The musician as critic rather than as supporter thus appears provocative, whether the criticism is directed toward military dictators, as in the case of the Nigerian Fela Anikulapo-Kuti, or toward elected leaders by some Senegalese rap artists. As documented by Olaniyan, Fela in particular cultivated provocation at many levels: politically, aesthetically, socially.

38. There are several examples currently of such socially conscious musicians who perform in a critical rather than an elegiac mode. I will mention only three here to illustrate: Tiken Jah Fakoly from Côte d'Ivoire, Awadi from Senegal, and Nneka from Nigeria.

39. These kinds of innovations can be developed in the first instance by individuals working alone without significant public funding, unlike innovations pertaining to the construction of infrastructure or emanating from medical research. Once the apps have been developed, the inventors gain publicity for their innovation by participating in regional and international tech competitions. For example, the developers of Afrinolly won the Google Android developer challenge award for sub-Saharan Africa in 2011. The Kenyan developer of the AroundMe app likewise took home the prize (75,000 Euros) for the "In the know" category of the global Nokia Create for Millions Challenge in August 2012. This app, which has its own Wikipedia page, has reportedly hit more than six million downloads around the world. It is also worth noting here that Africans more frequently develop apps for mobile phones, which are now ubiquitous across the continent, than for tablets like the iPad and the Kindle Fire, which remain relatively rare outside of the upper middle class. Thus, this kind of creativity does not feed into the kind of singularity that I have described for literature books. See my earlier comments on Afrinolly for an example of this.

40. Perhaps the best-known site dedicated to this cause is the site associated with MASSOB, or the Movement for the Actualization of the Sovereign State of Biafra (http://massob.org/). But there are several others, such as Biafra Nation (www.biafraland.com/). Contributors to other Nigerian-authored websites and blog sites that are not specifically dedicated to the rebirth of Biafra regularly call for secession and a breakup of Nigeria. Such articles are not uncommon on websites like Sahara Reporters (http://saharareporters.com/) or on Nigerian Village Square (http://www.nigeriavillagesquare.com/). Although I have not taken the time to search for such blogs and websites, I don't doubt that there are websites dedicated to such politically incorrect subjects as the reinstatement of Laurent Gbagbo as president of Côte d'Ivoire or alternative interpretations of the Rwandan genocide.

41. Producing socially conscious art requires interested performers to make strategic choices so they can enjoy a modicum of commercial success and avoid political trouble at home. While some musicians take the risk of getting involved in local politics, as has happened most recently in Senegal, many of the African musicians who would define themselves as socially conscious now tend to reserve their most explicit political critique for such broad themes as corruption, colonialism, war, the International Monetary Fund, tribalism, etc. Alpha Blondy, Tiken Jah Fakoly of Côte d'Ivoire, and Nneka of Nigeria come to mind. Though they are clearly critical of prevailing politics in their respective countries (Tiken Jah Fakoly even went into exile while Laurent Gbagbo was in power), they rarely go after local politicians and institutions in the kind of direct and confrontational manner adopted by the late Fela Anikulapo-Kuti. Musical heirs to Fela, like the Nigerian Afrobeat singer Lagbaja, have shown themselves to be much more culturally than politically engaged. Filmmakers like Tunde Kelani and lately Kunle Afolayan who have been trying to sidestep the overwhelmingly commercial dictates of Nollywood filmmaking in their own films are likewise trending toward an emphasis on Yoruba cultural nationalism in place of direct critique of the political class. Their films might be considered more aesthetically rather than politically provocative.

42. For Cowen, "genres that rely heavily on equipment and materials, which . . . [are] capital-intensive, tend to produce popular art" (40).

43. The performance poets come to mind again here as examples of verbal artists who have chosen to "self-publish" using You Tube rather than work with local publishers. So do authors who publish exclusively in online literary journals. For similar reasons, musicians whose audience is drawn mainly from one country sometimes elect to avoid contracts imposed by the

larger local recording companies, which are viewed as exploitative. This then means they have to worry about how to generate a profit from their music and how to prevent piracy. By contrast, and where possible, app developers partner with local and regional media companies in order to more effectively "monetize" their invention. What these app developers aim for is commercial viability rather than provocation of any kind.

44. I am referring here to publishers, newspapers, radio and television stations, and educational institutions, among others. To take a well-publicized example, support for the rights of gays and lesbians by such cultural brokers has been hard to come by in most African countries in the early twenty-first century. There are, however, private initiatives to foster creativity, especially in the area of media technology. One example that comes to mind is iHub, a web-based site and business in Kenya that describes itself as "an open space for the technologists, investors, tech companies and hackers in the area . . . with a focus on young entrepreneurs, web and mobile phone programmers, designers and researchers." See iHub home page: http://www.ihub.co.ke/.

45. See, for example, the following BBC reports on responses to the painting and cartoon, which were seen by some constituencies in South Africa as disrespectful for creating representations of President Zuma that focused on his genitals: http://www.bbc.co.uk/news/world-africa-18159204 and http://www.bbc.co.uk/news/world-africa-18743710. This was truly an opportunity for debating not just freedom of speech but what the freedom to create contributes to a society. The many popular and professional responses to what was described as the "Swedish circumcision cake controversy" outside Africa, but also to some extent within Africa, offer another fascinating illustration of the increased salience of sexual matters when it comes to art and provocation relating to contemporary Africa.

Works Cited

Adejunmobi, Moradewun. "Revenge of the Spoken Word: Writing, Performance and New Media in Urban West Africa." *Oral Tradition* 26, no. 1 (2011): 3–26.

———. *Vernacular Palaver: Imaginations of the Local and Non-native Languages in West Africa.* Clevedon, UK: Multilingual Matters, 2004.

Ali, Mohammed Naseehu. *The Prophet of Zongo Street.* New York: Amistad Books, 2006.

Allison, Simon. "The Caine Prize Controversy, How African Do You Have to Be?" *Daily Maverick*, July 11, 2013, http://www.dailymaverick.co.za/article/2013-07-11-the-caine-prize-controversy-how-african-do-you-have-to-be/.

Anyidoho, Kofi. *The Place We Call Home and Other Poems.* Banbury, UK: Ayebia Clarke Publishing, 2011.

———. *PraiseSong for the Land.* Accra, Ghana: Sub-Saharan Publishers, 2002.

Cowen, Tyler. *In Praise of Commercial Culture.* Cambridge, Mass.: Harvard University Press, 1998.

Cunningham, Stuart. "The Creative Industries after Cultural Policy: A Genealogy and Some Possible Preferred Futures." *International Journal of Cultural Studies* 7, no. 1 (2004): 105–15.

Gupta, Akhil. "The Song of the Nonaligned World: Transnational Identities and the Reinscription of Space in Late Capitalism." In *Culture Power Place: Explorations in Critical Anthropology*, edited by Akhil Gupta and James Ferguson, 179–99. Durham: Duke University Press, 1997.

Hartley, John, ed. *Creative Industries.* Malden, Mass.: Blackwell, 2005.

Keane, Michael. *Created in China: The Great New Leap Forward.* New York: Routledge, 2007.

———. "From Made in China to Created in China." *International Journal of Cultural Studies* 9, no. 3 (2006): 285–96.

Kao, John. *Innovation Nation: How America Is Losing Its Innovation Edge, Why It Matters, and What We Can Do to Get It Back.* New York: Free Press, 2007.

Klammer, Arjo. "The Value of Culture." In *The Value of Culture: On the Relationship between Economics and Arts,* edited by Arjo Klammer, 13–28. Amsterdam: Amsterdam University Press, 1996.

Kuria, Mike. "Speaking in Tongues: Ngũgĩ's Gift to Workers and Peasants through Mũrogi wa Kagogo." *Journal of Literary Studies* 27, no. 3 (2011): 56–73.

Lehrer, Jonah. *Imagine: How Creativity Works.* Boston: Houghton Mifflin Harcourt, 2012.

Lobato, Ramon. "Creative Industries and Informal Economies: Lessons from Nollywood." *International Journal of Cultural Studies* 13, no. 4 (2010): 337–54.

Maphoto, Mike. *Diary of a Zulu Girl.* http://diaryofazulugirl.co.za/.

Nyairo, Joyce, and James Ogude. "Popular Music, Popular Politics: *Unbwogable* and the Idioms of Freedom in Kenyan Popular Music." *African Affairs* 104, no. 415 (2005): 225–49.

Ogbechie, Sylvester. *Making History: African Collectors and the Canon of African Art.* Milan: 5 Continents Editions, 2012.

Olaniyan, Tejumola. *Arrest the Music! Fela and His Rebel Art and Politics.* Bloomington: Indiana University Press, 2004.

Pratt, Andy C. "The Cultural Economy: A Call for Spatialized 'Culture of Production' Perspectives." *International Journal of Cultural Studies* 7, no. 1 (2004): 117–28.

Rifkin, Jeremy. *The Age of Access: The New Culture of Hypercapitalism Where All of Life Is a Paid-For Experience.* New York: Putnam, 2000.

Selasi, Taiye. "Bye-Bye Barbar." *Callaloo* 36, no. 3 (2013): 528–30.

Szanton, David. *The Politics of Knowledge: Area Studies and the Disciplines.* Berkeley: University of California Press, 2004.

Tuakli-Wosomu, Taiye. "Bye-Bye Barbar." *The Lip,* March 3, 2005, http://thelip.robertsharp.co.uk/?p=76.

Wang, Jing. "The Global Reach of a New Discourse: How Far Can 'Creative Industries' Travel?" *International Journal of Cultural Studies* 7, no. 1 (2004): 9–19.

4 In Praise of the Alphabet

Patrice Nganang

Reformulating an Old Question

There has never been a better time for criticism than today. And critics of African literature in particular should be in a state of rapture. The reason for such a thrill is simple: the talk of "post" (as in, say, the postcolonial) marks the end of criticism of African literature as we know it—not the beginning but the end, since it would be ludicrous to expect the post-postcolonial, and then the post-post-postcolonial, to arrive one day. And yet the task of criticism is still so young! The void that criticism faces today is what puts me into a state of perpetual intellectual trance, since after all, nothingness is the land of all possibilities. *Ex nihilo omne ens qua ens fit*.[1] Critics should therefore hasten the dying of the dead and bury the rotten corpse without any sense of remorse. Facing the void left by the buried dead, we contemporary critics should be rubbing our hands happily. Most notably, we should avoid rushing to new materials—popular cultures, digital cultures, sexual orientation studies, masculinity studies, transnationalism, ecocriticism, animal studies, trash studies, star studies, and whatnot—with old questions. More than a call to look for new objects of study, the crisis[2] that criticism faces today should prompt a call to return to the basics. Thus, if there is a phrase I would like to transform into a call today, it would be "Back to the basics!"

The title of this essay, "In Praise of the Alphabet," falls under this motto. And since I will be arguing about two competing paradigms of African writing and criticism, the *global* and the *artistic* paradigms, it is important to first define what I mean by paradigm. A paradigm is simply *the conditions of possibility of a thought*.[3] The paradigm of a literature is the conditions of possibility of that literature, and so the paradigm of criticism is the conditions of possibility of that criticism. A paradigm not only lies at the foundation of creative writing and literary history but also dictates the grammar and the vocabulary of criticism. It is the a priori of any form of literary practice. Thus, it becomes legitimate to organize the history of African literature, as we have always done, around a precolonial literature that is predominantly oral, around an anticolonial moment that is militant, around the moment of a national literature, and even to single out a literature of disillusionment and emigration, which marks the beginning of contemporary postcolonial literature, *provided* we choose the global paradigm to be the condition of possibility of African literature. And the independence of African countries from Europe in 1960 becomes a turning point in the many-thousand-years-old intellectual history of the African continent *only because* of the global paradigm through the frame of which that history is read.

The global paradigm gives African literature a particular calendar, yet it does more than dictate its periodicity: it also defines its content.[4] In his canonical study of Cameroonian literature, *The African Quest for Freedom and Identity*—five hundred pages and monumental as it is—Richard Bjorson can therefore manage to mention the name of Ibrahim Njoya, the inventor of a writing system, only twice; to write extended chapters on Mongo Beti and Ferdinand Oyono; and to focus on many other obscure writers. Yet he never mentions the name of the scribe of the sultan, the calligrapher and drawer whose name was also Ibrahim Njoya,[5] who left us with books containing an alphabet we have yet to decipher. And Bjorson is certainly not the only critic to have labored strictly under the umbrella of the global paradigm, for the two volumes on Cameroonian literature published by *Notre Librairie* also pass over Njoya's writing system, of which the critic Claude Wauthier says that it remained "sans portée pratique."[6] Mongo Beti, who wrote thousands of words of outrage about the violence that was unleashed on the Bamileke region between 1956 and 1970, never mentioned the writing system of the Bagam. This reminder is not meant as a slander but as a remark on the capacity of a paradigm to close brilliant critical minds by sharply defining the kinds of questions they raise, their choice of material, and therefore the forms and the individuals who become important to them. It is an urge to reevaluate the *practice*, the *criticism*, and the *criticism of the criticism of African literature*,[7] as deep inside the global paradigm there is one simple question. It is the question that runs through V. Y. Mudimbe's acclaimed theoretical diptych, *The Invention of Africa* and *The Idea of Africa*: "What is Africa?" (*Idea* xiv).

Of a continent whose name has shifted so much—from Abyssinia to Africa, from Barbaria to Ifrikiya, from Ethiops to Nigritia—I will not pretend to know more than St. Augustine did in his *Confessions* or Apuleius in *The Golden Ass*. But I will contend that the question "What is Africa?," when applied to literature in the way the critic Obiajunwa Wali did during the famous 1962 Makerere conference,[8] when one could still discuss such topics without the qualifier "post," is rooted in the global paradigm: What is *African* literature?[9] We now know that Wali's question has resonated deeply in the labor of writing about the African continent and that, even when laughed at because of his implicit belief in an authentic African Self, or when overlooked because of his scorn of European languages, it profoundly dictates the grammar of the criticism of African literature, when it is summed up in Abiola Irele's dictum "Literature occurs within language" (43). The surge in the study of literatures in African languages certainly owes a lot to the line Wali violently drew in the sand. Because, when asking the question "What is African literature?," he insisted on the adjective "African," thus transforming his question into "What makes a literature African?," his quest still resonates in Mudimbe's own inquiry, which the Congolese writer summarized in the following terms: "How do we define African cultures?" (*Idea* xiv).

I start with Obi Wali's question because from the vantage point of the global paradigm, the criticism, historiography, and even a certain practice of African literature are understandable. And his question can easily become: What makes a text African? How do we define Africa? What indeed is that thing, Africa? A strange thing, I guess. Wali's question "What is African literature?," when it insists on the adjective "African," finds its prehistory in Léopold Sédar Senghor's critical pieces, particularly his influential "Ce que l'homme noir apporte,"[10] published in 1939, although, as we well know, Senghor's answer is drawn along racial lines. Obi Wali's answer is different: to him, the use of African languages is the defining factor. And he therefore traces a tradition of criticism that would be embraced by many writers and mainly popularized by Ngũgĩ wa Thiong'o. The issue of African languages is still hotly debated in Senegal, I have heard, and Boubacar Boris Diop discovered the pleasure of writing in Wolof, even though the genocide of 1994 that influenced him to write in his mother tongue should have warned him instead: after all, the people in Rwanda spoke the same language while killing each other, and languages, as we well know, do not unite—on the contrary, they divide people—but that is surely another matter.

Asking the question of Wali again, "What is African literature?," I would like to insist *not* on the adjective "African," since its definition either as "language" or as "race," from the Greeks to today, leads straight into an aporia, but rather on the word "literature," thus on the letters of the alphabet. The question that will lead me, a transformation of the original question asked by Wali, is simply: What is literature? Formulated differently, it becomes: *What is literature in Africa?* Considering the literary tradition that has been produced from the Mediterranean Sea to my own Cameroon, I will indeed have to look at African literature *not* from the point of view of language or race but from the point of view of writing. My question "What is literature in Africa?" can therefore easily be transformed into *What is writing in Africa?* And here, the most convincing and logical definition I have read so far comes from Ibn Khaldun, the famed Berber scholar, who writes this in his monumental philosophy of history, *The Muqaddimah*: "Writing is the outlining and shaping of letters to indicate audible words which, in turn, indicate what is in the soul. It comes second after oral expression. It is a noble craft, since it is one of the special qualities of man by which he distinguishes himself from animals" (327).

Ibn Khaldun's definition, written as early as 1377, is important for four reasons. First, it defines writing primarily in instrumental terms—it is an art, a notation technique,[11] for which one needs specific tools. Second, it locates writing inside a system of "crafts,"[12] as he says (the other crafts being book production, singing, music, medicine, weaving, tailoring, agriculture, architecture, midwifery, and carpentry). Third, it insists on the necessary scarcity of writing:[13] writing needs an intense training, thus, it is based on a system of admissions and exclusions, since it is at the basis of a bureaucracy, and therefore at the origin of power. Fourth, it depicts writing as a distinction[14] of humanness: humans versus animals is the separating line here. After all, he writes, "To man, God gave the ability to think, *and the hand*,"[15] distancing himself from Aristotle's coronation of the *logos*. "With the help of the ability to think, the hand is able to prepare the ground for the crafts," he writes. "The crafts, in turn, produce for man the instruments that serve him instead of limbs, which other animals possess for their defense" (Khaldun 46, my emphasis).

Above the multiplicity of crafts, Ibn Khaldun's framework gives writing a foundational position: "Writing is the most useful craft because, in contrast to the other crafts, it deals with matters of theoretical, scientific interest" (331). An instrumental definition of writing thus leads him to establish what I will call the artistic paradigm. The humanness of humans is distinguished by writing, yet the first constitutive character of writing in his definition is technical: "the outlining and shaping of letters." One cannot be simpler: *writing is the skilled drawing of lines and setting of dots on a space*, nothing more, nothing less. That writing is at the beginning of literature is self-evident and is exemplified in *The Muqaddimah* by an extended analysis of its relation to poetry. Yet "poetry was the archive of the Arabs," the text goes on to say, "containing their sciences, their history, and their wisdom" (455). But that writing is also at the beginning of cartography, of architecture, of bureaucracy too, and therefore of politics, will need further elaboration.

The Birth and Death of African Writing

If Ibn Khaldun began the artistic paradigm in 1377, Ibrahim Njoya, the sultan of Bamum, closed it in 1920, when the teaching of his alphabet was banned by the French colonial administration. The gap between both authors is immense, nearly six hundred years, and the Sahara desert lies between them. That Njoya drafted his *lewa* abecedary after seeing Arabic characters is not of minor consequence, even though, because of the breadth of knowledge that Ibn Khaldun mobilized, from Ptolemy, Averroes, Galen, and al-Idrisi to the Arabic translations of Aristotle, it would be an exaggeration to compare his *Muqaddimah* with the *Sang'aam*, Njoya's memoir,[16] since the first book of Cameroonian literature, which was started in 1908, was solely based on collected testimonies. Finished on Monday, June 19, 1921, in Mantum, West Cameroon, it was subsequently translated first into Njoya's secret *shümum* language as the *Libonare*[17] and then into French in 1945 as *Histoire et Coutumes des Bamum*. It is clear that Njoya never read any text written by Ibn Khaldun, but the history of ideas does not proceed by textual causality only, for it is also *a history of technologies*, and *a history of their diffusion*.[18]

The *Muqaddimah*'s definition of writing is very generous; so generous, in fact, that one would be hard-pressed to find any African culture that did not know writing. After all, writing includes divination, magical graffiti, esoteric symbols, mystic codes, and mathematical formulae, but also the formalized use of an alphabet. It starts with geomancy,[19] which Ibn Khaldun defines as "the craft called 'sand writing,'" *ilm al-raml*, whose goal is "to discover the supernatural and know the future" (87). If historically, writing mostly culminates in bureaucratic practices, particularly copying and book production, it is nevertheless understood not as a fixed category but as a skill that can be learned and forgotten, that is invented and can disappear. "The transformation of writing in man from potentiality into actuality takes place through instruction," he writes (327). And such transformation is not only individual, it is historical as well; after all: "The quality of writing in a town corresponds to the social organization, civilization, and competition of luxuries (among its inhabitants), since writing is a craft" (327). In other words, the scarcity of writing in certain cultures is not due to the essential *orature* of their way of living and doing but to the limits they impose on *themselves*[20] regarding the instruction of their writing system. Secrecy was a historical curse, and "for this reason," he concludes, "we find that most Bedouins are illiterate" (327).

This, without doubt, is a definition of writing that Ibrahim Njoya shared, he who after establishing the first abecedary of his alphabet, the *lewa*, proceeded to instruct the nobility of his sultanate. But let us listen to his own narration, as written in the *Sang'aam*: "Before," the text informs us,

> the Bamum did not know how to write: the script they use today was invented by King Njoya. One night he had a dream. One man came to him and told him: "King, take this board and draw a man's hand, wash your drawing and drink it." The king took a board, drew a man's hand as he was asked to. He then gave the board to the man who wrote signs on it and gave it back to him. There were many people in attendance, and all were students who had a piece of paper in their hand. They all wrote something on it and passed it along to theirs peers. The next day the king took a board, and drew a man's hand, washed the board and drank the water he had used, as he was asked to in his dream. The king then called many people and told them: "If you draw different things and name them, I will make a book that speaks in silence." "Why try?" the people answered, "even if we try, we will never succeed." "If you think about it,

you will succeed," the king responded.... They followed his advice, and soon came back to show him their work. He too had prepared drafts. He then called Mama and Adjia and asked them to help him compare the work that had been done. Five times he tried, but without good results. Only the sixth attempt was successful. The script was invented. The king then called everybody and taught them his new characters. People learned them, to the satisfaction of king Njoya. (Njoya 41–42)

The six abecedaries the text refers to are the original *lewa*, which probably was invented in 1895–96 and had 510 signs; the *mbima* of 1899–1900, which had 437 signs; the *nyi nyi nfa mfw* of 1900–1902 with 381 signs and the *rii nyi nfa mfw* of 1902 with 286 signs, both of them coinciding with the arrival of the first Europeans in Fumban, the Germans; then the *rii nyi mfw men* of 1907–08 with 205 signs; and the *a ka u ku* of 1910, which is also known as the final version of Njoya's alphabet. The *a ka u ku* has two versions, that of 1910 and the *a ka u ku mfemfe*, done in 1918.

Like most foundational texts, Njoya's narration of his invention process is quite unique and very rich in symbols; it underlines the significance of the hand in particular. A drawing by Ibrahim Njoya, the king's calligrapher, quite vividly illustrates the process of alphabetization. It presents a gathering of people dressed as noble Bamum men would be, sitting around an instructing sultan who faces a board. To my knowledge, nowhere else in African literature does writing appear as it does here, in its concretion as an art that always needs to be perfected, that is transmitted through instruction, and most important, that is related to other crafts, here drawing, in a very intimate way. I will not insist on the relation between dream works and writing, which is established here, too, although it is important to underline the fact that dreams defined not only Njoya's invention of a script but his most important political decision, accepting German colonization, in a preemptive fashion. Suffice it to mention that in 1906, Njoya opened schools in his sultanate, the first one having sixty-six students, thus starting an alphabetization that would subsequently culminate in the invention among the Bamileke of a parallel writing system, the *bagam* script,[21] of which a tentative vocabulary was established in 1922. Beyond all these developments, it is important to recognize that in his understanding of writing as a personal and collective struggle to transform a potentiality, a dream into an actuality, Njoya remained deeply rooted inside the paradigm that was inaugurated by Ibn Khaldun in 1377: the artistic paradigm. He was in fact the ultimate manifestation of *artistic reason*.

The artistic paradigm sets literature and writing apart, for it understands writing as a craft, as an art whose expression *can be* literature *but does not have to be*. Writing is the condition of possibility of literature, *but literature is not the only manifestation of writing*: esoteric, magical, religious, scientific, philosophical, and legal documents; cloth design; architecture; and city planning equally express the potentialities of writing. One can write on sand, walls, stones, wood, paper, or computer board.²² Furthermore, writing is related to other crafts, and in Njoya's narration, drawing is the one he specifically mentions, as is cartography and architecture in his artistic practice. Ibn Khaldun's system of the arts included some more crafts, and it divided them into the "necessary" and the "noble crafts," of which he says, "Crafts noble because of their object are midwifery, the art of writing, book production, singing, and medicine" (319). If it would be truly difficult to find a time in African history when writing has been that important, that central to the *polis,* it is because such a system is based on the scarcity of the craft of writing. But secrecy is its curse, too, and the death of Njoya's script is related to its banning by the French colonial administration in 1920, as well as to the restriction of its instruction to certain individuals only, as opposed to the compulsory character of French instruction for everyone. Still, its centrality is also related to the paradigmatic position of the arts. In the case of Njoya, this is exemplified by his understanding of the alphabet as the new a priori in Bamum life. Such a proposition is expressed in the *Sang'aam,* when Njoya narrates how he drafted the codex of his sultanate by collecting the testimonies of people: "After they talked," the text reads, "God took away their voice. No king can ever change these things again" (136). Writing is definitive: it seals lives. Njoya repeated the same procedure with his books, which he pointedly calls *lerewa:* "ce qui parle sans qu'on l'entende" (that which speaks without being heard) (41).

The artistic paradigm elevates the scribe, recognizes the relation of the *marabout* and *ifa* priest to writing, and sees a writer in the office secretary and an artist in the blogger; it underlines their shared craft. But it also declares all crafts as warranting preservation. If Njoya's vision relates them to the patronage of his palace (as he says about the goldsmith, "The goldsmith's son or the sculptor's son cannot become servants of the palace, because their craft would disappear" [101]), Ibn Khaldun has a different vision: "The crafts can improve only when they are needed and when they are in demand with many people," he writes. Rather than the sultan, it is demand, thus the public, which dictates the necessity or the nobility of a craft.

> When the condition of a city weakens . . . , luxury in the city decreases, and its inhabitants revert to restricting themselves to the necessities. The crafts belonging to luxury become few. The master of a particular craft is no longer assured of making a living of it. Therefore he deserts it for another, or he dies and leaves no successor. As a result, the institutions of the crafts disappear altogether. Thus, for instance, painters, goldsmiths, calligraphers, copyists, and similar artisans who cater to luxury needs disappear. (317)

Neither craft nor paradigm is eternal: both are subjected to learning and forgetting, to the flux of history, to the changing will of humans, and to the transformation of cultures. Writing systems sometimes cease being understandable. Like the Egyptian hieroglyphs, alphabets that were of large usage become esoteric and disappear; but as Njoya shows, new ones are also invented.

An Ongoing Critique of Global Reason

Fundamental to the artistic paradigm is an understanding of literature as being the product of a system of the arts, which itself is rooted in the nobility of certain crafts—of writing in particular. In such a system, the dominant position of the alphabet defines politics in a specific way. For Njoya, it was the legitimization of his family dynasty, and for Ibn Khaldun, it helped illuminate "how and why dynasties and civilizations originated" (7). For both men, the moral mandate of politics is *not* freedom; *it is happiness*. Njoya always insisted on the happiness of his subjects. Yet neither the nobility of writing nor the paradigmatic position of the arts can outbalance the fact that the artistic paradigm is overshadowed by the political system of inequality it sustains. African writers today cannot yearn for a time when only a few people could read—the *ifa* priest, the *marabout*, the nobility, scholars, copyists, calligraphers—even if writing was more important than it is today. The real challenge is therefore not restorative; on the contrary, it is to find a way to give writing a renewed meaning during our time of the triumph of *global reason*. Yet some questions remain: Can writing—and criticism—so easily obliterate the artistic paradigm?[23] And the question becomes more poignant, particularly when addressed directly to critics: Does not the artistic paradigm introduce a systematic framework through which one could easily relate writing to visual cultures, sculpture to trash, and thus connect all the crafts and arts to form a single whole? At what costs then do we forget "the question of technology,"[24] which the artistic paradigm raises, in the criticism of contemporary African arts? Is it really possible, when analyzing the "distribution of the arts,"[25] to do away with the concept of totality? And what about the thought of system, when we address the "reproducibility" of the work of art today through piracy?[26]

Because the demise of the artistic paradigm in contemporary African writing and criticism is related to the acquired ascendant of the global paradigm, it may be necessary to remember that the global paradigm was introduced into African literature only in 1789, with the publication of *The Interesting Narrative of the Life of Olaudah Equiano, or Gustavus Vassa, the African, Written by Himself*. Equiano's book appeared with the French Revolution and at the height of Enlightenment, published as it was eight years after Kant's *Critique of Pure Reason*, which elevated freedom into a cardinal principle of reason. One needs only read the introduction to Hegel's *Philosophy of History*, which was first delivered in Berlin in 1822–23, to see why the tradition of contemporary African literature, both in its essentialist and militant brands,[27] owes *The Interesting Narrative* a debt of gratitude. Without doubt, Hegel's text has an ambivalent position in African intellectual history. Vilipended as it is, it still provides propositions that the criticism and practice of African literature have not yet invalidated. Was Hegel's statement "Africa must be divided into three parts" (91) a philosophical prelude to the *divide et imperia* of the Congo conference of 1884–85? Yes, we too still divide our criticism and histories of African literature into Maghrebine, francophone, anglophone, and so on, literatures. Was his racialization of what he calls "Africa proper" (91) degrading? Without a doubt, yet in our studies we still highlight Africa south of the Sahara, in which "Black Africa" stands metonymically for the whole continent. If Hegel's defense of slavery (the clear blueprint of Marx's also infamous defense of colonization in "British Rule in India")[28] in the name of progress was classic bigotry, we seem to still be answering his slander after more than two hundred years. Although the first formalized writing system appeared in Africa, some of the latest "theories of the African"[29] still consider the continent to be on the threshold of the world, as Hegel did, and they too hold it to be infested with cannibalism or "necropolitics"[30] and are waiting for it to "sortir de la grande nuit," as the title of Achille Mbembe's book reads. After all, at what cost can contemporary African thought give up the concept of historical dialectics without causing a Foucaultian laughter?[31]

If we still labor under the shadow of Hegel, Equiano established the framework from which our responses make sense. He thus defined African literature as an ongoing critique of global reason. Starting with the Negritude movement, African personality, anticolonial literature, national literatures, literature of emigration in its most successful forms, black British literature, black Paris writing, the centrality of the "Black Atlantic" over the Indian ocean, Caribbean and African American literature, or mostly overlooked forms like testimonies, memoirs, essays, petitions, and manifestos, it would be truly difficult to *not* read all that is being written by Africans today as footnotes to Equiano's book. *The Interesting Narrative* not only mapped out the intellectual geography of African literature but embodied *African literature as a mandate to freedom,* as a tool that "in the smallest degree promotes the interests of humanity" (32), a proposition on which in principle it was in agreement with Hegel. Essential is that here, politics occupies the position that was occupied by the crafts in the artistic paradigm. More concretely, "language," "race," and later "nation," "identity," and "gender" all take the position that was occupied by writing. The fruits of this transvaluation are still blossoming, for African literature has never been as visible in the West as it is today. Not only are we experiencing a radical multiplication of African writers, but there are few major U.S., French, or British venues where they have not yet published a book and few major prizes they have not received, and I do not know of any leading newspaper that still does not review books published by African writers. Besides, many African writers have blogs, webpages, or a Facebook page to remind everybody of their words. Some African writers have become distinguished professors at Western universities, and the Internet allows writers who are based on the continent to be read worldwide. Yet the triumph of African literature has been achieved at the cost of writing, for writing has never been as *powerless* as it is today. That is the *true* paradox of contemporary African literature, a paradox that itself is a manifestation of the crisis of the global paradigm.

After all, what was the *worth* of an African writer's word in stopping the genocide that happened in Darfur? Some 4.5 million people died during the second Congo war between 1998 and 2002, while more than 1 million people were killed in Rwanda in 1994, *with all African writers silent.*

Since few books published by Africans today can match the success of Equiano's, it is necessary to look into *The Interesting Narrative* to find an early expression of that crisis and maybe the roots of its persistence in our current intelligence. If the artistic paradigm was based on a distinction of writing as the dividing line between humans and animals, the global paradigm is based on a rift between "the West and the rest of us,"[32] which becomes foundational to African literature. While Equiano introduces himself as "Gustavus Vassa, the oppressed Ethiopian" (232) when it is not "the African," his addressees are, he notes, "the candid and unprejudiced friends of the Africans" (14). No, his reader is not Baudelaire's "mon semblable, mon frère," for a literature installed in the global paradigm is per definition oppositional. In such a concept, African writing is the Other that answers back to the West: it "talks back." Yet the cost of such an answer is veiled, since even Equiano accepted the premises of the system that transformed him into a commodity. "As the inhuman traffic of slavery is now taken into the consideration of the British legislature," he writes, "I doubt not, if a system of commerce was established in Africa, the demand for manufactures would most rapidly augment, as the native inhabitants would insensibly adopt the British fashion, manners, customs, etc." And he concludes, drafting one of the very first defenses of colonialism ever written by an African: "In proportion to the civilization, so will be the consumption of British manufactures" (233).[33] The dearth of writing in the heart of the global paradigm results from subordinating the art of using the alphabet to political and financial systems whose historicity and violent rationality it does not control. By disconnecting itself from the history of technology, writing relinquishes its intimate connection to dreams, to *geomancy,* which characterized it in the artistic paradigm, and therefore its capacity to invent the future. It transfers such power to the politician or the banker, whom the writer can now insult with his books, numerous petitions, and open letters, as Equiano so well did.

Nothing exemplifies the dearth of writing inside the global paradigm more than its crippling of the arts, when crafts are defined in opposition to each other: prose against poetry, writing against theater, women writers against male writers, and, for the African case, writers living abroad against those still living in the country, anglophone against francophone writers, literature written in African languages against literature written in European languages. Yet these are just a few examples of a fight that initially opposed one language against another when it did not oppose one race against the other. If the global paradigm installs writing inside an agora, then one country where the insane dogfights, which such a disposition of the arts creates, are experienced vividly is Cameroon. After all in Cameroon, literature is effectively curtailed under a *literary apartheid*. It is perfectly natural there for a French-speaking Cameroonian to reach university without ever having touched, let alone read, a novel, a poem, or a play written by an English-speaking compatriot. Needless to say, the contrary is equally true for English-speaking Cameroonians. At the beginning of the year 2010, a Yaoundé-based daily, *Le Jour,* asked many Cameroonian writers about their references in African literature. The sole anglophone writer who was interviewed mentioned Chinua Achebe (and there is no surprise there), while francophone writers mostly referred to Ferdinand Oyono, Mongo Beti, or Cheikh Hamidou Kane, whom we all read in high school. Only one francophone writer mentioned English-speaking writers, and here again it was two Nigerian writers, Chris Abani and Chimamanda Ngozi Adichie, whose works have been published in Paris recently in French translation. How can one pretend as a writer to define the political horizon of a continent, or even of a country, when one is so clearly a victim of its intellectual vicissitudes? Ah, today still, our signature as writers remains Equiano's: "the oppressed Ethiopian."

In conclusion, I would like to come back to Ibn Khaldun's distinction of writing in his definition: "It is a noble craft," he wrote, "since it is one of the special qualities of man by which he distinguishes himself from animals" (327). I return to this distinction because it makes the critical insistence on the adjective "African," which introduced the question "What is African literature?," meaningless. After all, if Equiano defined himself as an Igbo, an African, and then as an "oppressed Ethiopian," for Njoya, Africa simply did not exist. He understood himself as a Bamum, as the son of Njapdunke, his mother, and certainly not as a Cameroonian. Cameroon referred to a city during most of his lifetime, "Kamerun-Stadt," which is today's Douala, and his self-identification may have been part of the reason why his writing has mostly been presented as having a "tribal" formulation in many a national history of Cameroonian literature. As for Ibn Khaldun, Africa was "Ifrikiya": the word "Africa" meant nothing to him, and it never appears in *The Muqaddimah*. How can one expect these three brilliant minds of a really large continent to provide an answer to the question of what African literature is, when indeed for all of them the very concept of "Africa" was problematic—as it is for me today?

It has become obvious, I hope, why Ibrahim Njoya could only be overlooked in the national histories of African literature: he asked the question of literature from the point of view of writing. Thus, instead of providing an answer to the question *"What* is African literature?" that nagged our best critics since 1962, or rather since 1939, what inspired him throughout his life was the drive to discover *how* literature can be produced on the African continent in the first place. Located beyond the *whatness* of the global paradigm, his artistic quest indicates a future we still need to investigate. His anguish in thinking through a writing system still lies ahead for us writers. Yet what about his calligrapher? Had both Ibrahim Njoyas only imagined that long before them, Ibn Khaldun had already transformed their instrumental understanding of writing into a qualitative one! But as we well know, the Sahara desert stretched between those geniuses, marking a barrier between minds that were otherwise rooted in the same paradigm. From the depth of his time, Ibn Khaldun's definition thus addresses us with vehemence and raises the need for an *artistic politics,* by which I mean a politics that appropriates the artistic paradigm *but addresses the challenges of our global present.* After all, if what distinguished us humans from animals was only our tongue, as was the belief in the tradition of Aristotle, if it is truly the *logos* only that is our distinction and our seal, then the "recurring cycle of human stupidity" (Soyinka 19)—and the genocide in Darfur is only the latest example—has shown that we have always overestimated ourselves. What remains is the need to go back to the basics and rediscover the simple truths of the alphabet.[34] Its endless permutation is what lies at the bottom of both the arts of divination and writing,[35] and as Njoya teaches us, the perfectibility of writing transforms it into a promise. "Writing is a noble craft," says Ibn Khaldun, and how true! for the alphabet can elevate us humans beyond our common animality. Yes, it has that potential; it truly does. After all, animals do not write.

Notes

1. "From the nothing all beings as beings come to be." Heidegger, *Was ist Metaphysik?* 43.
2. I use the term "crisis" in the sense of Husserl: to address the moment when a body of knowledge reaches the thresholds of its possibilities. See Husserl.
3. We may remember that Kant describes the quest for "the conditions of possibility" as being the primordial task of critique: "*Critique* . . . has as its first task to discover the sources and conditions of the possibility of such criticism, clearing, as it were, and leveling what has hitherto been waste-ground," he writes in *Kritik der reinen Vernunft 1,* 18. On the term "paradigm," see Kuhn 25.
4. Thus Irele can write: "To engage upon a discussion of the question of an adequate approach to the scholarly study and critical interpretation of African literature is to postulate at the outset a specific character of this literature which distinguishes it in some particular respects from other literatures and which for that reason requires such an approach." Irele, "Studying African Literature," in *African Experience,* 9.
5. See Tardits, "Un grand dessinateur: Ibrahim Njoya," in *Les dessins Bamum,* 53–64.
6. Claude Wauthier, *L'Afrique des Africains,* quoted in *Notre Librarie* 1, no. 100 (1990): 52. For a close analysis of some texts that use that writing system, see Schmitt but mostly see I. Dugast and M. D. W. Jeffreys and also Delafosse.
7. The first truly comprehensive criticism of African literary criticism has been written by Mudimbe, whose erudite exercise was preceded in the concrete field of literature by Mateso's *La Litterature africaine et sa critique.* In the tradition of similar studies, including the ones

written by Paulin Hountondji, Bernard Mouralis, Georges Ngal, and many others, Mateso and Mudimbe do not count the criticism written in Arabic in their corpus.

8. See Wali.

9. For the inscription of that question inside the global paradigm, see Ngũgĩ wa Thiong'o: "The language of African literature cannot be discussed meaningfully outside the context of those social forces which have made it both an issue demanding our attention and a problem calling for a resolution." "The Language of African Literature," in *Decolonizing the Mind*, 4–33, particularly 4.

10. Senghor, "Ce que l'homme noir apporte," in *Liberte 1*, 22–39.

11. The German language sees a difference between *Schreiben* (script), which is opposed to language, and *Aufschreiben* (notation), which insists on the technical dimension of writing. These two dimensions of writing open up two possibilities of analysis, the first followed by Jacques Derrida and the second by Friedrich Kittler. See Derrida, *Grammatologie*; Kittler, *Aufschreibesysteme*.

12. As such, he formulates long before McLuhan a definition of "craft" as "medium," the system of which is less restrictive and indeed purely instrumental. See McLuhan.

13. For a formulation of the use of scarcity in the transmission of knowledge in contemporary critical theory, see Foucault, *L'Archeologie du savoir*, 155ff.

14. I borrow the term "distinction" from Bourdieu but expand it from its limited use as a sociological analysis of economic and social conditions to encapsulate what singularizes humans as human. See Bourdieu, *Distinction*.

15. The French research program of mediology, the study of medial cultures and practices, as laid out by Debray, in the tradition of Leroi-Gourhan's study of gestures and instruments and Michel Serres's study of transmission, has now taken the task of analyzing instruments, from the hand to technologies, seriously. See Leroi-Gourhan; Debray. Also important is the German brand of media theory around Friedrich Kittler. See Kittler, *Gramophone, Film, Typewriter*.

16. The question of genre was polemically raised in the introduction of the book by the translator, Henri Martin. Martin later conceded that the book is indeed a memoir. See Martin, introduction, and "Le pays des Bamum et le Sultan Njoya," 5–40, particularly 24.

17. See Dugast.

18. The questions of periodicity in such a history is easy to solve when one remembers that a history of writing is a history of technologies of writing and a chronology of crafts. Such questions, which in this case concern African art history, have been addressed theoretically in Foucault, *Histoire de la sexualite 1*, 152; but mostly in Benjamin, "The Ring of Saturn or Some Remarks on Iron Construction," in *Arcade Project*, 885–87.

19. See Wim van Binsbergen, "The Astrological Origins of Islamic Geomancy," http://www.shikanda.net/ancient_models/BINGHAMTON%201996.pdf.

20. Cheikh Anta Diop theorized the "regression" of systems of formalized knowledge as being a consequence of religion, Islam in particular. See Anta Diop 171.

21. See Johnston's "Short Note on the Syllabic Writing of the Eyap," an article that announced the script but repressed the publication of collected vocabulary, but mostly see Tuchscherer.

22. A history of African literature from the point of view of writing has been attempted in the collected volume *Africa's Hidden Histories*, in which writing by clerks, teachers, catechists, school pupils, local healers, and entrepreneurs become the focus of analysis. It unearths letters, diaries, obituary notices, etc. See Barber.

23. The question of writing has certainly not been exhausted by deconstruction, although Barthes, *Le Degré zero de l'ecriture*, and Derrida, *Writing and Difference*, remain standard.

24. For an elaboration of that question, see Heidegger, "Die Frage nach der Technik," in *Gesamtausgabe*, and "Wozu Dichter?," in *Holzwege*, 259–96.

25. The concept of the "distribution" is from Rancière, but of course one should have a larger frame of reference than Schiller, whom he references, and include for instance Walter Benjamin's essay "The Work of Art in the Age of Mechanical Reproduction" but also Hegel's system of the arts as presented in his *Aesthetics: Lectures on Fine Arts* to trace its history. Equally important are Nietzsche's *Birth of the Tragedy* and the unique *Laocoön* of Lessing. See Rancière, *Politics of Aesthetics*, 24–25.

26. See Larkin.

27. For an elaboration on these two brands, see Mudimbe, *Invention of Africa*, 83; and Mbembe, "African Modes of Self-Writing."

28. See Hegel, *Philosophy* 99; and Karl Marx, "British Rule in India," http://www.marxists.org/archive/marx/works/1853/06/25.htm.

29. See Miller.

30. See Mbembe, "Necropolitics."

31. Let us remember the comments of Foucault: "Truly to escape Hegel involves an exact appreciation of the price we have to pay to detach ourselves from him. It assumes that we are aware of the extent to which Hegel, insidiously perhaps, is close to us; it implies a knowledge, in that which permits us to think against Hegel, of that which remains Hegelian. We have to determine the extent to which our anti-Hegelianism is possibly one of his tricks directed against us, at the end of which he stands, motionless, waiting for us." "The Discourse of Language," in *Archeology of Knowledge*, appendix, 235.

32. I borrow this formulation from the otherwise quite discredited Chinweizu, *The West and the Rest of Us*.

33. In contrast, the sentences of Jamaica Kincaid express the dead end of the former slave or of the one colonized in the present and his or her incapacity to imagine life beyond capitalism: "Do you know why people like me are shy about capitalists? Well, it's because we, for as long as we have known you, were capital, like bales of cotton and sacks of sugar, and you were the commanding, cruel capitalists, and the memory of this is so strong, the experience so recent, that we can't quite bring ourselves to embrace this idea that you think so much of." Kincaid 36–37.

34. For a very innovative study of the relation between writing, mathematics, and design, which draws on fractal geometry to build a system of architectural design and suggests roads for computer simulation, see Eglash.

35. A lesson that resonates with the German philosopher Gottfried Wilhelm Leibniz, who in his dissertation *Dissertation De Arte Combinatoria* (1666) not only set the principle of the endless permutation of the letters of the alphabet as the beginning of a word or verse but also rooted the principle inventivity in the art of geomancy while at the same time laying the ground for current mathematics and computer sciences.

Works Cited

Anta Diop, Cheikh. *L'Afrique noire précoloniale*. Paris: Présence Africaine, 1960.
Barber, Karin, ed. *Africa's Hidden Histories: Everyday Literacy and Making the Self*. Bloomington: Indiana University Press, 2006.
Barthes, Roland. *Le Degré zero de l'ecriture*. Paris: Le Seuil, 1972.
Benjamin, Walter. *The Arcade Project*. Cambridge, Mass.: Harvard University Press, 1999.

Bourdieu, Pierre. *Distinction: A Social Critique of the Judgment of Taste.* Cambridge, Mass.: Harvard University Press, 1984.
Chinweizu. *The West and the Rest of Us: White Predators, Black Slavers, and the African Elite.* New York: Random House, 1976.
Debray, Regis. *Cours de mediologie generale.* Paris: Gallimard, 1991.
Delafosse, Maurice. "Naissance et evolution d'un systeme d'ecriture de creation contemporaine." In *Revue d'Ethnographie et des Traditions populaires,* 3rd year, no. 9 (1922): 11–36.
Derrida, Jacques. *Grammatologie.* Frankfurt: Suhrkamp, 1992.
———. *Writing and Difference.* Chicago: University of Chicago Press, 1974.
Dugast, I. "La Langue secrete du Sultan Njoya." *Etudes Camerounaises* 3, nos. 31–32 (September–December 1950): 231–60.
Dugast, Idelette, and M. D. W. Jeffreys. *L'Ecriture Bamum. Sa Naissance, son evolution, sa valeur phonetique, son utilization.* Yaoundé: IFAN, 1950.
Eglash, Ron. *African Fractals: Modern Computing and Indigenous Design.* New Brunswick: N.J.: Rutgers University Press, 1999.
Equiano, Olaudah. *The Interesting Narrative and Other Writings.* London: Penguin Books, 2003.
Foucault, Michel. *L'Archeologie du savoir.* Paris: Gallimard, 1969.
———. *Archeology of Knowledge.* London: Routledge 1972.
———. *Histoire de la sexualite 1: La volonte de savoir.* Paris: Gallimard, 1976.
Hegel, Georg Wilhelm. *The Philosophy of History.* New York: Forgotten Books, 1899.
Heidegger, Martin. *Gesamtausgabe. Vorträge und Aufsätze.* Frankfurt am Main: Klostermann, 1972.
———. *Holzwege.* Frankfurt am Main: Klostermann, 1972.
———. *Was ist Metaphysik?* Frankfurt am Main: Klostermann Verlag, 2007.
Husserl, Edmund. *The Crisis of European Sciences and Transcendental Phenomenology.* Evanston, Ill.: Northwestern University Press, 1970.
Irele, Abiola. *The African Experience in Literature and Ideology.* Bloomington: Indiana University Press, 1994.
Johnston, H. H. "Short Note on the Syllabic Writing of the Eyap—Central Cameroons." *Journal of the Royal African Society* 20, no. 78 (1922): 127–29.
Kant, Immanuel. *Kritik der reinen Vernunft 1.* Frankfurt am Main: Suhrkamp, 1992.
Khaldun, Ibn. *The Muqaddimah.* Princeton: Princeton University Press, 2004.
Kincaid, Jamaica. *A Small Place.* New York: Farrar, Straus and Giroux, 1988.
Kittler, Friedrich. *Aufschreibesysteme, 1800–1900.* München: Wilhelm Fink Verlag, 1995.
———. *Gramophone, Film, Typewriter.* Stanford: Stanford University Press, 1999.
Kuhn, Thomas. *Die Struktur wissenschaftlicher Revolutionen.* Frankfurt: Suhrkamp, 1993.
Larkin, Brian. "Degraded Images, Distorted Sounds: Nigerian Video and the Infrastructure of Piracy." *Public Culture* 16, no. 2 (Spring 2004): 289–314.
Leroi-Gourhan, Andre. *Gesture and Speech.* Cambridge, Mass.: MIT Press, 1993.
Martin, Henri. Introduction to *Histoire et Coutumes des Bamum,* by Ibrahim Njoya. Yaoundé: IFAN, 1945.
———. "Le pays des Bamum et le Sultan Njoya." *Etudes Camerounaises* 3, nos. 31–32 (September–December 1950): 5–40.
Mateso, Locha. *La Litterature africaine et sa critique.* Paris: Karthala, 1986.
Mbembe, Achille. "African Modes of Self-Writing." In "New Imaginaries," special issue, *Public Culture* 14, no. 2 (2002): 239–75.
———. "Necropolitics." *Public Culture* 15, no. 1 (2003): 11–40.

McLuhan, Marshall. *Die Magische Kanäle: Understanding Media*. Dresden: Verlag der Kunst, 1995.
Miller, Christopher. *Theories of Africans: Francophone Literature and Anthropology in Africa*. Chicago: University of Chicago Press, 1990.
Mudimbe, V. Y. *The Idea of Africa*. Bloomington: Indiana University Press, 1994.
——. *The Invention of Africa: Gnosis, Philosophy and the Order of Knowledge*. Bloomington: Indiana University Press, 1995.
Ngũgĩ wa Thiong'o. *Decolonizing the Mind*. Harare: Zimbabwe Publishing House, 1987.
Njoya, Ibrahim. *Histoire et Coutumes des Bamum*. Yaoundé: IFAN, 1945.
Rancière, Jacques. *Aesthetics and Its Discontents*. Cambridge: Polity Press, 2009.
——. *The Politics of Aesthetics: Distribution of the Sensible*. New York: Continuum, 2004.
Schmitt, Alfred. *Die Bamum-Schrift*. Vols. 1 and 2. Wiesbaden: O. Harrassowitz, 1963.
Senghor, Léopold Sédar. *Liberte 1: Négritude et humanism*. Paris: Seuil, 1964.
Soyinka, Wole, ed. *Art, Dialogue, Outrage: Essays on Literature and Culture*. London: Methuen, 1988.
Tardits, Claude. *Les dessins Bamum: Marseille-Foumban, Cameroun*. Skira ed. Marseille: Musées de Marseilles, 1997.
Tuchscherer, Konrad. "The Lost Script of the Bagam." *African Affairs*, no. 98 (1999): 55–77.
Wali, Obiajunwa. "The Dead-End of African Literature?" *Transition*, no. 10 (September 1963): 13–16.

5 African Cultural Studies
Of Travels, Accents, and Epistemologies

Tejumola Olaniyan

IN CONTEMPORARY AFRICA, cultural creativity far outstrips cultural criticism, happily and sadly. *Happily,* because the continent is not, at least, losing out on *both* creative and critical production. Artists in all media, though many could do with more and better training to sharpen their native talents, are working prodigiously to shape form and meaning out of their demanding specific contexts and the intricate ways those contexts interact with the world. *Sadly,* because the conditions for the training of intellectuals and cultural critics are far less than adequate and because an overall healthy development of cultural creativity, the type that continually breaches accepted boundaries and invents new forms and suggests new meanings, depends on a robust interaction between talented artists and discerning critics, between the creative and the critical imagination. This is the large backdrop of my response to the challenge thrown to me, a challenge that noted, in perceivable and (understandably, I should add) wistful tones, "shifting paradigms" in the scholarly understanding of African cultural production and "a gulf between those living and working in Africa and those who live and work abroad, a gulf increasingly seen in their perspectives on the world and in the types of works they produce."[1]

I would like to begin with two stories. The first one is generic, as quite a few presentations in any African literature conference anywhere today would make clear. It is from the 2006 African Literature Association conference held in Accra, Ghana. One typical thread connecting the many discussions I participated in was what was lamented as the paucity of vigorous literary and cultural criticism on the continent. In one instance, the discussions drifted very quickly to charges and countercharges of an alleged "too theoretical" language of recent African literary and cultural criticism, "especially by scholars based in Europe and

America," to the "neglect of the political context" of the "literature itself, which is Africa." Contentious and overlapping multisided arguments ensued.

The "too theoretical" phrase was a coded polemical broadside against a particular way of doing African cultural studies, a way perceived as originating from Europe and America in the 1980s and as informed primarily by the then dominant high intellectual currents known as poststructuralism and postmodernism. The comment was not new to me. I had three years earlier published a chapter titled "Postmodernity, Postcoloniality, and African Studies" in which, in response to similar criticisms, I explored in detail the pros and cons of postmodernism and poststructuralism for the study of Africa. In response to the 2006 episode, though, I saw an opportunity for a new kind of self-reeducation. I wanted to engage in that self-reeducation by providing what I thought was sorely missing in the discussions, which it had not occurred to me to attend to in "Postmodernity" and which I could not find in existing scholarship: a portable but still broad historical accounting of the predominant modes of African cultural criticism of the last fifty years or so. My findings here constitute partly a cultural history of a scholarly method, partly an institutional history of cross-continental discourse formations, and partly an intellectual biography of a generation.

This takes me to my second story, a specific and true story. It happened in the United States, right at the moment of the explosion of what I had described as poststructuralist-informed postcolonial discourse in the 1980s. It was during the conference "Feminism and Cultural Imperialism: The Politics of Difference," held at Cornell University in April 1989 and attended by many leading scholars. A member of the audience, Omofolabo Ajayi-Soyinka, a Nigerian scholar visiting then at the Cornell Africana Studies and Research Center, commented during a general session that she did not find the literary theory known as deconstruction useful for her work. Gayatri Chakravorty Spivak, who had presented earlier during the conference and was not part of the session that just ended, stood up and responded with a lengthy monologue in defense of deconstruction and of theory, peppered with elliptical and condescending remarks about nativists, those who forget there are universities in Africa, and several other anti-theory targets. And then, without waiting for a response, she walked out of the packed hall. I was there, so I saw and heard it. It became some small scandal; the news and inevitable embellishments spread far and wide and across oceans: a leading female postcolonial scholar from India publicly humiliated a junior female scholar from Nigeria in the name of a rarefied Euro-American high theory. In a racialized American context, it quickly became the case of the Asian woman against the African woman in defense of male-dominated white, Eurocentric theory. Biodun Jeyifo, professor of English at Cornell at the time, put together a widely circulated response titled "'Race' and the Pitfalls of Ventriloquial Deconstruction: Gayatri Chakravorty Spivak's Regressive Monologue on Africa," which consisted of a transcript of Spivak's comments and Jeyifo's critical gloss. Although the action that triggered the controversy was regrettable, the outcome remained one of the most informative on the contested emergence of a new kind of what I will call a scholarly *accent* of speaking about the postcolonial and African worlds, by whom, and in what contexts.[2] *That* accent has since the 1990s become dominant, though far from hegemonic.

From these two stories, we can get a sense of how dramatic the perceived rift in theoretical orientation between and among scholars straddling postcolony-metropole divides could be and indeed was. And especially from the second story, we get a sense of the general global postcolonial character of the problem. It is not exclusively an African issue. The stories also tell us that unlike in the preceding era, in which heavy theoretical accent was implicitly or explicitly racialized as white and Euro-American,[3] some of the acknowledged carriers and most insightful bearers of that stereotyped, flashy theoretical accent in the new, post-1970s era are actually from the former colonies who have made names for themselves and now live in Europe and America or circulate frequently between there and their native countries. They include Spivak, yes, but more to the point in the African studies context Valentin Y. Mudimbe (*The Invention of Africa; The Idea of Africa*), Kwame Anthony Appiah (*In My Father's House*), and Achille Mbembe ("The Banality of Power"; *On the Postcolony*), to cite just three examples for now. The question of different, differential, and antagonistic accents became very complicated. It became implicated in a messy, tangled manner by factors such as changed and changing locations, travels, epistemologies, ideologies, and politics—all kinds of politics: race, status, gender, nation . . . Let me briefly unpack some of these.

* * *

Up until the late 1970s and early 1980s in the African academic world (and, indeed, the postcolonial world generally), one unchallenged orthodoxy was that ideology, conceived primarily in social science terms as a set of rough-and-ready ideas and beliefs shared by a group and performing explanatory, prescriptive, evaluative, orientating, and pragmatic functions, was immediately and ultimately the main determinant of (perceived) differences in intellectual thought. I would have labeled this general perspective "Marxist," and indeed Marxism had a key influence in it and provides the classic examples, but such a specific label would needlessly circumscribe the vast spectrum of ideas that I aim to capture here. The originating catalyst of the view was the anticolonial struggle beginning in the first half of the twentieth century. It was nourished by the Cold War and the division of the world into "worlds" based on "development," very ideologically driven terms. Even the supposedly "non-aligned" international organ of most of the formerly colonized territories, the Non-Aligned Movement, did little—in its political and propaganda success of the 1960s and 1970s—but, ironically, helped to entrench in the scholarly consciousness the idea of starkly divided global and local terrains ruled by warring ideologies. The same functional effect was achieved by the Organization of African Unity (OAU), later the African Union (AU).[4] Intellectual production could not but be acutely conscious of the macro-political issues that spectrally dominated the life of the nations. Especially among the academic left—a minority everywhere in Africa but with a loud moral voice though little political power—it became common sense not just to *see* particular ideological traits embedded in particular intellectual production but also to make public identification and critical evaluation of those traits the major canons of critical reading and social criticism.

Beginning in the 1980s, this common sense in the discursive characteristics of African intellectual production began to be troubled, challenged. And the prime cause was travel and location. First, there was the significant migration of intellectuals from Africa to settle in Europe and America, and second, there were those who received their advanced degrees in Europe and America and who settled there thereafter. The subsequent inevitable transnational recirculation of these intellectuals and their ideas to and from their professional locales and their homelands engendered an intellectual reengagement with their at-home colleagues that was in general unlike any previous relationship they had ever had—highly critical and contentious, yes, but with a new twist: *the location of scholarly production began to be figured as a central, acute determinant of orientations and positions, even ideologies.*

Such testy engagements were not just, as would be expected, among ideological opponents but very frequently among acknowledged ideological bedfellows. Whatever happened to the old assumption that only ideology—whether disputations across competing ones or among orientations within one—could engender such division? What could have been responsible for this "peculiar" new kind of fragmentation of an erstwhile roughly shared discursive accent?

I will give some illustrative examples and then go on to propose one way of understanding the state of affairs. To responsibly consider complex intellectual configurations that are, additionally, never completely fixed for all time, I need to make a few clarifying and demarcating caveats. Of course, ideology still remains a central marker of accents among the scholars, whether they have traveled or not. Otherwise, there would be no way to substantively account for the vigorous and polemical engagements among Chinweizu, Wole Soyinka, and Kwame Anthony Appiah during the 1970s and 1980s on such matters as the nature of the aesthetic, politics, and art and the supposed proper response of postcolonial cultural production to unrelenting Western cultural imperialism.[5] Chinweizu was the inveterate cultural nationalist against the liberal humanist Soyinka for being too liberal humanist and less African cultural nationalist; and Appiah was the cosmopolitan liberal humanist against both Chinweizu and Soyinka for being cultural nationalist, though one more so than the other. But even here, travel and migration were involved, complicating further the lines of division. Chinweizu was trained in and lived for a time in the United States but lived thereafter mostly in Nigeria, while Appiah, of mixed Ghanaian and British parentage, lived mostly in the United Kingdom and the United States. Soyinka had lived abroad, too, on and off but resided mostly in Nigeria; he is no doubt the most-traveled of the three, and indeed the most-traveled African I know. For Chinweizu, that was part of the problem, literally and metaphorically. One of his most polemical attacks against Soyinka and other African writers he dismissively called "euro-modernists" was titled, very evocatively, "Prodigals, Come Home!" Paradoxically, it was Chinweizu's overtly racialist Afro-cultural nationalism, borrowed as it was from the 1960s and 1970s Black Power movement in the United States, that was hardly "at home" in Nigeria.

Let me add even more demonstrably straightforward examples. Take the case of the intellectual itineraries of some notable African Marxist intellectuals. The extent and depth of self-revision that we witness in the works of the Nigerian Biodun Jeyifo and the Kenyan Ngũgĩ wa Thiong'o after they relocated outside the continent in the 1980s have no parallel in the works of other Marxist cultural critics who remained on the continent, such as Edwin Madunagu, Omafume Onoge, or Chidi Amuta. In Jeyifo's post-departure work, the rigor and passion still remained but the polemical intensity waned considerably; the implicit conception of the social space became far less stark and the work as a whole less orthodox Marxist and more adventurous. Even the stock of citations and footnotes changed character too.

Jeyifo is the leading scholar of Wole Soyinka, and when we compare his earlier readings of Soyinka, such as "Soyinka Demythologized" (1974) or the essays collected in *The Truthful Lie* (1985, but many published earlier), with samples of his later U.S.-based work, such as the famous 1988 essay "Wole Soyinka and the Tropes of Disalienation," his edited book *Perspectives on Wole Soyinka* (2001), or his monograph *Wole Soyinka: Politics, Poetics, Postcolonialism* (2004), we cannot but note a distinct *discontinuity* in theoretical and intellectual accent, even when there is ideological continuity. What distinguishes the new criticism is an openness that is alert to the complexities of representation of culture, difference, and their politics. Paradox, contradiction, aporia, and so on, are no longer irritations, irrationalities, or bourgeois sleights of hand to be transcended or forced into conformity by dialectical materialism, but all yield useful, indispensable insights of and on their own. Thus Jeyifo, who earlier pronounced Soyinka's mythologizing as "illusory" and the "rout of . . . true revolutionary potential" ("Soyinka Demythologized" 53), can now propose that "if the gods of mythology and traditional religious ritual and their attributes yield central ideas of traditional African thought, what Soyinka has done is to return to these ideas in order to revitalise them for contemporary society" ("What Is the Will of Ogun?" 174). Consider also his spirited efforts to show how Soyinka makes "*his* rationalisation of African traditions consistent with the will to liberation and revolution in contemporary Africa" (176; Jeyifo's emphasis). Soyinka's objectionable "rarefied" mythic constructs, Jeyifo now discovered, actually demonstrate a convergence with history in a manner as potent as it is culturally rooted ("Wole Soyinka" xx–xxi). Before, Soyinka's worldview was undialectical and conservative; now, it is constituted by complexity and a willful aporia that is immensely suggestive in reading the contemporary African condition (xxviii–xxix).

A trajectory similar to Jeyifo's could be seen in the pre- and post-exile scholarly production of the distinguished Kenyan writer and Marxist cultural critic, Ngũgĩ wa Thiong'o. We can put side by side, as a quite remarkable example, his book of essays *Writers in Politics: Essays,* which he published in 1981 shortly before he was forced into exile by the Kenyan state, and a revised and enlarged edition of the same book published in 1997, after sixteen years in Europe and America. The new title did not change much: *Writers in Politics: A Re-engagement with Issues of Literature and Society.* However, as with Jeyifo, while the ideological commitment remained, the balloon of polemical intensity had lost considerable air, and the language now embodies a greater sense of possibilities than of unnegotiable starkness. Part 1 of the earlier book, with its unmistakable oppositional title, "Literature, Education: The Struggle for a Patriotic National Culture," has become in the new edition a disarmingly commonplace but also much more accommodating "War of Images." The second part, "Writers in Politics," becomes in the new edition a more generalizing and less threatening "Words and Powers," while Part 3, with its confrontational title "Against Political Repression," now becomes a smoochy, futuristic "Links of Hope." Very "postcolonial" in tone, to invoke a stereotype. And these changes are just the tip of the iceberg. In fact, Ngũgĩ had to make clear in the preface to the new edition that "this collection of essays is more a new book than a revised edition." And the reasons for the extensive changes? In less than four lines, Ngũgĩ explains them all: outdated data and data that "seemed to cloud the central issues" (ix). Nothing at all about the significant issue of tone or accent that is my major concern here. Or, rather, we could consider accent itself as "data" whose usefulness or otherwise is subject to the vagaries of place and time.

Enough of examples. The important question now is how to make sense of these differences in accents of postcolonial African cultural studies. I have in this essay been using "African cultural studies" and "African cultural criticism" interchangeably. That is because I am invoking their more capacious meaning as the transdisciplinary study of African cultural forms and practices and the modes and contexts of their production, dissemination, consumption, and apprehension. I am using "accents" in two ways: both as *a distinctive manner of expression* and as *emphasis*. The accents of African cultural studies are many, and only a microscopic study can do thorough justice to the variety. For this occasion, I have decided to take a broad sweep and divide contemporary expressions of African cultural criticism into two large categories: the *affirmative* and the *interstitial*.[6]

By affirmative African cultural studies, I mean those studies that are more or less nationalist in character and affirmative of indigenous traditions and cultures against Euro-American cultural imperialism. This scholarly formation is of course heterogeneous in expression and orientation and in varying degrees of refinement and theoretical sophistication. In predominant terms, it is characterized by a general conception of the West as antagonist, to which the studies direct varying degrees of militancy. Expressions of affirmative African cultural studies are more likely to affirm and defend given or invented differences and identities than to interrogate them. The formation's epistemology, though of differing inflections, is overwhelmingly realist, and there is a particular privileging in its critical canons of a self-authorizing personal and collective experience. Whether produced in Africa or abroad, the accent of African cultural studies before the 1980s was principally affirmative.

Interstitial African cultural studies, on the other hand, is characterized by a sustained critique and interrogation of both the "center" and the "periphery," to borrow the old social science language. It may not be anti-nationalist, but it is by no means nationalist; rather than affirm and defend given differences such as "continent," "race," "class," "nation," and "foreign-indigenous," it tries to relativize and deconstruct them, showing how the binary oppositions can produce only not-enabling identities but disabling, identitarian positions. It very often constructs an in-between "interstitial" space supposedly subversive against the great binary absolutes of the West and the non-West. Complexity, aporia, calibrations, ambivalence, and the like are some of the key concept-themes of interstitial African cultural criticism. Its conception of resistance is more agonistic, while that of affirmative African cultural studies is antagonistic. Some of the leading names I would associate with this interstitial formation include a few that I have already mentioned—Mudimbe, Mbembe, Appiah, Jeyifo—and also Benita Parry, Simon Gikandi, Robert Nixon, Anne McClintock, Kenneth Harrow, Ato Quayson, and Neil Lazarus, among others, all living (or did at one time) in Europe or America. (I am myself sympathetic to this formation, to be critically self-conscious here.) This list is just a very adumbrated sample. Interstitial African cultural studies currently reign supreme in the powerful academic world of Europe and America, while the affirmative formation remains dominant in Africa. I am suggesting that a major marker of difference between the affirmative and discursive formations is travel, migration. This suggestion remains valid in spite of many notable exceptions I can point to, distinguished scholars resident in Europe or America whose accent is much closer to the affirmative formation dominant outside those regions. I mean scholars such as Micere Mugo, Isidore Okpewho, Abiola Irele, Eustace Palmer, Paul Zeleza, Niyi Osundare, Carole Boyce Davies, Oyekan Owomoyela, Obioma Nnaemeka, and others. They share the same orientation with the wide spectrum of mostly Africa-based scholars such as Eldred D. Jones, Omolara Ogundipe-Leslie, Ambroise Kom, Njabulo Ndebele, and Mary E. Kolawole, just to name a few.

I need to reiterate that accents are never free-floating or divorcible from the contexts that produce and give them meaning; neither are they hermetically yoked to those contexts. By "context" I mean not just spatial but also temporal; that this makes our task—as cultural theorists—more complex and challenging is not the usual standard rhetoric of difficulty. As I have argued, interstitiality as a theoretical, discursive orientation in African cultural studies began to flower in the 1980s and 1990s. The preceding era, marked by decolonization, national liberation, and anti-dictatorship struggles—and antiracist and civil rights struggles in the United States—was characterized by very stark and momentous social divisions. That binary context produced scholarship that was far more temperamentally affirmative of particular positions, irrespective of the particular ideological character of each position, than it was interstitial. Take, for instance, two instructive examples. Biodun Jeyifo trained in the United States toward the end of the civil rights–Black Power era and therefore was profoundly influenced by that foundationally binary period. Chinweizu, too, trained in the United States at about the same time. In this regard, the difference in ideological orientation between Chinweizu's Afrocentric, specifically Black Power, cultural nationalism, and Jeyifo's earlier overly exacting Marxism is less interesting than the fact that they shared a lot in the very stark nature of their formative contexts and the positively affirmative character of their cultural theorizing at that time. Both of them returned to Nigeria, though at different times, while Jeyifo relocated to the United States in the late 1980s.

The emergence and dominance of interstitial thinking in Europe and America was predicated in part on the success of decolonization and civil rights struggles. These led to an epochal opening up of the social space—Africans began governing themselves and racial apartheid eventually ended, the color bars came down in most places, and women and minorities had rights. The middle classes everywhere expanded, though with far more glittering economic benefits and privileges in Europe and America. The epochal post–World War II "opening up of the social space" turned out not to mean the end of the existing structure of *economic* inequality both between and within nations. On the contrary, the unequal remained not just firmly in place but also widening steadily. Democratization of the social space, it turned out, can happen in the context of its economic opposite. In this context, *culture* largely became the main apparently equal and equalizing weapon for interacting in that opened-up space. Everybody has a culture, and so the great binary struggles, represented most somberly by the Cold War and its underlying competing economic visions, became supposedly obsolete.[7] Europe and America had the wealth and the potent means of dissemination of ideology to exult in the affluence of the few and to persuade the majority to patiently await their turn. And "everyone" could see it was working, for the middle class was expanding, even if slowly. What inequality? But in most postcolonial African contexts, the much more speedily widening gap coupled with negative state performance could just not be hidden, and no state rhetoric was potent enough to Vaseline its craggy, venal, and nincompoop face. In these contexts, no flashy, sophisticated theoretical term could imagine a less than loud binary social space. For those of us in Europe and America, this is the reason our colleagues at home squint so much at our theorizing, stereotypically so less invested, so satisfied in tone, and so wealthy in its references. Just consider the starkly opposed ecologies of scholarly production. Imagine no electricity for twenty-four hours, or having to drive for miles in heavy traffic to a commercial Internet café to check your e-mail. You get there and the computers are unbearably slow while your money is burning out at full pace. You finally open your inbox, and the pdf of that latest article that your guilty colleague in the United States kindly sent to you cannot open because the computer is too slow—its memory too small, unstable Internet connection, outdated version of Adobe Acrobat, whatever. By this time you are tired; you yawn and scratch your head . . . *interstitial* what? Who says binarism is dead? And we have not even considered the mind-numbing scale of political corruption with impunity, from Cape to Cairo. The continued resonance of the affirmative vision in Africa today is sponsored by this reality. The interstitial accent of African cultural studies could only have been invented in and sponsored by Europe and America.

The struggle is still on between the two accents of African cultural studies about who speaks for Africa and where. Statistically, those who practice interstitiality, no matter where they are, are in the minority. The affirmative accent still dominates African cultural studies. However, in terms of social capital, the interstitial orientation is still firmly dominant in Europe and America. The scholars of that orientation hold the most prestigious positions in the most prestigious schools and publish in the most prestigious journals and for the most prestigious university presses. In the Western academy today, it is the interstitial accent, with its "refined," sophisticated discourse and seemingly less belligerent attitude toward the West, that has the greater power to speak for the African world and for African cultural studies as a practice of critical cultural self-understanding.[8]

Yes, at the level of reputation, interstitial African cultural studies reigns supreme in the West, but that does not mean it is not already gaining an aggressive and very solid foothold in Africa itself. The reasons are not hard to find. First, there is the glitter of this accent, supported by the wealth of the Euro-American academy and reproduced in tons of books, journals, fellowships, conferences, lecture invitations, and both permanent and visiting appointments. There is no hardcore affirmative-oriented scholar in Africa who can resist this in the long run. This is power. Second, as I explained earlier, unlike before, when "race" was a differentiating factor in the struggle between foreign and indigenous epistemologies and their promoters, now a number of the leading articulators of theoretical positions and languages whom many in the affirmative camp would label as "foreign" are not foreigners at all but natives, even if of a kind that are nonresident in the native land. And third and finally, the nonresident natives who now and then return speaking in a different theoretical accent are not always ideological opponents of their at-home colleagues but frequently allies. Sooner or later, their colleagues at home will be compelled to make sense of their strange but comparatively more powerful accent. Of course, we have for three decades now been living in that "sooner or later" time. Colleagues on the continent are not just listening intently to us, whether they like it or not; they are now positively awed by our scholarship—yes, by its flamboyance, but also by its *superiority* and our privilege. And if you are scandalized by what I just said, let me reiterate that our superiority is real. Just how could it be otherwise, given our many publishing outlets, our well-stocked libraries, the regularity and quality of our scholarly exchanges, our comparatively ample research funds, the generally stable and entrenched nature of our peer review system, our secure workplace, our working health care system, and more? We would have to be disingenuous to assume that these mean nothing qualitatively to what we produce compared to a context in which the factors do not exist or are rudimentary. We are obviously not born smarter at this end, only much more enabled to be smart, and so we appear to be smarter. The task is not to deny this but to ask what the responsibilities are that our privilege demands of us. In any case, just guess why Europe and America are the primary destinations of desire for many African scholars in Africa today; for many of us in Europe and America, that desire was once our own too. There are innumerable problems of racism and discrimination in our context here, but if we think that overall we have things worse than our colleagues at home, then we should be bold enough to go back and exchange places with them.

One of the characteristic features of interstitial African cultural studies is its readiness to authorize an unending list of differences to account for in criticism: not just race, class, gender, nation, and ethnicity but also language, sexuality, ecology, disability, human rights, age, region, animal rights, trash generation and disposal, and many more. From the affirmative point of view, all of this fragmentation is overwhelming and distracting. But which of these cannot be related to the "serious" political issues and the political arrangements of our African societies? None, absolutely. In fact, that fragmentation has really expanded our intellectual landscape, leading to relentless experimentation not just in critical but also in creative production. Dispersal itself has become a tool and a source of knowledge, if only we can rise up to the challenge.

My own lament is that the two accents of African cultural studies are mapped not just spatially but unequally, generally speaking: interstitial here in Europe and America, affirmative there in Africa. In spite of the generally global nature of scholarship (we study more or less the same canonical texts in foundational areas), scholarly socialization everywhere still bears strong regional imprints, and that is the way it should be. Edward W. Said calls these imprints "irreducibly first conditions" (237). There should be and ought to be different accents, in response to differences of the contexts of intellectual production. The problem comes when accents *unequally* cross borders. This is more so where there is an in-border lack of access to adequate intraregional scholarly research and publishing opportunities—opportunities through which a region can critically nurture its own views of the world in vigorous interaction with other accents. Were there long-standing and flourishing African publishing outlets that Africanists all over the world could interact with routinely, there would not be the current orphan mentality that structures the relationship of scholarship in and on Africa to Euro-America. I was talking to a senior European Africanist some time ago, and he reflected on a time forty or so years ago when the shiniest publication on one's CV was that article published in a journal in Africa: the journals were not many, but they were all well known, highly regarded, and circulating regularly. Because the scholarly exchange was active multidirectionally at the time, there was little perception of some inscrutable difference of accents across borders. Now, all those journals are dead, more or less, and there is a generation or two now of younger Africanists in Europe and America who are actually getting away without language mastery study, much less looking to the continent to publish or to keep abreast of the scholarship coming from there, once their "primary materials" have been gathered. And now, when scholars on the continent send articles to journals at this Euro-American end, many of them sound so, civilly speaking, different.

The interstitial formation is energetically dynamic and not static at all. Some might think that because such clichés as "hybridity" and "Homi Bhabha" are now infrequently bandied around, the interstitial formation is thereby waning. Nothing could be further from the truth. What has happened is that its internal transformations have actually enabled more fanciful and more (updated) politically correct terms such as "global" and "world." Again, the insights of the best manifestations of these frameworks have been useful, even if the inclusivity promised is head-scratchingly deceptive. It is the inclusivity proposed by the powerful in an unequal relationship.

So, what does this all mean? That there will soon be a time when the interstitial accent will be dominant in Africa? It is already germinating in a few universities in South Africa today. No, I do not think that there will soon be a time when the interstitial accent will be continentally dominant, so long as the sociological peculiarities that produced the distinctive accents in the different areas remain. But it is to be expected that the instinctive suspicion with which the interstitial accent is greeted in those regions will wane considerably over time, and indeed has been waning. It is because of that waning that the term "postcolonial" is now widely used by scholars based in Africa. Just remember the massive opposition to it a mere dozen years or so ago; the few holdouts sound so archaic today. Let them keep their accent and eat it; we just won't publish them or give them visiting fellowships. We in Euro-America are probably truly as mean as this sounds. But I know we are not proud of it, and we ought to change and increase our do-gooder philanthropic efforts. Even so, at the risk of sounding contradictory, I will say that an increasing embrace of the interstitial accent by scholars in Africa is far from desirable, so long as the generative center of that discourse remains outside of Africa. Since the academic and scholarly interaction between Africa and Euro-America remains unequal, a growing embrace of the interstitial accent in Africa could only be sponsored less by the conviction of its insights, appropriateness, or utility and more by the blinding glitter of its attractions—those fellowships and teaching positions abroad, big grants, and conference funding. Equality is the indispensable first condition for the productive mutual abrasion of accents. I am sure we can and will get to that point; I just do not know when.

Notes

1. Frieda Ekotto and Kenneth Harrow, conference invitation letter, February 24, 2010. My gratitude to all attendees for the vigorous discussion of my keynote address. I also specially acknowledge Ekotto's and Harrow's perceptive comments on this version.
2. In addition to Jeyifo's response, see Ajayi-Soyinka's own description of

> a controversy I inadvertently generated during a conference . . . at Cornell University in 1989, when I made an analogy between the reserved reception of white-based feminist criticism among African and African-American women. My observation that because feminist critical perspective is framed by colonialism in Africa and racism in America, deconstruction theory is an inadequate analytical tool, provoked a sharp response from Gayatri Spivak, and later, a spate of private and public rejoinders between some African critics, Spivak, and myself. ("Black Feminist Criticism and Drama" 161)

For a longer reference, see her "Transcending the Boundaries of Power." At the beginning, Spivak invoked the gender specter, professing anger at her being made "an object of a widely circulated scurrilous smear campaign by men, professing outrage for a silent woman of color, who do not want to acknowledge the responsibility of their own positioning in the US" ("Reading" 93). Later on, though, and as gestures of rethinking herself, she did begin to make affirmative side references now and then to Ajayi-Soyinka's work—see her interview with Robert J. C. Young, "Gayatri Chakravorty Spivak," and her essay "How to Read a 'Culturally Different'

Book," first published in 1994 and now included in the big collection of mostly previously published essays, *An Aesthetic Education in the Era of Globalization*. Even so—and this remains strange and meaningful—Spivak seemed to become kinder only after persuading herself that Ajayi-Soyinka was an artist rather than a scholar. In the interview, Ajayi-Soyinka was "a Nigerian dancer who teaches dance at the moment in the United States" (12), and in "How to Read," Ajayi-Soyinka was "a renowned dancer from Nigeria" (90).

3. For a now classic account of this problematic, see Jeyifo, "Nature of Things." See also, in a vaster context, his "In the Wake."

4. Rich background contexts could be found in texts such as Alavi and Shanin, *Introduction*; July, *African Voice*; Escobar, *Encountering Development*; Freire, *Pedagogy of the Oppressed*; Mohammed, *Africa and Nonalignment*; and Willetts, *Non-Aligned Movement*. On the OAU/AU, see Francis, *Uniting Africa*; and Akokpari et al., *African Union*.

5. See Chinweizu, Jemie, and Madubuike; Soyinka; and A. Appiah. See also Chinweizu's *The West and the Rest of Us* and *The Anatomy of Female Power*.

6. I am adapting these terms from Jeyifo, "For Chinua Achebe," but I bear full responsibility for their particular extensions in this context.

7. See Olaniyan, "What Is Cultural Patrimony?"

8. In other words, there is an unmistakable theoretical alliance between interstitial postcoloniality and postmodernism, in spite of the differences carefully sketched out in Appiah's famous essay "The Postcolonial and the Postmodern." See also Bhabha's less famous essay of the same title.

Works Cited

Ajayi-Soyinka, Omofolabo. "Black Feminist Criticism and Drama: Thoughts on Double Patriarchy." *Journal of Dramatic Theory and Criticism* 7, no. 2 (Spring 1993): 161–76.

——. "Transcending the Boundaries of Power and Imperialism: Writing Gender, Constructing Knowledge." In *Female Circumcision and the Politics of Knowledge: African Women in Imperialist Discourses*, edited by Obioma Nnaemeka, 47–80. Westport, Conn.: Praeger, 2005.

Akokpari, John, Angela Ndinga-Muvumba, Tim Murithi, and Salim A. Salim. *The African Union and Its Institutions*. Auckland Park, South Africa: Jacana Media, 2009.

Alavi, Hamza, and Teodor Shanin, eds. *Introduction to the Sociology of "Developing" Societies*. New York: Monthly Review Press, 1982.

Amuta, Chidi. *The Theory of African Literature: Implications for Practical Criticism*. London: Zed Books, 1989.

Appiah, Anthony. "Soyinka and the Philosophy of Culture." In *Philosophy in Africa: Trends and Perspectives*, edited by P. O. Bodunrin, 250–63. IleIfe: University of Ife Press, 1985.

Appiah, Kwame Anthony. "The Postcolonial and the Postmodern." In *In My Father's House: Africa in the Philosophy of Culture*, 137–57. New York: Oxford University Press, 1992.

Bhabha, Homi. "The Postcolonial and the Postmodern." In *The Location of Culture*, 171–97. New York: Routledge, 1994.

Chinweizu. *Anatomy of Female Power: A Masculinist Dissection of Matriarchy*. Lagos: Pero Press, 1990.

——. "Prodigals, Come Home!" *Okike: An African Journal of New Writing* 4 (1973): 1–12.

——. *The West and the Rest of Us: White Predators, Black Slavers, and the African Elite*. New York: Vintage, 1975.

Chinweizu, Onwuchekwa Jemie, and Ihechukwu Madubuike. *Toward the Decolonization of African Literature, Vol. 1: African Fiction and Poetry and Their Critics.* Washington, D.C.: Howard University Press, 1983.
Davies, Carole Boyce. *Black Women, Writing, and Identity: Migrations of the Subject.* New York: Routledge, 1994.
Escobar, Arturo. *Encountering Development: The Making and Unmaking of the Third World.* Princeton: Princeton University Press, 1995.
Francis, David J. *Uniting Africa: Building Regional Peace and Security Systems.* Burlington, Vt.: Ashgate, 2006.
Freire, Paulo. *Pedagogy of the Oppressed.* Translated by Myra Bergman Ramos. 1973. New York: Continuum, 1993.
Irele, Abiola. *The African Imagination: Literature in Africa and the Black Diaspora.* New York: Oxford University Press, 2001.
Jeyifo, Biodun. "For Chinua Achebe: The Resilience and Predicament of Obierika." In *Chinua Achebe: A Celebration,* edited by K. H. Petersen and A. Rutherford, 51–70. Oxford: Heinemann, 1990.
———. "In the Wake of Colonialism and Modernity." *Anglophonia/Caliban* 7 (2000): 71–84.
———. "The Nature of Things: Arrested Decolonization and Critical Theory." *Research in African Literatures* 21, no. 1 (Spring 1990): 33–48.
———, ed. *Perspectives on Wole Soyinka: Freedom and Complexity.* Jackson: University Press of Mississippi, 2001.
———. "'Race' and the Pitfalls of Ventriloquial Deconstruction: Gayatri Chakravorty Spivak's Regressive Monologue on Africa." Texts from the "Feminisms and Cultural Imperialism: The Politics of Difference" conference, Cornell University, April 22–23, 1989.
———. "Soyinka Demythologized: Notes on a Materialist Reading of *A Dance of the Forests, The Road,* and *Kongi's Harvest*" (1974). Ife Monographs on Literature and Criticism. Department of Literature in English, University of Ife, Nigeria, 1984.
———. *The Truthful Lie: Essays in a Sociology of African Drama.* London: New Beacon Books, 1985.
———. "What Is the Will of Ogun?" *Perspectives on Nigerian Literature: 1700 to the Present.* Vol. 1. Edited by Yemi Ogunbiyi, 169–85. Lagos, Nigeria: Guardian Books, 1988.
———. "Wole Soyinka and the Tropes of Disalienation." In *Art, Dialogue and Outrage: Essays on Literature and Culture,* vii–xxxii. Ibadan, Nigeria: New Horn Press, 1988.
———. *Wole Soyinka: Politics, Poetics, and Postcolonialism.* Cambridge: Cambridge University Press, 2004.
July, Robert W. *An African Voice: The Role of the Humanities in African Independence.* Durham: Duke University Press, 1987.
Lazarus, Neil. *Nationalism and Cultural Practice in the Postcolonial World.* Cambridge: Cambridge University Press, 1999.
Mbembe, Achille. "The Banality of Power and the Aesthetics of Vulgarity in the Postcolony." *Public Culture* 4, no. 2 (Spring 1992): 1–30.
———. *On the Postcolony.* Berkeley: University of California Press, 2001.
McClintock, Anne. *Imperial Leather: Race, Gender, and Sexuality in the Colonial Contest.* New York: Routledge, 1995.
Mohammed, Bala. *Africa and Nonalignment: A Study in the Foreign Relations of New Nations.* Kano, Nigeria: Triumph, 1978.
Mugo, Micere Githae. *Writing and Speaking from the Heart of My Mind: Selected Essays and Speeches.* Trenton, N.J.: Africa World Press, 2012.

Ndebele, Njabulo. *Rediscovery of the Ordinary: Essays on South African Literature and Culture.* 1991; Scottsville, South Africa: University of KwaZulu-Natal Press, 2006.
Ngũgĩ wa Thiong'o. *Writers in Politics: A Re-engagement with Issues of Literature and Society.* Rev. and enlarged ed. Oxford: James Currey, 1997.
———. *Writers in Politics: Essays.* London: Heinemann, 1981.
Okpewho, Isidore. *Once Upon a Kingdom: Myth, Hegemony, and Identity.* Bloomington: Indiana University Press, 1999.
Olaniyan, Tejumola. "Postmodernity, Postcoloniality, and African Studies," In *Postmodernism, Postcoloniality, and African Studies,* edited by Zine Magubane, 39–60. Trenton, N.J.: Africa World Press, 2003.
———. "What Is Cultural Patrimony?" In *Marvels of the African World: African Cultural Patrimony, New World Connections, and Identities,* edited by Niyi Afolabi, 23–35. Trenton, N.J.: Africa World Press, 2003.
Parry, Benita. *Postcolonial Studies: A Materialist Critique.* New York: Routledge, 2004.
Quayson, Ato. *Calibrations: Reading for the Social.* Minneapolis: University of Minnesota Press, 2003.
Said, Edward W. "Traveling Theory." In *The World, the Text, and the Critic,* 226–47. Cambridge, Mass.: Harvard University Press, 1983.
Soyinka, Wole. "Neo-Tarzanism: The Poetics of Pseudo-Tradition." In *Art, Dialogue and Outrage: Essays on Literature and Culture,* 315–29. Ibadan, Nigeria: New Horn Press, 1988.
Spivak, Gayatri Chakravorty. "How to Read a 'Culturally Different' Book." In *An Aesthetic Education in the Era of Globalization,* 73–96. Cambridge, Mass.: Harvard University Press, 2012.
———. "Reading *The Satanic Verses.*" *Public Culture* 2, no. 1 (Fall 1989): 79–99.
Willetts, Peter. *The Non-Aligned Movement: The Origins of a Third World Alliance.* New York: Nichols, 1978.
Young, Robert J. C. "Gayatri Chakravorty Spivak: Neocolonialism and the Secret Agent of Knowledge: An Interview with Robert J. C. Young." 1991, pp. 1–44, http://robertjcyoung.com/spivakneocolonialism.pdf (accessed June 27, 2012). Originally published in *Oxford Literary Review* 13 (1991): 220–51.
Zeleza, Paul. *Manufacturing African Studies.* Dakar, Senegal: Codesria, 1997.

6 *Le* Freak, *C'est* Critical and *Chic*

North African Scholars and the Conditions of Cultural Production in Post-9/11 U.S. Academia

Lamia Benyoussef

IN AN INTRODUCTORY English composition class I taught a few years ago, an African American student asked me if she could write her comparative essay on the immigration and integration experiences of Arab and Caucasian Americans. When I pinpointed that the U.S. Census Bureau classified Arab Americans as Caucasians and suggested that she drop the racial categories in favor of a geographic terminology (that is, Middle Eastern and European immigration), in total shock and disbelief she exclaimed: "Arabs do 9/11 and they are still whites?" For a moment I froze there, not knowing what to say. I was not sure if she was angry at me because I was guilty by association or at her own self for still failing to be "white," even though she was no evildoer like me, her teacher. That life-altering teaching moment repatriated me in W. E. B. Du Bois's discourse on the Negro veil in *The Souls of Black Folk*. "It dawned upon me with a certain suddenness" that North African women academics too (alias *moukéres* or *les négresses des sables*) "are different from Others; or [like them perhaps] in life and longing, but shut out from their world by a vast veil." If the point of this essay can be summed up in one sentence, it is the desire to tear down that veil, to creep through the silences and wonders of the academic world "and live above in the blue sky," free from the pitfalls of colorisms and the haunting shades and "shadows"[1] of diversity. This chapter is inspired not only by my own experience as an Arab and Muslim academic in the South but also by the scholarly work and experiences of other North African scholars who find themselves, like me, in the double bind functioning as a native informant (after all, Islam keeps enrollment high) while remaining on the threshold of American academia because their physical presence is as critical as the critical languages they teach.

In contrast with the commonly held thesis that African writers living abroad are more likely to be "experimental" and explicit about sexuality and inclusive of "marginal groups"[2] than their colleagues at home, this essay argues that in the context of the Maghreb, this dichotomy, far from being based on any tangible reality, is in fact a patronizing Eurocentric construct that infantilizes African writers as suppliers of raw materials (plays, films, and novels) for Western metropolitan consumption, that is, literary criticism and theory. Such a position wrongly assumes that only the African author in Europe or North America has the freedom to be creative, avant-gardist, and inclusive of others, as if "creativity" or "morality" could crop up only on "Western" soil. Even if it is true that publications in North and sub-Saharan Africa have been largely realist, this realism translates less the absence of creativity than the integration of African writers within their social and academic environment. In the context of Tunisia, Algeria, and Morocco, for example, the last decade has seen a surge in the production of both literary theory and fictional works like plays, novels, and films in both Arabic and French. Relying on the literature produced by North African expatriate scholars in the last decade, I will demonstrate that the focus on language and sexuality of expatriate Maghrebi writers is less an indication of their newly found liberty than a sign of their academic ghettoization after 9/11. Under the corporate (and imperial) notion of diversity as spectacle, the only place for a North African scholar/author in American academia, in particular, is that of the exhibitionist-voyeur who unveils ad nauseam the Muslim female body, the Arab mind, and Islamic patriarchy while remaining on the threshold of the American dream. Things are worse for expatriate North African women scholars who find themselves confronted with new forms of patriarchal and sexual violence in the workplace. The first section of this essay addresses not only the conditions of cultural production for North African academics in Western universities but also the nascent engagement of Maghrebi writers in the ongoing debates over the Holocaust, the Spanish Inquisition, the genocide of Native Americans, and immigration. The central argument here is that these trends are the direct outcome of ghettoization and identification with former/current marginalized groups rather than a sudden ennoblement by the Western values of tolerance, freedom, and diversity, which are endemic to their host countries.

Focusing on the articulation of gender in the production of knowledge about the Maghreb, the second section argues that the new interest in women academics in North Africa and the Middle East is not so much a reflection of the plight of university women outside the United States as it is a sign of the increasing haremization of American academia. Just as Simone de Beauvoir used the female body of Moroccan women to forge for herself a place in the manly world of

French letters, some American women scholars, inheriting the imperial and hegemonic discourse of French feminism, have also erected their own academic careers by writing/appropriating the bodies and voices of Muslim women residing abroad. Except for a few, the ghettoization and intellectual violence against their Arab American or Muslim sisters in Western universities remain of no interest to them. This ideological scotoma can be explained by a combination of factors ranging from the silence of complicity, fear of retaliation, and political naïveté to the uncritical adoption of French feminism in which Muslim women often appear as bodies and voices but always missing a brain, a history, and an individual agency. Whereas some American women academics are still writing about the North African female body, Assia Djebar, Nina Bouraoui, and Malika Mokeddem, women scholars in the Maghreb, are de facto the new agents of change in their countries, not the mascots of diversity, as is often the fate of their expatriate sisters, who are subjected to all forms of policing and surveillance.

Immigration and the Legacy of Colonial Rule in Western Academia

While most scholarship by Africans and non-Africans focus on the legacy of European colonialism in Africa, little has been written about the transfer of the racial hierarchy common to French and British colonial societies into the heart of metropolitan universities in the postcolonial era. In *Citizen and Subject*, Mahmood Mamdani argues that one of the main obstacles to the democratization of African societies in the postcolonial era is the inherited legacy of colonial indirect rule between subjects (natives) and citizens (Europeans), which persisted in the postcolonial period in the form of a bifurcation of power disproportionately shared between the individual and the African state. Extending Mamdani's argument to postimperial European societies, this chapter argues that with globalization and the migration of Africa's skilled labor to Western countries, the colonial legacy of indirect rule has also found its way into Western academia, as noticed in the bifurcated power structure between tenured and tenure-track faculty citizens (mostly whites and male) and nontenure-track or part-time faculty subjects (mostly women minorities and new immigrants). While American women earned 52.3 percent of all doctoral degrees in 2009 ("Fast Facts"), only 23.9 percent of women were in tenure-track positions in 2010 ("Table 11"). Women in academic positions in 2012 in the United States earned 93 percent of men's salary at the instructor's level, 91 percent at the assistant professor level, 92 percent at the associate professor level, and 90 percent at the professorial level ("Almanac"). According to the same source, out of the total number of assistant professors, 60,407 were white men; 57,211 were white women; 4,607 were black men; 6,035 were black women; 10,037 were Asian men; 7,253 were Asian women; 3,265 were Hispanic men; 3,064 were Hispanic women; 298 were Native American men; 381 were Native American women; 8,182 were nonresident foreign men; and 4,175 were nonresident foreign women ("Number"). Although they do not tell us much about the actual number of faculty of North African origin, these statistics leave us with two lingering questions: What legal protections are extended to Arab and Muslim faculty of North African or Middle Eastern origin when they are classified as white/Caucasian by the U.S. Census Bureau? What does diversity mean when the skin of a faculty member is too brown to teach Shakespeare or too white to teach Wole Soyinka or serve on a school diversity committee? Because Islamophobia is recognized neither in its individual nor institutional manifestations, Muslim or Arab faculty in U.S. academia are the least protected minority against discrimination in employment, salary, and career opportunities. The appropriation or classification of Arab Americans as Caucasians not only de-Africanizes the achievements of ancient North African civilizations but, more important, conceals the institutionalized forms of discrimination against Arab and Muslim Americans today.

While Mamdani leaves out gender in his study of citizenship and indirect rule in postcolonial Africa, I would like to add gender to my discussion of the colonial legacy of indirect rule in Western academic institutions. The haremization of the humanities, in particular, has taken the form of a racialized, gendered, and sexualized pyramid that recalls the racial and gender segregation in fin de siècle French and British colonial societies. When located in the West, the caste-system characteristic of colonial societies in Africa is renamed diversity. In the aftermath of 9/11, the academic ghettoization of Arab and Muslim scholars in U.S. universities has become more blatant since the Patriot Act legalized discrimination against Arab Americans and Muslims in the name of national security and public safety. As soon as Arab Americans or legal alien scholars of Middle Eastern or North African origin dare invoke the principle of gender or racial equity in the workplace, the specter of Islamic terrorism is invoked, and they are immediately branded safety threats.

In the aftermath of 9/11, a career in English, French, or Middle Eastern studies has been almost foreclosed for many Maghrebi scholars residing in the United States.[3] Even though they hold PhDs in English or French, to survive, many of them are now forced into teaching positions where they have to teach and advertise Arabic as a critical language—that is, their mother tongue as a dangerous/terrorist/treacherous/unsafe/satanic language. Through their multilingual and interdisciplinary skills, North African scholars in American universities are now expected to unveil to their young American students "the secrets of the Muslim mind" under the noble objectives of global citizenship and cross-cultural understanding. While corporate academia presents bilingualism as an invaluable asset to prospective students, the trilingualism of Arab and Muslim faculty of North African origin is often an impediment to their tenure and promotion. While faculty are often encouraged to spread themselves thin in the name of interdisciplinary and enrollment, this well-roundedness becomes a liability for Arab or Muslim faculty who find themselves denied tenure and promotion under the vulgar excuse that they have "leur cul entre deux chaises," that is, because their position is not clearly defined in one field as those of their non-Arab or non-Muslim colleagues.

One could argue that throughout U.S. academia, French programs have come under the gun because of state budget cuts, but this alone does not explain why only a few tenure-track dual positions in Arabic and francophone studies have been opened over the last years to answer the increasing demand for Arabic classes. Because Nietzsche's noble Arab is "generous," one Arab faculty member is more than enough to build an entire academic program gratis, that is, through independent studies. While Spanish departments have on average six or seven full-time faculty to run their academic program, only one full-time faculty member at best is hired to build the Arabic program. Even though Africa is the future of France, as former French president Nicolas Sarkozy put it a few years ago, the U.S. undergraduate French curriculum remains highly Eurocentric and includes only francophone African texts that have been decontaminated from their Africanness to fit into the narrative frame of the French civilization mission. Just as Léopold Sédar Senghor remains included because of his *éloge de la francité*, Assia Djebar's texts are carefully selected to show how French language liberated Arab women in Algeria from Islamic tradition (Redonnet et al. 190). If the number of students in upper-level French programs is today shrinking, it is because very few French classes address the challenges of the twenty-first century. A French class on François de La Rochefoucauld or a class module on the Cajun culture of New Orleans is less likely to prepare students for the job market than a French course in contemporary African politics, yet there is a strong resistance in some universities to broaden the French curriculum to include francophone literatures, histories, politics, and cultures of the African world, even if this decentering could help save French programs by attracting students from international studies, political science, business, engineering, and the health sciences. Very few French programs have hybridized the content of their curriculum or attempted to strike a balance between liberal arts education and francophone classes for specific purposes.

Scheherazade in Diversistan

In response to Zora Neal Hurston's statement that the black woman is the mule of the world (14), I would like to suggest that institutional racism and sexism has not disappeared from U.S. academic institutions; it has just changed its target. State budget cuts alone do not also explain why in some U.S. institutions only Arab and Muslim women faculty are required to publish like tenure-track faculty do while not being on a tenure-track. State budget cuts alone do not explain why the very few tenure-track Arab and Muslim women faculty have to wait three years to teach one course in their research areas while their colleagues are allowed to do so nearly every semester. State budget cuts alone do not explain why instructors with no educational background in either North African or Middle Eastern studies are appointed directors of such academic programs and are trusted with the task of observing the teaching of tenured and tenure-earning Arab or Muslim female faculty. In other fields, such positions are usually assigned to senior faculty in the field, not to instructors with a master's degree in a nonrelated discipline.

Should they complain that their research areas have been given to part-timers, Arab and Muslim women faculty are told, "Our institution is egalitarian. It does not discriminate in research between part-timers/full-time instructors and tenured/tenure-track faculty." This expedient notion of equity finds antecedent in French colonial policies in North Africa. In 1895, Victor de Carnières, a colonial settler from Le Parti des Prépondérants, opposed the extension of French citizenship to Tunisian Jews under the excuse of preserving equity between the Muslim and Jewish indigenous population: "We are adamant to combat with all our strength the Tunisian Jews' tendency to isolate themselves from the native population and to form, thanks to some special institutions, a sort of a state within a state."[4] Just as in colonial times, the principle of equality among natives was used to deny Tunisian Jews equity with French colonial settlers, in postimperial times, the principle of equality between part-timers/full-time instructors and tenured/tenure-track Muslim faculty is there only to conceal the inequities between Muslim and non-Muslim tenure-earning faculty.

The plight of Arab and Muslim women expatriate academics recalls the biblical story of Jacob and Laban's two daughters. Just as Laban deceived Jacob by substituting Leah for Rachel in order to extend his servitude another seven years, U.S. corporate academia often deceives Muslim women faculty into signing job contracts that indefinitely dangle and postpone their tenure. While most assistant professors get tenured between four and eight years after their original tenure appointment, many expatriate Arab/Muslim women faculty are tricked into a system that requires that they toil for an initial period of seven years as a non-tenure-track research assistant professor (with the same duties and obligations in teaching, research, and service as tenure-track faculty but with the lower pay of an instructor) before being given the equal opportunity to be on track for tenure. Should *la négresse des sables* protest these Western-style Dhimmi Laws, she becomes a toxic waste, a cancer that must be surgically removed lest it contaminate the purity of Haran's well and flock. As long as the North African girl strokes our imperial ego by constantly reassuring us (through her teaching, scholarship, and service) how our French language gave her a voice and rescued her grandmother from the yoke of Arab culture and Islamic tradition, and as long as she develops safe courses that increase enrollment, such as Sexuality in Islam, Human Rights in the Muslim World, the Sociology of Islamic Terrorism, Islam vs. Modernity, Male vs. Female Honor in the Middle East, and the Belly-Dancer and the Sheikh, her presence can only add spice and flavor to the humanities. The moment North African women faculty mention on the syllabus Bigeard's shrimps and death flights, or the "enfumades" of Pélissier and Bugeaud, the Muslim/Arab "girl" is placed under surveillance lest she hurt herself and others (let's not forget the 9/11 terrorist attacks and Nidal Malik Hassan). At best, she is told, "Your research endeavors clearly fall outside the realm of French culture and civilization. You don't have a place in our department. We need a faculty who is happy to teach French culture and civilization."

Over a hundred years ago, the French novelist Jules Lemaître wrote that the Algerian Moorish woman was "a child" with "no more soul than a flower" (qtd. in Lazreg 40). Similarly, in many North American universities, the expatriate North African woman scholar is infantilized in the position of child star/mascot/entertainer who sings "wild and pretty" (qtd. in Lazreg 40) to increase enrollment but has no career prospects of her own. While being themselves denied equal opportunity in employment because they are "Arabs" and "Muslims," under the oppressive capitalist structure of corporate academia, North African scholars are expected to be the salesmen who sell Arabic language courses (and in the long run the natural resources of the Middle East) in the same package as global ethics: buy Arabic 101, and you have the Caves of Ali Baba.

While in North African state universities, women scholars have equal pay for equal work, Barbara Petzen, curriculum specialist and outreach director for the Middle East Policy Council, is organizing workshops for schoolteachers at UCLA to tell them that in the Middle East, "a young woman would be under enormous pressure to make perfect stuffed grape leaves for the family of her fiancé. [The grape leaves] should be as thin as a pinkie finger, stuffed so they do not burst when cooking, and spiced to the future mother in-law's tastes" (MacVan). The grape leaves lesson is an American vision of the Middle East "which has become objectified" rather than a Middle Eastern authentic cultural practice. In this lesson plan, while the subject of discussion is absent (no people of the Middle East are interviewed or invited to the classroom), it is the American teachers and policy makers who are writing the script and performing what they believe Middle Eastern culture is. In this classroom, the Middle East is literally and metaphorically a spectacle produced by the West for Western consumption, a performance that tells us more about gender relations in American academia than women's conditions in the Middle East.

Unlike American female teachers who transfer their domestic culinary skills into the workplace to "earn . . . points toward salary increases" (MacVan), in North African universities, the boundary between academic work and domestic chores cannot be crossed. Women female faculty are neither forced to cook for their students and male colleagues for cross-cultural understanding nor reprimanded for lack of collegiality if they refuse to cook, sing, or dance for their colleagues and students. North African women scholars like Olfa Youssef, Raja Benslama, Nawal Saadawi, Fatima Mernissi, Assia Djebar, Amal Grami, Boutheina Ben Hassine, Nejet Mchala, Aroussia Nalouti, Fatma Ben Mahmoud, and Saloua Charfi Ben Youssef are loved/hated/promoted/denied promotion for their intellectual work, not for their cooking skills. The corporate coax of inclusiveness has caused a sense of false consciousness or misrecognition among many American women academics: to secure their jobs, they can only project themselves onto other spaces and write about the female body in the East; they do not have the freedom to write about their own.

Are Arab and Muslim Americans the New Jews or the New Blacks? Emerging Topics in North African Exilic Literatures

Because of the aforesaid academic ghetto, many expatriate Maghrebi scholars in the United States have recently engaged in interethnic dialogues over the Holocaust, immigration, slavery, Jim Crow, and the concentration camps for Japanese Americans during World War II. Their intent is not to relativize or minimize the horror of the Holocaust/slavery/Jim Crow or to make a career for themselves but to theorize and come to terms with their own social, economic, and academic ghettoization. Magical realism, irony, and avant-gardist forms not only are therapeutic but are shields against censorship, institutional isolation, and political persecution. In his book *How Does It Feel to Be a Problem?*, a title that derives from a question raised in Du Bois's *Souls of Black Folk*, the Egyptian-born scholar Moustapha Bayoumi interviews many young Arab Americans about their experiences in post-9/11 America. As if to seek confirmation, Sade, one of the interviewees, says to Bayoumi: "We're the new blacks. . . . You know that, right?" (2). In this book, Bayoumi also establishes a parallel between the detention centers for Arab Americans after 9/11 and those for Japanese Americans (or other compound nationalities) in the aftermath of the 1941 Pearl Harbor attack (40). Similarly, Steven Salaita in *Anti-Arab Racism in the U.S.* calls for a new form of political positioning for Arab Americans, one that would be in alignment with the struggles of other minorities, arguing that the political racism against them is deeply rooted in political and theological institutions related to the history of Western imperialism and the "dispossession of Indians. . . . Anybody serious about combating racism should approach American society with a cyclical rather than a linear methodology" (213–14).[5]

Just as in *À la Recherche du Temps Perdu*, Proust inhabits the body of Scheherazade to come to terms with his marginalization as a Jew and a homosexual in fin de siècle France, many North Africans in the United States and Europe are now symbolically inhabiting the body of the Jew in the interwar period to come to terms with their own experience of suffering and alienation in post-9/11 Western academia. In *We Are All Moors: Ending Centuries of Crusades against Muslims and Other Minorities,* the Moroccan-born Anouar Majid argues that the specter of the Moor not only shaped and fueled the extermination of Amerindians and later the Jews in World War II but also continues to provide the hidden text that forms the current perception of Hispanics and other immigrants in the United States. As Majid puts it,

> The paradox of minorities in any national unit is that their presence is practically indispensable to shaping national identity, yet their vilification inevitably escalates into calls for expulsion or deportation—measures that rarely, if ever, produce the sort of tranquility imagined in the early phases of intolerance and persecution. To cite two of the most famous examples in history: The expulsion of Moriscos in Spain and the deportation and annihilation of Jews in Germany did not strengthen either nation; on the contrary, both nations were weakened and, in the case of Germany, even defeated by such pathological measures. (Majid 46)

One cannot ignore the implicit analogies Majid makes between the Mudéjar's status in seventeenth-century Spain and the status of Muslims and Arab Americans under the twenty-first-century Patriot Act. Both the Arizona Senate Bill 1070 and Alabama House Bill 56 anti-immigration laws have stigmatized the Mexican population and sanctified the legal expression of racism against all brown people, including Arabs. If section 13 of Alabama's anti-immigration law makes it a crime for religious sanctuaries to harbor "illegal immigrants" (a common practice hitherto in churches and synagogues), it is for the purpose of deterring Muslim illegal immigrants (that is, terrorists) from seeking shelter in mosques. It is the common history of racism and marginalization between Mexicans and Arab Americans that has made Majid and many other Arab American scholars organize against institutional discrimination in Arizona and Alabama. This explains why, despite the fear of deportation, so many young Arabs and Muslims in Alabama participated in the demonstrations against HB 56.[6]

Although based in France, the scholarship of the Tunisian-born psychiatrist and scholar Fethi Benslama has not, lately, been immune to the kind of constraints encountered by his colleagues in North America. In his 2002 book *Psychoanalysis and the Challenge of Islam,*[7] Benslama departs from the Judeo-Christian framework that underlies Freud's and Lacan's psychoanalytic formulation of the father-son conflict and argues that the God of Islam has neither sons nor daughters. Instead of the father son-conflict, he holds the father's abandonment (of his wives or children) as the primary trauma in the Muslim psyche, from the story of Abraham's abandonment of Hagar and Ishmael in the desert, to Muhammad's status as an orphan and his symbolic abandonment (through death) by his biological and adoptive fathers.[8] In his recent article "The Agony of Justice," on suicide attacks and martyrdom in Islam, he posits the secularization of death in the West through the substitution of the divine father (*pater*) with the fatherland (*patrie*) (126–27) and self-sacrifice or martyrdom for God in the Muslim world. Even though he is quite right in observing that the three-letter prefix in *istchhadi* (demander of sacrifice) entered the Arabic language only in the 1980s[9] with the Israeli occupation of southern Lebanon, he abandons altogether his 2002 thesis that the Muslim psyche is haunted by the absence of the father. Indeed, he resurrects/invents a new Muslim father who is none other than Hussein, son of Ali and Muhammad's son-in-law. These suicide attacks, he argues, constitute a new invention, even though they masquerade as an Islamic tradition, for the Shi'i *Istishhadi* is today reproducing rather than remembering the martyrdom of Hussein.[10] Benslama's resurrection or invention of a Muslim *pater* in 2010 illustrates the ideological constraints that frame the conditions of cultural production and reception of works of North African writers in the West. Benslama's seminal work on Islamic psychoanalysis, which was ignored in the anglophone world over the last twenty years, is now being translated into English and will certainly be used in the next decades or centuries to come as a flashlight to map out and illuminate the darkness of the Muslim and Arab psyche. Can a North African "Muslim"[11] scholar residing in the West have the freedom *not* to speak about Islam or Muslim women's bodies? My answer is "no" because we are still enmeshed in the nineteenth-century anti-Semitic rhetoric[12] that defines the Jew/the Muslim/the Arab solely through his or her monotheistic beliefs and relationship with women. It is that same secular racism that continues to govern cultural production of North African writers in the American diaspora.

In the aftermath of 9/11, the word "dialogue" came to be constructed in the U.S. media and academia as the bridge between East and West, the desert and the forest. High school and university curricula were revised to emphasize intercultural dialogues and global citizenship ethics. Fulbright grants were given to American and foreign scholars to foster exchange and engage otherness in Africa, Europe, Asia, and Latin America, with particular emphasis on the Middle East. This intercultural dialogue, which stems from the ethos of global responsibility, is built on many silences: Who is included or excluded from these dialogues? What issues are present or absent in these round tables? Who is being silenced in the name of global responsibility? What complicities are there between academic responsibility and the irresponsibility of global capital?[13] What patterns of gendered and racialized responsibilities undergird state-funded research projects in the sciences and humanities? Why do we teach culture and not the economy or the environment? The notion of global and/or academic responsibility seems to be based on an invisible epistemic violence, all the more oppressive because it is veiled in the noble rhetoric of human rights and global ethics. As a Tunisian academic residing in North America, I feel silenced by the ghetto of diversity that emphasizes my culture but not my history, my vagina but not my brain. How do North African women academics survive, challenge, subvert, and deviate from the institutional corporate script when the only course they are encouraged to develop is on the male honor of their father they hide between their Muslim thighs? What a strange wording! I did not invent this strange language. I was asked once to develop a course on Islam in North Africa. A male supervisor suggested that I include a unit on the location of male honor in Islam: "You know, how in your culture, a man's honor is between the thighs of his sister, mother, and daughter. You know what I am talking about . . ." That day, I understood the humanities' complicity in institutionalizing racism and buttressing sexual violence against women.

French Imperial Legacy and the Crisis of Translating Maghrebi Women's Literature in the Anglophone World

There is a considerable incongruity between the Arabic cultural production by North African women scholars at home and its translation or lack thereof in the anglophone world. The gap comes from the Eurocentric interest in francophone literature and dismissal of Arabic cultural production. For instance, two articles in Cybelle H. McFadden and Sandrine F. Teixidor's collection *Francophone Women: Between Visibility and Invisibility* reproduce the kind of Eurocentric feminism that silences rather than reveals the full scope of North African women's writings. Written from the point of view of French *écriture féminine*, the titles of the two essays are almost identical: the first is Mary Ellen Wolf's "After Images of Muslim Women: Vision, Voice, and Resistance in the Work of Assia Djebar," and the second is Adrienne Angelo's "Vision, Voice, and the Female Body: Nina Bouraoui's Sites/Sights of Resistance." The current silence regarding Arabic literature produced by Tunisian, Moroccan, and Algerian women academics is astounding. The silence concerning the new generation of Tunisian women scholars of Arabic expression stems not only from the anglophone scholars' ignorance of Arabic but, more important, from their bias toward Arabic and refusal to see that it is the Arabic women scholars who are the real agents of change in their communities. Unlike their expatriate sisters in the United States, Tunisian women scholars (whether they teach Arabic, French, or English) have more opportunities to work their way up the academic ladder. The most seminal works in Tunisia are produced by young *docteurs d'état* in Arabic who publish in Arabic (although many of them also master French and English). To name only a few: Amal Grami is one of the outspoken advocates of equal citizenship for Egyptian Copts, Raja Benslama is a strong proponent of *laïcité* in the Muslim world, and Olfa Youssef pioneered the new school of Islamic psychoanalytic feminism. In *The Bewilderment of a Muslim Woman*,[14] Youssef does not shy away from finding hospitality for gay people in certain Qur'anic verses or from conversing with medieval and contemporary male scholars on "unfeminine" debates on halal or haram sex. In an earlier work, *Weak in Mind and Religion: Chapters in the Prophet's Hadiths*,[15] she does not hesitate to use Lacan's concept of the *qadhîb* (phallus) to reinterpret on the symbolic level the Qur'anic verses often used to deny women equal rights in inheritance and political leadership. Reinterpreting the word *din* (religion) as political power, she argues that it is on the symbolic level (that is, political power, not faith) that women are feeble. The silence regarding the achievements, respect, and recognition of Tunisian women scholars by their colleagues, students, and communities in their home countries speaks volumes about the complicity of Western feminists with global power as they continue to run the broken record of French *écriture féminine* to study North African women's literature. Also, the national and international success of Jalila Baccar's play *Khamsun* (Fifty)—which is an indictment of the postcolonial state and the secular elite's responsibility in the rise of the *integrist* movement in Tunisia—is a clear indication that in the twenty-first century, North African Muslim women are the agents, not the symbols, of change. Similarly, the work of Aroussia Nalouti (novelist) and Fatma Ben Mahmoud (poet) as high school teachers did not prevent them from becoming widely respected literary critics in Tunisia and beyond: while the former is one of the pioneers of the feminist political novel, the second is the first to create an Arabic *écriture féminine* that appeals to both men and women. Similar changes have been observed in Morocco by Fatima Sadiqi and Moha Ennaji.[16]

If francophone scholarship on the Maghreb is stuck in the trope of "the North African woman without a voice," it is simply because Western scholars do not like what Maghrebi women are saying; to use a Tunisian proverb, "They hear with one ear." The exclusive focus on francophone North African women's literature, far from showing that Arabic is an oppressive language preventing women from expressing themselves as they can in French (the liberating language of their colonial masters), reveals on the contrary the complicities between state power and corporate academia. The most important scholarly works written in Tunisia in the last decade were, in fact, by the new generation of university women who received their academic training in Arabic and Islamic studies in Tunisia, not in France or North America. Writing one's subjectivity through the detour of the other is not new; it is the hidden text of Simone de Beauvoir's *écriture féminine*. In August 1938, on the eve of World War II, Beauvoir and Jean-Paul Sartre organized a vacation together to Morocco. The journey came after the French publisher Grasset rejected Beauvoir's first work of fiction, *La Primauté du spirituel* (*The Prime of Life*).[17] Even though the book reviewer, Henry Müller, found her description of certain intellectual milieus quite accurate and commended her for "her intelligence" and her ability "to observe and analyze" the condition of postwar young French women under "the intellectual currents of their day," he rejected her manuscript for lack of "originality" (Beauvoir, *Prime* 262–63).

Beauvoir's 1938 trip to Morocco can be read, therefore, as a quest for originality—how else could she forge herself a position in the male-dominated world of French academia? In Casablanca, Beauvoir and Sartre got bored with "the European Quarters" and decided to visit the native shantytown or ghetto. In contrast with the American feminist writer Edith Wharton, who praised General Lyautey for the "Torch of Civilization" he brought to North Africa, Beauvoir felt ashamed and attributed these horrible conditions (which Wharton and many others constructed as native traditions of dirt and uncleanliness) as the direct outcome of French colonialism and segregationist policies in Morocco (Beauvoir, *Prime* 261). Beauvoir's criticism of French imperialism did not prevent her from stepping in the footsteps of Gide, Larbaud, and Morand and adopting their male orientalist, scopic drive through which the world is produced as an exhibition:

> All manner of delights awaited us. We adored Fez: it combined extremes of secrecy and riotous extroversion—on the one hand veiled women, shuttered places, and impenetrable *medersa* and mosques; on the other, lavish displays of goods, with hawkers and shopkeepers shouting and gesticulating fit to beat the band. But secrecy won out over openhandedness: as we walked back up the main street at dusk, with torches flaring, on both sides we observed officers barricading the dark alleyways with chains; first the gates of the souks, then those of the town itself were closed behind us. (262)

It was the interplay of things accessible and inaccessible, the visible and the invisible, the sacred and the forbidden that made Sartre and Beauvoir's stay in Morocco delightful. It was lack or prohibition (the castrating officers and their chains) that fueled their desire to penetrate the labyrinthine female body of Fez, emasculating its male-gendered souks and raping its female-gendered alleyways. In Bous-bir, the Jewish and Arab quarters were compared to those imperial fairs and "exhibitions" in Western metropolitan centers.

What Beauvoir observed in those "model villages" exhibited in France "were not just exhibitions of the world" but, in the words of Timothy Mitchell, "the ordering up of the world itself as an endless exhibition" (218, 220). As "picture," a model native village, or what we refer to in academia today as "a model language village," the world is "before an audience on display—to be viewed, investigated, and experienced" (220).

It is as spectacle, as an imperial exhibition for French tourist consumption, that Arab women appear in the feminist literature of the mother of French feminism. Beauvoir recalls her trip with Sartre to the native bordello of Bous-bir: "I was amazed to find cafés and grocery shops there. We met an Arab woman who was heavily tattooed and swathed with long flowing robes, over which she wore masses of heavy, *clashing* jewelry. She took us to a bistro, and then to her room, where she undressed, *did a belly dance,* and smoked a cigarette through her vagina."[18]

Many questions come to the fore. Primary among these are the following: What does it mean for a French woman scholar to stand and gaze at the gendered subaltern's "smoking" vagina in the company of a male companion and fellow academic, who is no other than Jean-Paul Sartre, the father of French existentialism? Why did Beauvoir's feminist scholars remain silent over these scenes within the pages of their scholarship on *écriture féminine*? Is it perhaps because in 1961 Beauvoir helped bring to trial the rapists of Djamila Boupacha?[19] Is it perhaps because of the silence of shame and complicity in the violation of the gendered subaltern's body? What does it mean for the mother of French feminism to gaze at the vaginas of her "*soeurs musulmanes*" to claim for herself a place in French academia? Just as the Arab woman masculinizes and empowers herself by putting the phallic cigarette in her vagina, the French woman masculinizes and empowers herself by putting the phallic pen in her hand. It is only by objectifying the female body of the gendered subaltern as spectacle that Beauvoir was able to forge for herself a career in the male world of French letters. The illiterate Moroccan prostitute and the educated aristocratic French woman reach the same conclusion: the freak is an instrument of social, economic, and gender inscription; while the first exhibits her body for survival, the second exhibits the gendered subaltern's body for scholarly recognition.

This French imperial imaginary not only has found its way in the U.S. rhetoric of multiculturalism but also has conditioned the topics that North African women scholars can teach or produce in the diaspora. If they are allowed to teach anything besides their dangerous mother tongue, it is usually courses on excision, honor killings, human rights in the Muslim world, and the like. In other words, we have not moved far from Beauvoir's spectacle of the Muslim vagina with a cigarette, a freakish synecdoche that still shapes our scholarly and voyeuristic thirst for undressing the subaltern female body and the infamous *phallus Islamicus*.

Mitchell observes that at the 1889 Paris Universal Exhibition, French organizers displayed Egyptian girls, dervishes, Oriental perfumes, and donkeys at the Cairo Pavilion in order to show France's imperial grandeur. Just as the Egyptian delegation to Paris at the turn of the last century felt objectified, disgusted, and degraded by the stare of Europeans, Arab or Muslim woman faculty feel today violated by the insidious form of institutional violence that exhibits their bodies and "dangerous" Muslim/Arab minds on the noble Pavilion of Ethic and Civic Responsibility yet allows them no position to generate new meanings for diversity other than that of the spectacle.

In conclusion, I would like to draw a parallel between the current condition of the North African scholar teaching in Western academia and the portrait of the "freak" in Leslie Aaron Fiedler's *Freaks: Myths and Images of the Secret Self*:

> There is, that is to say, no agreement among these traditionally called freaks about what they would like for programmatic reasons to be called now; only a resolve that it *be something* else. Those who still earn their living by exhibiting themselves inside shows apparently prefer to be known as "entertainers" and "performers," like tightrope walkers and clowns. But larger numbers of

strange people do not want to be considered performers or indeed anything special or unique. They strive, therefore, to "pass," i.e., to be assimilated into the world of normals. (11)

Fiedler draws a distinction here between the performer and the freak: while the first performs and exhibits himself or herself and others for *le fric* (for a living), the second refuses to be exhibited. In the first case, self-exhibition is a choice, and in the second, normalcy and acceptance are sought, not the spectacle to be made of oneself. Fiedler's distinction between the freak and the performer does not take into account cultural, gender, and racial differences. In our commodified world (including that of academia), racial, ethnic, sexual, social, or cultural differences have been transformed into an exhibition or spectacle. Through the flow of global capital, the corporatization of academia, and the immigration of African scholars into Europe and the United States in the last forty years, the old colonial indirect rule has shifted inward to the center of Western academia. In corporate academia, expatriate North African women scholars are the new freaks displayed on the stage of cultural diversity. Being themselves the spectacle, they neither write nor edit the corporate script; they are exhibitionist-*voyeuses*, not *metteuses en scène*. Sartre's and Beauvoir's bordello has moved center stage, from the colony to the center of empire, from the jungles of Africa to the theater of civilization. Like the Moroccan prostitutes in French colonial Morocco and the nineteenth-century colonial exhibitions in Paris, London, and Chicago, in the twenty-first-century Western Harem of Arts and Letters, expatriate North African women scholars are expected to excise their brains and exhibit their bodies, that is, to discuss, teach, and write about their vaginas (the locus of the male honor of their fathers, brothers, and husbands) for cross-cultural understanding. The only tenure-track position they can aspire to is that of the exhibitionist-*voyeuse* or the "*striptiseuse* of the Muslim mind."[20] What can my cultural production be in these conditions? I have no choice but to laugh at myself and from time to time wage therapeutic razzias on the excising scalpels of academia.

Notes

1. The reference is to W. E. B. Du Bois's "Of Our Spiritual Strivings" in *The Souls of Black Folk* 2008, The Project Gutenberg Book, http://www.gutenberg.org/files/408/408-h/408-h.htm#chap01 (accessed February 15, 2014).

2. From the announcement of "Conference on Critical Theory Concerning Cultural Production of African Literature and Cinema," sponsored jointly by Michigan State University and the University of Michigan, proposed by Kenneth W. Harrow and Frieda Ekotto, October 29–30, 2010.

3. While American media continue to demonize Arabs and Muslims by presenting them as primitive, bloodthirsty, and women-haters, the "American dream" is ironically shifting eastward to the Arab/Persian Gulf. Because of the current economic crisis, many American

scholars, architects, businessmen, and engineers are immigrating to Bahrain, Qatar, the United Arab Emirates, Saudi Arabia, and Kuwait, where they enjoy the "Neo-colonial Third"—an economic privilege given exclusively to European and American citizens who are not cursed with Arab names. "Arabic is certainly a great career if you are an American student," I sometimes find myself (*malgré moi*) advising my favorite Arabic students and cynically laughing at myself.

4. "Un danger," *La Tunisie Française,* June 15, 1895, cited in Annabi.

5. Even though Steven Salaita is a Palestinian American, I will include him in this essay because anti-Arab racism in U.S. academia has targeted not just Muslim Arabs but also Christian Arabs like Salaita, Edward Said, and Joseph Massad.

6. In spring 2013, a twenty-year-old undergraduate Iraqi student majoring in international studies at the University of Alabama at Birmingham was selected by the Birmingham Civil Rights Institute (BCRI) as the Outstanding Youth Honoree of the year in recognition of her leadership role in raising awareness of Alabama's new anti-immigration law (HB 56) and in organizing the Students for Justice in Palestine Movement on campus. This recognition, which coincided with the fiftieth anniversary commemoration of the Sixteenth Street Baptist Church bombing in Birmingham, became quite controversial when the BCRI received letters protesting that the award went to an "anti-Semite." See Sutten.

7. The book was published in 2002 as *La Psychanalyse à l'épreuve de l'Islam.* In 2009 it was translated into English under the title *Psychoanalysis and the Challenge of Islam.*

8. Benslama's insight throws light on many North African folktales and on Abdelwahab Meddeb's "Poème d'Auschwitz," where the Jew appears as an Ishmael, i.e., an abandoned child, not in the desert this time but in the "concrete" slabs and crematory ovens of the death camps where God "has withdrawn." See Meddeb 164–65. It is unfortunate that Benslama abandoned that theory to focus on Islamic martyrdom.

9. It is neither from the Middle Ages nor from the Qur'an, as both Muslim fundamentalists and the experts on terrorism argue (Benslama, "Agony of Justice" 130).

10. Benslama's focus on Shi'i and Sunni male suicide attackers overlooks the role of gender in the articulation of the "Self-putting to death of the Other." As a matter of fact, the first woman suicide bomber in the Middle East was neither a Shi'i Lebanese nor a Sunni Muslim; she was a Christian woman. The cross of Santiago de Compostela that the Spanish soldiers dispatched to Iraq in the summer of 2003 puts into question Benslama's claim about the secularization of death in the West.

11. I am using here Fethi Benslama's definition of "Muslim" as one who belongs to Islamic civilization (poetry, philosophy, rationalist traditions, poetry, sciences, etc.) rather than to the Islamic faith. See Benslama, *Déclaration d'insoumission.*

12. See Renan.

13. I am indebted here to Spivak's insightful questions in "Responsibility," 23.

14. The title *The Bewilderment of a Muslim Woman: In Inheritance, Marriage and Homosexuality* is my translation. The original Arabic title is *Hayratu muslima: Fi al miraath, wa al zawaaj, wa al jinsiya al muthlaa.*

15. My translation of the Arabic title, *Naaqisaatu 'aqlin wa din.*

16. See Sadiqi and Ennaji, *Women in the Middle East and North Africa.*

17. Published in 1979 under a new title, *Quand prime le spirituel.*

18. The original French text reads differently: "Une Arabe couverte de tatouages, de bijoux bruyants et d'une longue robe nous emmena dans un bistrot, puis dans sa chambre: elle ôta sans robe, fit trembler son ventre et fuma une cigarette avec son sexe" (*La Force de l'âge* 338). In the original French text, we find neither "belly dancing" nor "clashing." Why had the original French expressions ("bijoux bruyants," jingling jewelry, and "fit trembler son ventre," moving/trembling her stomach, been changed into "clashing jewelry" and "belly dancing"? Here, the

English translator is not translating but rather recreating and reinventing the sentence to make it fit the American visual arrangement of the world.

19. Boupacha was an Algerian woman tortured and raped with a bottle by fascist members of the French army during the Algerian Revolution. See Beauvoir, Halimi, Alleg, and Audin.

20. I am very grateful to the few colleagues and friends at work who helped me escape whenever they could the psychological violence of ghettoization through genuine acts of religion. I am very thankful, in particular, to my former chair, Dr. Sheri Spaine Long, who stood up for me and gave support to my teaching assistant and Arabic students in my darkest hours. I extend my gratitude as well to those who did not, do not, and will never feel comfortable with the fact that I am a Muslim and an Arab woman. They also allowed me to see that I, Sycorax, mother of Caliban and daughter of Hannibal the Cannibal, I forgive, not "despite" my North African "Muslamic" culture but because of it, "and I refuse to go anywhere" (Salaita 29).

Works Cited

"Almanac of Higher Education." *Chronicle of Higher Education,* April 8, 2012, http://chronicle.com/article/faculty-salaries-data-2012/131431#id=144050 (accessed October 1, 2012).
Annabi, Hassan El. "L'Autre' à travers le journal de la Tunisie Française: Le sangsue, l'Abruti, et le Chinois de l'Europe (1892–1900)." *Cahiers de la Méditerranée* 6 (2003), http://cdlm.revues.org/index1000.html#ftn14 (accessed October 12, 2012).
Baccar, Jalila. *Khamsun.* Tunis: Dar al Janub li al nashr, 2007.
Bayoumi, Moustapaha. *How Does It Feel to Be a Problem? Being Young and Arab in America.* New York: Penguin Press, 2008.
Beauvoir, Simone de. *La Force de l'âge.* Paris: Gallimard, 1960.
———. *The Prime of Life.* Translated by Peter Green. Cleveland: World, 1962.
———. *Quand prime le spirituel.* Paris: Éditions Gallimard, 1979.
Beauvoir, Simone de, Gisèle Halimi, Henri Alleg, and Maurice Audin. *Djamila Boupacha.* Paris: Gallimard, 1962.
Benslama, Fethi. "The Agony of Justice." In *The Israeli-Palestinian Conflict in the Francophone World,* edited by Nathalie Debrauwere-Miller, 123–40. New York: Routledge, 2010.
———. *Déclaration d'insoumission: A l'usage des musulmans et de ceux qui ne le sont pas.* Paris: Champs Flammarion, 2005.
———. *La Psychanalyse à l'épreuve de l'Islam.* Paris: Aubier, 2002.
———. *Psychoanalysis and the Challenge of Islam.* Translated by Robert Bononno. Minneapolis: University of Minnesota Press, 2009.
Djebar, Assia. *Algerian White: A Narrative.* New York: Seven Stories, 2000.
"Fast Facts" National Center for Education Statistics, http://nces.ed.gov/fastfacts/display.asp?id=72 (accessed October 6, 2012).
Fiedler, Leslie Aaron. *Freaks: Myths and Images of the Secret Self.* New York: Simon and Schuster, 1978.
Greĭgoire, Henri, and Rita Hermon-Belot. *Essai sur la reĭgeĭneĭration physique, morale et politique des Juifs: Ouvrage couronneĭ par La Socieĭteĭ Royale des Sciences et des Arts de Metz, Le 23 Aoʾt 1788.* Paris: Flammarion, 1988.
Hurston, Zola Neale. *Their Eyes Were Watching God.* New York: HarperCollins, 1998.
Lazreg, Marnia. *The Eloquence of Silence: Algerian Women in Question.* New York: Routledge, 1994.

MacVan, Mary. "Teachers Learn a Lesson in the Cultures of Food." *Los Angeles Times,* August 12, 2009, http://articles.latimes.com/2009/aug/12/food/fo-teach12 (accessed June 25, 2012).

Majid, Anouar. *We Are All Moors: Ending Centuries of Crusades against Muslims and Other Minorities.* Minneapolis: University of Minnesota Press, 2009.

Mamdani, Mahmood. *Citizen and Subject: Contemporary Africa and the Legacy of Late Colonialism.* Princeton: Princeton University Press, 1996.

McFadden, Cybelle H., and Sandrine F. Teixidor. *Francophone Women: Between Visibility and Invisibility.* New York: Lang, 2010.

Meddeb, Abdelwahab. *L'Exile occidental.* Paris: Albin Michel, 2005.

Mitchell, Timothy. "The World as Exhibition." *Comparative Studies in Society and History* 31, no. 2 (1989): 217–36.

"Number of Full-Time Faculty Members by Sex, Rank, and Racial and Ethnic Group, Fall 2007." *Chronicle of Higher Education,* August 24, 2009, http://chronicle.com/article/Number-of-Full-Time-Faculty/47992/ (accessed October 5, 2012).

Proust, Marcel. *À la Recherche du Temps Perdu.* Saint Amand: Gallimard, 1997.

Redonnet, Jean-Claude, Ronald St. Onge, Susan St. Onge, and Julianna Nielsen. *Héritages francophones: Enquêtes interculturelles.* New Haven: Yale University Press, 2010.

Renan, Ernest. *Études d'histoire religieuse.* Saint Amand: Gallimard, 1992.

Sadiqi, Fatima, and Moha Ennaji. *Women in the Middle East and North Africa: Agents of Change.* Milton Park, Abingdon: Routledge, 2010.

Salaita, Steven. *Anti-Arab Racism in the U.S.: Where It Comes From and What It Means for Politics Today.* London: Pluto University Press, 2006.

Spivak, Gayatri Chakravorty. "Responsibility." *Boundary* 2, no. 21 (1994): 19–64.

Sutten, Marie. "DFLL Student to Be Honored by Civil Rights Institute." *UAB News,* April 22, 2013, http://www.uab.edu/news/student-experience/item/3395-uab-student-to-be-honored-by-civil-rights-institute (accessed February 16, 2014).

"Table 11: Percent of Faculty in Tenure-Track Appointments and Percent of Faculty with Tenure, by Affiliation, Academic Rank, and Gender, 2011–12." *American Association of University Professors* (2012), http://www.aaup.org/NR/rdonlyres/33D4FF44-CEF5-45F7-8845-00E5D40525BB/0/Tab11.pdf (accessed October 1, 2012).

Wharton, Edith. *In Morocco.* New York: Nabu Press, 2010.

Youssef, Olfa. *Hayratu muslima: Fi al miraath, wa al zawaaj, wa al jinsiya al muthlaa.* Tunis: Dar Sahar li al nashr, 2008.

———. *Naaqisaatu 'aqlin wa din.* Tunis: Dar Sahar li al nashr, 2003.

7 Reading "Beur" Film Production Otherwise

The Poetics of the Human and the Transcultural

Safoi Babana-Hampton

IN HIS ANALYSIS of the cinema verité of the 1960s both in Europe and Quebec, especially as practiced by French filmmaker and ethnologist Jean Rouch, Italian filmmaker Paolo Pasolini, and Quebecois filmmaker Pierre Perrault, Gilles Deleuze proposes a new viewpoint from which to understand the distinction of fiction versus truth or subjective versus objective: "Objective and subjective images lose their distinction, but also their identification, in favor of a new circuit where they are wholly replaced, or contaminate each other, or are decomposed and recomposed" (149). As a consequence, Deleuze continues, "the cinema can call itself *cinéma-vérité*, all the more so because it will have destroyed every model of the true so as to become *creator and producer of truth:* this will not be a cinema of truth but the truth of cinema" (151, my emphasis). As Deleuze's lines suggest, the conventional boundaries governing our understanding of the two notions of "truth" and "fiction" collapse and disappear in favor of a new notion of "truth" as being primarily a *construct*, or a situated act of formalizing human experience. This act characterizes the very essence and raison d'être of the cinematic enterprise, whose field of application Deleuze extends even to works traditionally defined as documentary reportages or ethnographic investigations, such as those produced by Rouch and Perrault (149). Deleuze thus develops a view of the cinematic work as a visual field within which the poetic, the lyrical, and the aesthetic as well as the documentary and ethnographic elements are intertwined and interdependent and cross-fertilize each other in order to depict a multilayered reality or lived experience. All these considerations of the cinematic work are deeply inscribed in his conception of the artist, of whom he offers the following definition: "What the artist is, is *creator of truth*, because truth is not to be achieved, formed, or reproduced; it has to be created. There is no other truth than the creation of the New" (146–47).

In this essay, I examine the implications of critical approaches to Franco-Maghrebi film productions, which usefully integrate Deleuze's view of the artist and of the cinematic work. It is only by integrating formal/aesthetic approaches to "Beur" cinema, or what could be more appropriately called "transnational" cinema (following Hamid Nafici's use of the term below), that complement and enter into dialogue with cultural, sociological, and political approaches that one can fully understand them in their complexity and broad significance. Aesthetic approaches to these films consisting of a methodical study of the creative processes engaged by the artists are susceptible to delivering an understanding of the role of art in affirming the subjectivity and agency of the artist. They help us gain a unique insight into the ways that the artist's work shapes his or her milieu, as well as discern the forces that condition, inspire, and nourish the artist's cinematic imaginary.

When one examines the critical discourse associated with the reception of cinematic works by filmmakers of the Maghrebi diaspora or representing French minorities of North African origin, it is clear that the model of social cinema is a privileged paradigm. Critiques grounded in descriptive labels such as "banlieue cinema," "Beur cinema" (Tarr), or "urban cinema" generate readings that are sociorealist in their bent and attribute a primarily ethnographic value to these films. These cinematic works have been widely perceived as a means of raising social awareness about the living conditions of immigrants and cultural minorities of North African origin and about the failure of French urban planning politics in securing their successful social and economic integration. Films such as *Hexagone, Douce France,* and *Voisins, voisines* by Malik Chibane, *Le Gone du Chaaba* by Christophe Ruggia (adapted from Azouz Begag's eponymous novel), and Mehdi Charef's *Le Thé au Harem d'Archi-Ahmed* seem to be recognized almost exclusively for their documentary value. Indeed, this is precisely what explains the rare success of *Le Thé au Harem d'Archi-Ahmed* and its recognition as Best First Film by the French film academy in 1986. After the booming success enjoyed by his first film, Mehdi Charef sought to chart new frontiers in his cinematic adventure by attempting through his 2007 film, *Cartouches gauloises,* to disassociate his artistic activity from the reductive labels "banlieue" and "Beur." However, this film was not met with the same critical interest enjoyed by his first one (Milleliri).

The oppressive nature of the label "Beur cinema" or "banlieue cinema" drives some filmmakers such as Karim Dridi to describe it as "the ghetto of social cinema." Echoing Deleuze's and Charef's view of cinema, Karim Dridi maintains that social cinema does not exist and that it is a mere invention of professionals of the film market who impose a false hierarchy among elitist auteur films, politically correct films, and, at the extreme end of the spectrum, intellectually shallow commercial films. He asserts that as an artist he never sets out to make social cinema through his films but to make films that question the social order. Though produced in a different cultural context, Charef's and Dridi's films increasingly mirror the same aesthetic concerns expressed by filmmakers from the Maghreb such as Algerian Merzak Allouache, Tunisian Ferid Boughedir (also a film critic and film historian), and Moroccan Laila Marrakchi. Films such as *Bab El Oued City, Un été à la Goulette, Villa Jasmin,* and *Marock* ushered in filmmaking trends devoted to forging new conceptions of the cinematic image and promoting a vision of the cinematic practice rooted in the recognition of the interwoven character of its militant and aesthetic elements. Boughedir affirms in an interview with Radio France International that what filmmaking means to him is that "nous pouvions, nous aussi, devenir des *créateurs* de l'histoire du cinéma, et non seulement ses admirateurs" ("we too can become *creators* of the history of cinema and not merely its admirers") (Lequeret, my emphasis).

In a recent and well-documented study attending to the limitations of prevailing critical approaches to African film productions, Olivier Barlet rightly devotes a substantial portion of his analysis to the problematic occlusion of the agency and subjectivity of filmmakers from the African continent in critical discourses developed around their filmic productions. Through an extensive and probing critique of a wide range of cinematic works from the African continent and critical discourses attached to them, Barlet takes issue with approaches that either confine African film productions to what he terms the "ghetto of Otherness," reducing their meaning and horizon of possible interpretations to a perceived ethnic difference and cultural essence, or to the Sartrian notion of political engagement, defining the task of the artist essentially in terms of a moral imperative to change the world. In contrast to these two narrow perspectives, Barlet makes a case for redefining the role of the film critic in terms of a responsibility to recognize the African filmmaker-artist as being first and foremost a *creator* of images—that is to say, as a subject who expresses a certain way of seeing and thinking about the world and engages the viewer to participate in the process of meaning-making to transform not so much the world but rather images of or ways of thinking about the world that continue to nurture and legitimate endemic forms of alienation and suffering in the human condition (*Les cinémas* 22–29). As can be seen, Barlet's account of critical discourses applied to filmic productions from the African continent finds strong resonance in the experience of filmmakers of the North African diaspora in France. On a related level, his proposed model for reading differently film productions from the African continent bears relevance to works produced by filmmakers of the North African diaspora in France, as will be shown below.

As one of the first Franco-Maghrebi films from the first decade of the third millennium, Ismaël Ferroukhi's *Le Grand Voyage* is an understated yet powerful expression of the artist's desire to foreground and enact his primary role as *creator* of image in Deleuze's sense. As will be shown through specific examples in this analysis, what the film achieves through its singular formal features, transcultural setting, and thematic content is a sustained and multidimensional meditation on creativity and on the way in which Ferroukhi's poetics of the transcultural and the human spur his cinematic imaginary. Indeed, what unfolds before our eyes is vaguely reminiscent of Baudelairean poetics (see Baudelaire, "Le Peintre de la vie moderne"), insofar as it is engaged in extracting beauty and harmony from the indifferent, prosaic, and ugly (sub)urban landscape inhabited by cultural minorities of North African origin. I will study the way this cinematic production develops narrative and visual motifs that evoke a desire to understand, parody, or resist contradictory sides of territorialized conceptions of identity. It will be shown that the contemporary reinvestment of the traditional rite of Muslim pilgrimage or "journey" through the displacement of time and space as anchors of identity ushers in the return of humanist thought and the crystallization of a transcultural consciousness, which dispel sectarian views of identity.

Set in the city of Aix-en-Provence, not far from Marseille (in southern France), which is home to an important number of Muslim minorities of North African origin, Ferroukhi's award-winning film examines the physical, psychological, and spiritual journey undergone by a father and a son, estranged from each other in the complex postmodern world of the Moroccan diaspora in France. In this film, Ferroukhi draws on the Islamic rite of pilgrimage to frame the two characters' attempts to negotiate specific identity dilemmas, deriving largely from their diasporic status. The story is centered on the character Réda, who grudgingly yields to his father's order to take him on a road trip across Europe toward Mecca, their final destination. The aging father's ultimate purpose is to perform one of the most sacred pillars of Islam and foundational enactments of Muslim identity, namely pilgrimage, which he hopes to complete before he dies. Forced to abandon his secret love as well as interrupt his school schedule before the end of the academic term (missing his *baccalauréat* exam in the process), Réda is forced to reach deep into his soul and draw closer to his father by being literally stripped off all the exterior markers of his modern and Westernized daily life (his cell phone, his French passport, and his right to privacy and personal freedom confiscated by his authoritarian father are but a few examples). I argue that the film examines generational differences by depicting the ways that Muslim minorities (re)define their bearings in a (post)modern Western multicultural context and by assessing how these differences are negotiated inside the family structure as well as in the larger French society. Additionally, emphasis will be laid on how different generations come to terms with them in order to preserve their individual integrity and to ensure their spiritual salvation.

Drawing on various perceptions of pilgrimage and travel in the context of Morocco, I will show how the film modernizes this sacred rite by highlighting the individual, psychological, and intersubjective dimensions of the journey, as opposed to the institutional connotations it has historically carried (that is, as an act of affirmation of collective belonging to a community of believers or of affiliation with a doctrine, and so on). Abdelkébir Khatibi, Abdallah Hammoudi, Abdellatif Laâbi, and Rita El Khayat, some of Morocco's most important intellectual voices whose works focus on the study of relations between Islam and modernity, underline the vital importance of the notion of "journey" and "travel" around the world in traditional as well as in modern constructions of Muslim identity. The thematic emphasis of some of the narratives they have produced in recent years is on "pilgrimage" and "travel," attesting to a growing interest among Moroccan intellectuals and artists in rethinking Islamic identity in (post) modern and multicultural Western societies by appropriating the richly evocative Arabo-Islamic trope of *rihla* (the Arabic word for "journey" or "travel") and endowing it with new layers of meanings in order to bring out its contemporary relevance.

The French title of the film *Le Grand Voyage* is a literal translation of its Arabic counterpart, *a-rihla al-koubra*, which appears on the screen as the credits roll on. The French word *voyage*, however, does not quite capture the intellectual, spiritual, and historical roots of the word *rihla*. Historically, the *rihla* often evoked in the Muslim imagination the experience of religious pilgrimage and the image of the Muslim pilgrim as the archetypal traveler. In his study of travel accounts by Muslim pilgrims from Morocco, Abderrahmane El Moudden notes that the *rihla* carries two meanings: on the one hand, it designates actual travel, and on the other hand, it refers to "travel accounts" or narratives (69). El Moudden identifies three types of *rihlas* that dominated in Morocco before modern times: first, *rihlas* within Morocco; second, *rihla hijaziyya* (referring to travel to the Hijaz or Arabia for pilgrimage), which "resulted in oral or written comprehensive reports on the travel and on the various aspects of the pilgrimage" (70); and third, *rihla sifariyya* (including embassies and missions) "in which the writer reported on his travels in foreign lands" (70). Among these three types of *rihlas*, pilgrimage is considered the most important. According to El Moudden, the *rihla* had an ambivalent impact on the Moroccan Muslim traveler. This ambivalence is reflected in the fact that it enables both a sense of belonging and integration in a wider Islamic nation and also a sense of self-conscious identification that allows the traveler to become conscious of his or her own difference:

> Over many Islamic centuries, travelers, pilgrims, scholars, and ambassadors felt themselves linked to the wider community of Muslims. While this trend continued of course, at the western edge of the umma [Islamic nation] from the sixteenth century onward, historical trends favoured the more conscious expression of a distinct identity for Morocco.... Travelers and travel accounts refer, from then on with greater frequency, to a more precise and self-conscious geographical, socio-cultural, and political homeland. (82)

El Moudden's words are significant insofar as they they outline the historical development of the *rihla* (the "spiritual journey") and its encounter with modernity. As a film that openly appeals to the familiar Islamic motif of *rihla*, *Le Grand Voyage* can be understood by engaging both meanings of the word *rihla*: on the one hand, Réda's journey with his father can be described as a *rihla* in El Moudden's sense, that is to say as a personal experience representing a "long and enriching, though risky, voyage" (El Moudden 73) linked to the process of self-knowledge that reinforces both a sense of belonging and the sense of distinct identity. On the other hand, the film itself can be seen as a signifier or a travel narrative conveying the meaning of Réda's journey, thus emphasizing the filmmaker's serious preoccupation with questions of interpretation, meaning, and creativity, as will be shown in the examples analyzed below.

Other Moroccan film directors, such as Farida Belyazid in *A Door to the Sky* and Mohamed Ismaïl in *Adieu mères,* also have used the motif of travel (though in different historical and thematic contexts) as an ultimate spiritual journey associated with personal struggle; self-transcendence; search for meaning in an absurd, broken, or unjust world; ultimate self-fulfillment; and the birth of a new self. Belyazid's female protagonist Nadia, a Westernized young Moroccan immigrant living in Paris, turns her seemingly duty-bound trip to Fez, historically considered to be the spiritual heart of Morocco, into a life-transforming event, insofar as what originated as an unenthusiastic act of physical displacement from modern life to traditional life to visit her terminally ill father blossoms into an intense Sufi mystical experience of union with the self and the Divine. Nadia's enchantment with the beautiful voice of Kirana, an elderly wise woman filling the symbolic role of guardian of tradition, chanting Qur'anic verses and sharing her Sufi knowledge, takes on the allegorical form of a thoughtful dialogue between tradition and modernity. This is attained by the self-conscious transformation of her grieving, and ultimately of her deceased father's ancestral home, into a legacy of healing and the building of a profound and unshakable sense of fellowship with other less fortunate women. Nadia thus becomes an agent of positive change in other people's lives.

Though developing in the context of long-existing interfaith ties between Muslims and Jews in Moroccan society, Ismaïl's film, loosely inspired by the real historical event of the tragic death of forty-four Moroccan Jews in the fatal shipwreck of the *Egoz,* similarly evokes the theme of self-redemption achieved through the cultivation of fellowship with other human beings and by embracing conflicting sides of one's identity. Compelled to seek better living conditions for his family in Israel, with dire economic circumstances afflicting many Moroccan Jews in the aftermath of independence (in the broader context of growing pan-Arabism and Arab-Israeli political tensions in the Middle East in the 1960s), the main protagonist, Henry, a Moroccan Jewish businessman, never reaches his destination, owing to a tragic shipwreck. Before his departure, he premonitorily entrusts his family to Brahim, his Muslim close friend and business partner, who later becomes the father figure of Henry's two children when their mother loses her battle with cancer. Though Henry's journey of hope to Israel is brutally cut short, the film recasts this emblematic spiritual image of pilgrimage to the Holy Land, a sanctified rite in the Jewish collective imaginary, as a journey of self-reconciliation of the Muslim and Jewish identities of Moroccan society—identities challenged by the troubled political climate of the Arab-Israeli conflict in the Middle East.

The discourses of the Moroccan intellectuals and artists cited above allow us to see in each of them a modern-day Ibn Battuta, travelers (in real or imaginary landscapes) and travel writers. A legendary Moroccan writer, traveler, and pilgrim who lived in the fourteenth century and traveled extensively across all continents, Ibn Battuta is regarded as one of the most important medieval travelers and travel writers whose vision was inspired by his vast legal knowledge and the Sufi doctrine (Wolf). Michael Wolf notes that "[h]e traveled longer and farther, and wrote more, than Marco Polo. Jammed with vivid description and adventure, his book, exceeding a thousand pages, is the longest and most complex travel work in Arabic to survive the Middle Ages" (51). According to Wolf, Ibn Battuta was part of "a large class of mobile professionals" that included scholars, judges, lawyers, and teachers (52) who often crossed paths, if not traveled the same roads through large trading networks. As a lawyer and mystic, Ibn Battuta was "[s]haped by the world he traveled" and incarnated the reconciliation of two competing Islamic doctrines: Sufi mysticism and Sunni orthodoxy. "For Ibn Battuta," writes Wolf, "Mecca marked the first leg of a much longer journey. His hajj was a precipitating event, a catalyst that transformed him into a world traveler" (53). Ibn Battuta's biography closely links the spiritual journey of pilgrimage with the much bigger journey of life perceived as an ongoing process of understanding one's place in the world and one's relations with others. These complex secular and spiritual dynamics at the core of the experience of pilgrimage have been duly noted by other scholars such as Sam Gellens, Patrick Haenni, Raphael Voix, and Muhammad Khalid Masud.

Ferroukhi's film finely incorporates representational motifs that evoke the symbolic import of Ibn Battuta's *rihlas*. Like Ibn Battuta, Réda's journey with his father is replete with strife, confrontation with adversity, competing perspectives on Islam, and, finally, the desire to continue the journey they embarked on to reach their destination despite the various physical and symbolic hurdles they encounter on the way. This is perhaps most manifestly evident in the importance given by Ferroukhi to the multifaceted thematization of movement, virtually present throughout the film. The opening scene shows Réda riding his bicycle, moving away from the city toward an undefined countryside. The camera follows the rugged terrain he crosses, ultimately leading toward a junkyard where he is about to meet his older brother, who is in turn repairing the driver-side door of the car that Réda will drive on his journey. A brief conversation ensues centering mainly on the journey itself, Réda's misgivings, and his sense of helplessness in the face of his imminent long journey. Unsurprisingly, the story hurtles toward its denouement as soon as the destination is reached, only to present the end of the story as the beginning of a new journey back to France, which Réda undertakes this time as a changed young man, matured by his travel and mystical experience.

Réda's brother's ominous warning in the beginning of the film characterizes the journey in categorical terms: "It won't be a picnic," he says. His words are echoed by the father's own voice, much later during the trip, when Réda implores him to stop at Naples to visit the city and take pictures on the way. The father gives the following sardonic answer: "You think we're tourists?" The significance of these words lies in the emphasis they place on the actual travel as being primarily an *inward* journey. This is perhaps why Réda appears disgruntled in his reaction to his father's command to drive him to Mecca. Other plot details further highlight Réda's anxiety about undergoing this journey, which becomes associated with the unknown and the uncertain. First, he feels doubly bewildered and disarmed by the command itself. Initially, the task of driving his father to Mecca was to fall upon his older brother, but a misdemeanor on the part of the latter involving drunk driving resulted in his arrest and the revocation of his driver's licence. Without offering the least explanation, Réda's father takes him by complete surprise one day by announcing that they will leave on the weekend, granting Réda no more than four days to get ready for this monumental trip. Réda is forced, therefore, to embark on a journey that is not of his own choosing and for which he is not prepared in the slightest. He protests in vain to his silent mother: "Qu'est-ce qu'il veut que je foute là-bas; il veut pas prendre l'avion comme tout le monde? Moi je te préviens, je peux pas partir comme ça; j'ai mon bac à passer, je l'ai déjà raté une fois; c'est ma dernière chance" (What does he want me to do there? Why can't he take the plane like everyone else? I'm telling you, I can't just leave like this; I have my exam to take. I already failed it once, and it's my last chance). Having no power to resist his father's authoritative order, Réda clings to the only means that ensure his ties with the world that is familiar to him: his cell phone; a picture of his girlfriend, Lisa; his French passport; and a world map. Interestingly enough, Réda is seen studying the world map in his room right before his departure, which he intends to use as his main guide during the trip, as though it will provide him with the reassuring feeling of finding the way back to his familiar world.

During the farewell scene, Réda and his father are seen off by family members and neighbors in a typical working-class and immigrant suburban area in the city of Aix-en-Provence. Réda, out of bitterness and apprehension, is visibly aloof and indifferent to his family's good-byes. His older brother's words indirectly recall again the *inward* journey theme when he hands him a camera and asks him to bring back pictures from Mecca and then reminds Réda to "prends bien soin de la voiture" (take good care of the car), referring to the car whose gear shifter can be dysfunctional but is otherwise reliable: "elle peut faire le tour du monde sans problème" (it can go around the world without any problem).

The reference to the prolonged external journey across Europe and through the Middle East effectively underlines the immense void and generational gap existing between Réda and his father, which urgently needs to be bridged. As soon as they begin their trip, the viewer is struck by the heavy silence that settles between father and son. There are no real conversations taking place between the two during the drive itself or during the frequent rest stops and meal breaks. Foregrounding the image of the two characters caught up in frequent traffic jams or lost in the back roads underlines their inability to connect, even when they can not escape from each other. Intriguingly, it is also a way of exploring various forms of interaction between Islam and modernity: this is seen at first when the father interrupts his son's secular time and enactments of his French identity (his school life, his exam calendar, and his personal freedom/romantic life) and imposes an exclusively religious calendar (the time to perform daily prayers and the Islamic religious rite of pilgrimage). Choosing an unlikely and rather primitive means of travel from France to Mecca and discarding his son's cell phone that connects him to his love (and by extension to the modern world he is more familiar with) are two other revealing examples. During the trip, the father is seen stopping for prayer right after passing a customs checkpoint, despite his son's imploration to reserve his prayers for a more appropriate and private place. The father also prevents his son from resorting to the modern highway system guided by the road map and oddly insists on taking vague back roads and random detours. Through a thoughtful character study of the authoritative father, the film raises the question of what it means to be a Muslim and how one can be a Muslim in French society, a symbol of European modernity. Can the two be reconciled? The accrued importance and growing urgency of this question has now become apparent from the highly publicized political and intellectual debates stirring and dividing European societies today around the perceived "threat" of the religious (and especially the Islamic) phenomenon in Europe.

By portraying a father whose religious time conflicts with the secular time of the modern world in which he lives and who refuses to endow his journey with a meaning that is conveyed through the symbols of modernity that structure his son's French life, the father figures as a character who inhabits a parallel world while making no conscious attempts to integrate himself meaningfully into the larger French society. Depicting the father and son crossing different time zones, countries, and languages allows a study of the father/son relationship that displaces and transcends the binary opposition of Islam and modernity, allowing a more complex and differentiated reading of the two to unfold. As they push farther into Eastern Europe through the treacherous and convoluted back roads, they finally get lost and find themselves facing a fork in the road as a result of the father's eccentric choices, not knowing which direction to follow from there. Since he has been stripped of any decision-making power, Réda asks his father which way to go—right or left? The father decides to take a rest stop overnight at that spot. When they resume their trip the next morning, the father comments on Réda's apparent absentmindedness: "You're here but your mind is elsewhere," to which the latter replies, "We still don't know where we're going." These lines stress not only the continued absence of a sense of inwardness in Réda's journey but, more paradoxically still, and against all expectations, the lack of a sense of direction on the father's part as well. There are repeated scenes of the father asking for directions from anonymous people on the way or prompting his son to do so, a task complicated by their inability to understand the language in which the directions are given (as when they ask a Bulgarian man with whom they cross paths). Ironically, the father is seen at one point ordering his son to pick up an old Serbian woman entirely clad in black, whom they happen to spot on the roadside, and give her a ride, when they themselves are lost and worse still can't even communicate with her through a language they mutually understand. However, this same ironic scene of the father and son, lost in the middle of nowhere and facing a fork in the road, is especially significant since it shows the two characters positioned between two roads, two choices, and ultimately two worldviews. The two characters face one of the many unmarked travel paths and crossroads across Europe and are compelled to negotiate which direction to take. This well-crafted and highly evocative image of two lost souls with no sense of direction conveys that their journey of self-knowledge and new birth starts right there, in this in-between space that negates territorial views of identity, but also through the connections they weave with other spaces they cross and with other human beings from different parts of the world with whom their journey brings them into contact. Réda and his father are thus portrayed as wandering characters who struggle to find their way but who also have the potential of reinventing their relationship and their identities by negotiating and choosing together the road to take.

In addition to physical obstacles and natural adversities (as when they are snowed in and the father suffers from hypothermia as a result), the film shows that the two characters' sense of direction is shaped by and eventually develops from their encounters with other people with whom they engage in a significant degree of interaction, such as the Turkish character Mustapha. Mustapha is a middle-aged man who helps them extricate themselves from a complicated customs situation and soon strikes up a good friendship with Réda, to the father's clear displeasure, who immediately distances himself from him. Mustapha soon joins them in their journey and gains Réda's trust. His life story and perspective on Islam inspired by Sufi knowledge contrasts with the rather austere and orthodox views of Islam upheld by Réda's father. During a rest stop overnight, Mustapha takes Réda out to a café, and when Réda hesitates to order alcohol though visibly interested, Mustapha tells him a Muslim Sufi tale that validates Réda's individuality and desire: "One day, someone asked a Sufi master who drank wine if alcohol was forbidden by Islam; the Sufi master replied, 'It depends on the greatness of your soul.' He said, 'Pour your glass of wine into a basin of water, and the water will change colors; but pour this same glass of wine into the sea, the sea's color remains unchanged.' You understand?" Mustapha's voice represents another perspective on Islam that challenges the unitarian and authoritarian voice of Réda's father, which is perhaps why the latter distances himself from Mustapha in the first place. Mustapha's tale portrays Islam as a heightened form of individual self-awareness of the Divine, and to that effect it is perceived and lived as an inclusive and plural religion, just as the wine mixes with the ocean without ever changing its constancy and integrity. In his close study of the notions of "oneness" and "manyness" in Islamic thought, William Chittick makes this point very clearly when he writes that "*tawhid* [the assertion that God is one] begins with the recognition of diversity and difference. The integrated vision that tawhid implies must be achieved on the basis of a recognized multiplicity" (203). Citing the work of Persian Sufi mystic Farghani, Chittick notes that "oneness and manyness cannot be distinguished from one another in any absolute way, since both qualities belong to the reality of God" (209–10). Réda's encounter with Mustapha can be understood in this case as an experience of Sufi humanism, whose luminous light begins to seep into his soul and makes his reconciliation with his own father and, consequently, with the other side of his identity possible.

One morning, however, Mustapha myteriously leaves the hotel before Réda and his father wake up. And when the father can not find the money he kept inside a pair of socks, he immediately suspects Mutapha of being the culprit. Later in the film, viewers discover that Mustapha is innocent and that the father is mistaken in his claims. By casting doubt on the father's sense of judgment, the film does not seek to condem him or wholly dismiss the legitimacy of his worldview but rather emphasizes the common humanity he shares with his own son as well as with other characters with whom he comes into contact. This encounter reveals yet another instance that relativizes the father's worldview and his sense of judgement without totally discrediting him.

The increasing emphasis on the commonality of the father and son's experiences is achieved by the portrayal of confrontational scenes where one or the other threatens to part ways. These are also the instances that make it possible for the two of them to eventually carry on genuine conversations in which Réda learns more about his father's past—one unguarded moment ultimately culminates in reconciliation and personal redemption. Réda and his father are seen in one scene in a state of spiritual communion, pondering the deeper meaning of their journey, following Réda's question, "What's so special about Mecca?" Réda draws closer to his father and comes to the realization that his world will not be complete nor meaningful without his father's presence. Although he is finally granted permission by his father to return to France as they near Mecca, Réda chooses to continue to accompany him through the rest of the journey.

It is significant that it is during this stage of the journey, as both are only moments away from Mecca, that Réda invokes his girlfriend's name by writing it on the Arabian desert sand. Lisa never really appears in the film. She is merely evoked by name and through a photograph and partially heard over the phone. She therefore fulfills the structurally important function of according Réda's trip qualities that are reminiscent of a Sufi journey toward the Beloved and is therefore an outgrowth of Réda's encounter with Mustapha and his Sufi wisdom. It is interesting that Lisa's image remains constant in Réda's mind, even when he almost reaches Mecca; writing her name on the sand could be read as an attempt to unite the two conflicting allegiances or components of his identity (his modern/ Western self and his Muslim and spiritual heritage). Indeed, "[a] characteristic of Sufism is its use of the earthly language of love and passion to express ecstatic communion with the Divine" (Fatemi 96). The film shows that the father/son relationship (and by extension, the Islam/modernity relationship) is redeemed through constructive dialogue: "What's so special about Mecca?" asks Réda in French, to which his father replies in Arabic, "It's the heritage of Abraham . . . every Muslim who can needs to go on hajj . . . to purify his soul . . . we're only guests on this earth . . . without you, I never would have been able to get here . . . God bless you . . . I learned a lot in this trip." "So did I," replies Réda. Self-knowledge as illustrated by this dialogue is portrayed as being simultaneously knowledge of the Other.

As with previous scenes of cross-cultural encounters confronting Réda and his father with individuals from different nationalities and religious traditions across Eastern Europe and the Middle East, the film features the father and son's contact with, and opening up to, the impressive flow of the whole humanity in Mecca as a keystone experience for reaching a greater sense of self-awareness and for forging sustainable and meaningful human relationships. When they arrive at Mecca, Réda sees his father one last time, right before the latter joins throngs of pilgrims, a remarkable sea of human diversity, to perform the *tawaf* (a pilgrimage rite consisting in walking around the Kaaba seven times). His father is seen chanting in unison with other pilgrims, answering the call of God, or the Beloved, facing away from his son, who says to him "à ce soir" (see you tonight). As Réda waits for his father's return, he catches a glimpse of a herd of sheep whisked away by its shepherd, then utterly disappearing into the night. The image of the shepherd leading the way and the clouds covering up the moonlight is imbued with mystical allusions. It can be interpreted both as prefiguration of the father's looming death, and thus a confirmation of his mortality, but also as a moment of self-realization marking Réda's spiritual rebirth through his subsequent reconciliation with his father and the embrace of his legacy. Réda's survival through his toilsome trip and his father's death are two sides of the same coin. They both signify the death of the old self and the birth of a new one. Réda carries his father's heritage with him, and, more important, the journey of self-knowledge and discovery of his roots does not stop there because he returns to France with this newfound knowledge. The film begins with a representation of movement and ends with it as well, as Réda is seen preparing for his journey back to France. Réda's voyage with his father can be seen as an allegorical Sufi tale of personal rebirth and transcendence in a modern and transcultural world, highlighting the ambivalent construction of Muslim pilgrims as modern transcultural travelers, whose inward journey approximates the reality of their mobile lives and leads to a fuller sense of being, belonging, and becoming while cultivating a heightened "sense of self-conscious identification" (El Moudden 82).

Though theoretical approaches to cinema in general have substantially evolved over the years, they still lend credence to Deleuze's perspective on the artist as "creator of truth" evoked above. Like many contemporary theoreticians of transnational cinema, Hamid Naficy duly stresses the auteurist vision of most transnational filmmakers, according prime importance to such representational frameworks and perceptual determinants as "transnationality, liminality, multiculturality, multifocality, and syncretism" (204). To Nafici, "the authority of transnationals as filmmaking authors is derived from their position as subjects inhabiting transnational and exilic spaces, where they travel in the slip-zone of fusion and admixture" (207–8). It can be argued in this light that their very transnational subjectivity is what sets in motion the process of creative molding of their art in order to generate images of possible worlds, craft new subjectivities, and imagine the breaking-through of new beginnings. As seen in *Le Grand Voyage,* the interest of film productions from the Maghrebi diaspora in France lies in their densely textured narratives, which are best understood as individual and creative expressions of the ongoing social and cultural transformations experienced by the North African diaspora in France. It is instructive in this regard to recall Deleuze's view evoked above, which makes it possible to ascertain the fruitfulness of such an approach. Insofar as it complicates the lens of sociopolitical analysis, which dominated francophone postcolonial film criticism, a critical approach attentive to questions of form effectively shines light on those creative processes at work in cinematic productions that allow for pushing the frontiers of human understanding to new heights.

Works Cited

Barlet, Olivier. *Les cinémas d'Afrique des annés 2000: Perspectives critiques.* Paris: L'Harmattan, 2012.

———. "The Forbidden Windows of Black African Film: Interview with Ferid Boughedir." June 1998, http://www.africultures.com/anglais/articles_anglais/Boughedir.htmParis.

Baudelaire, Charles. "Le Peintre de la vie moderne." In *Curiosités esthétiques: L'Artromantique et autres Œuvres critiques de Baudelaire,* edited by Henri Lemaitre. Paris: Éditions Garnier Frères, 1962.

Chittick, William. "Spectrums of Islamic Thought: Sa 'id al-Din Farghani on the Implication of Oneness and Manyness." In *The Heritage of Sufism: The Legacy of Medieval Persian Sufism (1150–1500),* edited by Leonard Lewisohn, 203–17. Oxford: Oneworld Oxford, 1999.

Deleuze, Gilles. *Cinema 2: The Time-Image.* London: Athlone, 1989.

Dridi, Karim. "Des réalisateurs contre le ghetto du 'cinéma social.'" August 26, 2008, http://www.rue89.com/le-making-of-de-karim-dridi/des-realisateurs-contre-le-ghetto-du-cinema-social.

El Khayat, Rita. *Les Arabes Riches de Marbella.* Casablanca: Editions Aïni Bennaï, 2002.

El Moudden, Abderrahmane. "The Ambivalence of *rihla:* Community Integration and Self-Definition in Moroccan Travel Accounts, 1300–1800." In *Muslim Travellers: Pilgrimage, Migration, and the Religious Imagination,* edited by Dale F. Eickelman and James Piscatori, 69–84. London: Routledge, 1990.

Fatemi, Nasrollah S., et al. *Sufism: Message of Brotherhood, Harmony, and Hope.* New York: A. S. Barnes, 1976.

Gellens, Sam I. "The Search for Knowledge in Medieval Muslim Societies: A Comparative Approach." In *Muslim Travellers: Pilgrimage, Migration, and the Religious Imagination,* edited by Dale F. Eickelman and James Piscatori, 50–65. London: Routledge, 1990.

Haenni, Patrick, and Raphael Voix. "God by All Means . . . Eclectic Faith and Sufi Resurgence among the Moroccan Bourgeoisie." In *Sufism and the "Modern" in Islam,* edited by Martin van Bruinessen and Julia D. Howell, 241–56. New York: I. B. Tauris, 2007.

Hammoudi, Abdellah. *A Season in Mecca: Narrative of a Pilgrimage.* Translated by Pascale Ghazaleh. New York: Hill and Wang, 2005.

Khatibi, Abdelkébir. *Pèlerinage d'un artiste amoureux.* Paris: Editions du Rocher, 2003.

Lequeret, Elisabeth. "Ferid Boughedir: 'le Fespaco doit être militant et festif'" (interview). February 23, 2005, http://www.rfi.fr/actufr/articles/062/article_34314.asp.

Masud, Muhammad Khalid. "The Obligation to Migrate." In *Muslim Travellers: Pilgrimage, Migration, and the Religious Imagination,* edited by Dale F. Eickelman and James Piscatori, 29–49. London: Routledge, 1990.

Milleliri, Carole. "Touche pas à mon pote! Le Thé au harem d'Archimède." October 6, 2009, http://www.critikat.com/Le-The-au-harem-d-Archimede.html.

Nafici, Hamid. "Phobic Spaces and Liminal Panics: Independent Transnational Cinema." In *Multiculturalism, Postcoloniality, and Transnational Media,* edited by Ella Shohat and Robert Stam, 203–26. New Brunswick, N.J.: Rutgers University Press, 2003.

Tarr, Carrie. *Reframing Difference: Beur and Banlieue Filmmaking in France.* Bolton: Manchester University Press, 2005.

Wolf, Michael. "Ibn Battuta: Morocco 1326." In *One Thousand Roads to Mecca,* edited by Michael Wolf, 51–67. New York: Grove Press, 1997.

Filmography

Adieu mères [Goodbye Mothers]. Dir. Mohamed Ismaïl. Perf. Marc Samuel and Rachid El Ouali. Maya Films, 2008.
Bab El Oued City [The Door of Bab El Oued]. Dir. Merzak Allouache. Perf. Nadia Kaci and Mohamed Ourdache. Flashback Audiovisuel, 1994.
Cartouches gauloises [French Cigarettes]. Dir. Mehdi Charef. Perf. Mohamed Faouzi and Ali Cherif. K. G. Productions, 2007.
A Door to the Sky [*Bab Al-Sama Maftuh*]. Dir. Farida Belyazid. Perf. Zakia Tahiri, Chaabia Laadraoui, and Eva Saint-Paul. Interfilms, SATPEC, 1989.
Douce France [Gentle France]. Dir. Malik Chibane. Perf. Frédéric Diefenthal. Ciné Classic, 1995.
Un été à la Goulette [A Summer in La Goulette]. Dir. Férid Boughedir. Perf. Sonia Mankaï and Ava Cohen-Jonathan. Canal+, Cinares production, La Sept Cinéma, Lamy Films, Marsa film, Radio Télévision Belge Francophone (RTBF), 1996.
Le Gone du Chaaba [The Boy of the Chaaba]. Dir. Christophe Ruggia. Perf. Bouzid Negnoug and Nabil Ghanem. Films Christiani, Orly Films, 1998.
Le Grand Voyage [The Big Journey]. Dir. Ismaël Ferroukhi. Perf. Nicolas Cazalé and Mohamed Majd. Ognon Pictures, Arte France Cinema, 2004.
Hexagone. Dir. Malik Chibane. Perf. Jalil Naciri. Ciné Classic, 1994.
Marock. Dir. Laila Marrakchi. Perf. Morjana Alaoui and Matthieu Boujenah. France 3 Cinéma, Canal+, 2005.
Le Thé au Harem d'Archi-Ahmed [Tea in the Harem]. Dir. Mehdi Charef. Perf. Kader Boukhanef and Rémi Martin. CNG, 1985.
Villa Jasmin. Dir. Férid Boughedir. Perf. Luc Béraud. Image et Compagnie, 2008.
Voisins, voisines [Neighbors]. Dir. Malik Chibane. Perf. Frédéric Diefenthal. Ciné Classic, 2005.

8 Revealing the Past, Conceptualizing the Future On-Screen

The Social, Political, and Economic Challenges of Contemporary Filmmaking in Morocco

Valérie K. Orlando

THIS ESSAY OFFERS an analysis of Morocco's contemporary cinematic industry and focuses on films produced and distributed from 1999 to the present.[1] In the last decade, notably since 1999 and the death of King Hassan II, which ended "Les Années de plomb" (the Lead Years, 1963–99), Morocco has transformed itself, socioculturally and politically.[2] These transformations have been shown in film and on television. Both have proved to be the media of choice for depicting the sociocultural and political issues in contemporary Moroccan society. Encouraged by the more openly democratic climate fostered by young King Mohammed VI (popularly known as "M6"), men and women filmmakers explore the sociocultural and political debates of their country while also seeking to document the untold stories of a dark past. The themes they present to audiences explore some of today's most pressing questions in Moroccan society. Topics of films fluctuate between restoring suppressed or obfuscated memories and critiquing contemporary sociocultural challenges. Certain films tell the stories of the past that have not been told until recently. The themes include the torture and imprisonment of countless victims during the Lead Years, the exodus of thousands of Jews to Israel in the early 1960s, and the hard realities of the present, such as domestic violence, acute rural poverty, and the dismal plight of street children. In today's cinematic oeuvre, no subject is too controversial. Filmmakers seek to describe a country that has come to be known as "Le nouveau Maroc" (the New Morocco), a term fraught with conflict. Often schizophrenic in how it views itself, Morocco is a nation caught in debate over unanswered questions that persist from its past while it strives to plot new strategies for moving forward.

In my work, notably my book *Screening Morocco: Contemporary Film in a Changing Society*, I argue that film in Morocco acts as a *lieu de mémoire* (memory space), wherein untold historical events of the past and the filmmakers' remembrance of this same past are merged in order to contribute to a new vibrant collective consciousness.[3] Their films attest to the fact that visual cultural production of the present can help heal the wounds of the past, or at least make certain that formerly untold events are now remembered in the present so that they may be debated in public forums. The Moroccan filmic text also proves that the medium is an effective tool for bridging historical events with popular culture. Whether fiction based on historical events or actual real-life stories, the films made in Morocco in the new millennium "possess the potential to generate and mold images of the past which will be retained by whole generations" (Erll 389). Film and its more proletarian twin, television, are the perfect forms to sustain the "media of cultural memory" because they are accessible to the schooled and the unschooled, the rich and the poor (390). As elsewhere in Africa, these media also lend themselves to facilitating cultural memory through oral traditions that are already inherent in Moroccan culture and that are a predominant form of narrative.

Pierre Nora emphasizes that if a nation is able to define its relationship to its past, "it shapes the future" (11). The duty of the individual is to acknowledge the "law of remembrance," which "has great coercive force: for the individual, the discovery of roots, of 'belonging' to some group." Remembering thus becomes "the source of identity" for the nation, important for both the individual and his or her society (11). In general, Moroccan filmmakers' *travail de mémoire* (memory work) has produced films and documentaries in the last decade that are significantly more critically candid about sociocultural and political issues in their depictions of Moroccan life than in the past. During the most repressive years of "Les Années de plomb," films would metaphorically or symbolically put forward ideas criticizing social woes, but filmmakers rarely dared to be overtly critical, as filmmaker Mustapha Derkaoui suggests: "We don't want to make subversive cinema ... it's more that we must make cinema an adequate means of denunciation, and not a force with the goal of blind and intolerable subversion.... [In the past] ... cinema was constrained by the government's fears at the time.... Officials allowed much less experimentation and innovation in films" (qtd. in Carter 68).[4]

Since 1999, films have increasingly probed the societal realities of contemporary Morocco unfettered and uncensored, despite having become more subversive. Films such as Hassan Benjelloun's *La Chambre noire* (The Black Room, 2004), Leila Marrakchi's *Marock* (2005), Hicham Lasri's *L'Os de fer* (The Iron Bone, 2006), Zakia Tahiri's *Number One* (2008), and many others embrace an engaging social-realist cinematic discourse, one that is critical and analytical of contemporary society. In keeping with trends in filmmaking across Africa, Moroccan filmmakers' films exemplify what Manthia Diawara propounds in his book *African Cinema: Politics and Culture* as the quintessential themes of African social-realist cinema. Filmmakers working within the social-realist paradigm draw on contemporary experiences in order to "oppose tradition to modernity, oral to written, agrarian and customary communities to urban and industrialized systems, and subsistence economies to highly productive economies" (141). Similar to other filmmakers on the continent, Moroccan cineastes couch their narratives in two camps. The first critically engages certain forms and practices of modernity, which tend to be neocolonialist (Western consumerism, IMF and USAID regulations placed on the country, the international drug trade and its impact on Morocco, and the like). The second focuses on critiquing the debilitating traditional practices that persist in Moroccan society that hinder productive dialogue concerning how best to live in a globalized world (these include, for example, arranged marriages, local customs that impede the emancipation of women, and animist beliefs).

The Movement of the 20th of February and Morocco's Culture Wars

Currently, as the period now known as the "Arab Spring" unfolds across the Arab world, Morocco is witnessing social and political upheaval fostered particularly by its younger generations who have been at the forefront of "The Movement of the 20th of February." Like the rest of the Arab world, 65 percent of Morocco's population is under the age of thirty-five. Young people are more educated than their parents, more secular, and more driven by capitalism and global markets than older generations. Since February 20, 2011, from Marrakech to Casablanca, reoccurring demonstrations have been held on the twentieth of every month. Now popularly (and officially) recognized as "The Movement of the 20th of February," the monthly demonstrations have been overwhelmingly peaceful, despite some police repression of demonstrators in May 2011. The forceful action taken by the police was quickly condemned in the Moroccan press, and higher-ups were told to back off by the monarchy.[5]

Films, short documentaries uploaded to You Tube, Twitter feeds, and interviews conducted by young filmmakers working the urban streets of Casablanca and Rabat are capturing the crucial social issues that are now at the heart of The Movement of the 20th of February. Filmmakers are dedicated to accurately depicting the events of their time as well as the angst of young people who are concerned with how to navigate living in the global world while still holding on to certain traditions that are the backbone of Moroccan society. Filmmaker Aziz Salmy's film *Hijab al-Hob* (Veils of Love) is one of the most recent films that serves as an example of some of the culture wars raging in the New Morocco. Although made in 2009, the film predicts many of the issues and societal topics of debate that two years later were integrated into the political platform of The Movement of the 20th of February. Most controversial are the debates focused on religious versus secular purviews in Morocco's burgeoning millennial democracy and women's place in public space. These topics have been widely discussed in the Moroccan press and have opened up meaningful discussions between men and women, young and old, educated and unschooled Moroccans.[6] Salmy's film, about a young woman torn between the values of her traditional family and the endless possibilities presented by a more secular, modern world, articulates the overarching concerns shared by many Moroccans of all social milieus who find themselves caught up in the throes of globalization. As The Movement of the 20th of February is captured and documented by cameras, Twitter, iPhones, Facebook, and You Tube more than ever before, Moroccans are aware of the crucial role that film and new media will play in vocalizing the most pressing questions and issues of debate in Moroccan society.

In an interview in June 2009, filmmaker Hassan Benjelloun, attesting to the critical role of film in fostering debate in society, told me that "we don't have the luxury of making luxurious films" or "films for pleasure."[7] For Benjelloun, the filmmaker's principal duty should be to make films that are socially engaged and thought provoking and perform the function of safeguarding accurate depictions of the past. All of Benjelloun's films are critically probing and tackle such subjects as the random disappearance and torture of hundreds in Moroccan prisons during the Lead Years (as depicted in *La Chambre noire*) and the exodus of thousands of Jews from Morocco in the early 1960s (*Où vas-tu Moshé?* [Where Are You Going Moshé?], 2007). Domestic violence and a woman's right to divorce was the subject of *Jugement d'une femme* (The Judgment of a Woman, 2000), a film that was highly praised by social activists and feminists in Morocco. Indeed, filmmakers such as Benjelloun, Lahcen Zinoun (*Faux pas* [False Steps], 2003), and Farida Benlyazid (*Casablanca*, 2003; *Women's Wiles*, 1999), among many others, have become the keepers of memory, charging themselves with accurately depicting a cinematic discourse that reconfigures the past for present generations so that it will not be lost. These filmmakers promote what French scholar Jacques Le Goff remarks is "the idea of memory [as] an intersection" of multiple viewpoints (51). Moroccan filmmakers act as chroniclers of the past and reveal what Le Goff characterizes as a concern for "collective rather than individual memories . . . because Memory . . . refers first of all to a group of psychic functions that allow us to actualize past impressions or information that we represent to ourselves as past" (51).

Screening Memory Spaces

Collective memory as formed at an intersection of multiple layers and viewpoints of remembrances—those of the individual filmmaker, of the collective, of individual male and female prisoners and survivors of gross infractions of human rights abuses—has provided the signature themes of this decade. Kamal Kamal's *Tayf nizar* (Nizar's Ghost, 2001) tells the story of a doctor whose professional work entangles him in an investigation in Casablanca that eventually uncovers mass graves of political dissidents killed during the Lead Years. Jilali Ferhati's *Mémoire en détention* (Memory in Detention, 2004) recounts the story of political prisoner Mokhtar Alyouni (played by Ferhati), who was incarcerated for being a communist dissident in the 1970s and who in the early 2000s is still in prison, mainly because he has become an amnesiac and has no family and nowhere to go. Even the guards cannot remember exactly when Mokhtar was imprisoned and have let him stay so that he can tend the surrounding gardens, which he so enjoys. The amnesia of Mokhtar metaphorically mirrors the amnesia of a whole country as man and nation struggle to put in perspective the thousands of people who were detained in Morocco's prisons.

Ferhati's film encourages audiences to think about their relationship to the past throughout the film. When at one point Mokhtar leaves the prison, accompanied by a younger prisoner, Zoubeir, incarcerated three years for stealing cars, the warden charges the younger man with helping Mokhtar relocate his family. As the men crisscross Morocco following the *bribes de mémoire* (memory snippets) revealed on occasion to Mokhtar, they happen upon the crumbling prison where the old man was first detained. Zoubeir, also an aspiring theater actor, hoping to jar Mokhtar's memory, delivers a monologue as the older man wanders in the dark, abandoned halls: "They poured cold water on my head, they hurt me. . . . What did they want? What did I do to them? God help me." The delivery does succeed in opening up the old man's mind from which emerges scenes of his own torture. These become more vivid when Zoubeir tells him that the abandoned prison is actually "the first prison where you were taken the first time." Ironically, the young man notes, "they now want to make it into a cultural center." He closes his soliloquy, poetically adding: "If only memories would die before the bodies that house them do."

Films made about human rights abuses and the imprisonment of thousands of innocents during the Lead Years have been inspired by *la littérature carcérale* (prison literature), which has become an increasingly popular literary genre as Morocco delves into the egregious violations committed in its past. Testimonies overwhelmingly written in French by authors residing in Morocco, such as Ahmed Marzouki's *Tazmamart: Cellule 10*, Belkassem Belouchi's *Rapt de voix* (Abducted Voice), Abdelfettah Fakihani's *Le Couloir: Bribes de vérité sur les années de plomb* (The Hallway: Snippets of Truth about the Lead Years), and Aziz Binebine's *Tazmamort: dix-huit ans dans le bagne de Hassan II* (Tazmamort: Eighteen Years in the Prison of Hassan II),[8] are only a few of the many titles found on the bookshelves in small bookstores across Morocco. Prison accounts in Arabic, although fewer in number, have also become more prevalent as narratives are uncovered and retold. *Ufoulu al-layl: Yawmiyat Lm'arif wa Ghbila* (The Extinction of Night: Journal of Lm'arif and Ghbila) by Tahar Mahfoudi recounts the suffering of prisoners in two detention centers in Casablanca during the Lead Years, and Fatna El Bouih's *Une Femme nommée Rachid* (A Woman Named Rachid, first published in Arabic and then subsequently in French) is one of the first prison testimonials written by a woman. Literature about the abuse of human and civil rights in the country have created tangible, culturally produced memory spaces.⁹

A telling example of critically reclaiming the past in order to reveal flagrant abuses is Hassan Benjelloun's 2004 film *La Chambre noire*. Based on Jaouad Mdidech's 2002 autobiography of the same title, the film offers a condemning and compelling look at torture and disappearance under Hassan II. Although Mdidech collaborated on the screenplay, the film diverges from the book by focusing on the love story between Kamal and his fiancée, Najat, who are only briefly mentioned in Mdidech's autobiography. In the film, both protagonists work at the airport and seem apolitical and oblivious to the impending doom that awaits them. The 1970s era (the backdrop for the film's plot) represents some of the most repressive years of Hassan II's reign, during which the hunt for and incarceration of Marxist-Leninist supporters was in its heyday. Benjelloun emphasizes the randomness of kidnappings and interrogations. From one moment to the next, people disappear without a trace. Although he had left his militant student days behind him, is a respectable airport employee, and professes to be apolitical, Kamal is abducted from his place of employment and sequestered. He is interrogated about his years as a rebel at the university and his activity as a leader of the "March 23rd" Marxist-Leninist group. The filmmaker inserts real footage of television clips from the Green March, a nationalist propaganda stunt orchestrated by Hassan II on November 6, 1975. Nearly 350,000 unarmed Moroccans were urged to march to the border of the Western Sahara and cross over the line, symbolically claiming the region for Morocco from Spain. The green flags waved by participants also symbolically demonstrated national unity, allegiance to the king, and faith in Islam. The Green March became the monarchy's symbol for Islam, openly countering Marxist-Leninist ideology that supported pluralist party politics and secular institutions.

Without trial or access to a lawyer, Kamal is thrown in prison at Derb Moulay Chérif (which is also the Arabic title of the film). While there, he is forced to reveal the names of his former comrades, even though he confesses not to have seen them for years. Kamal ends up spending fourteen years in prison and tells Najat to "marry someone else." The two lovers are separated forever. The second half of the film concentrates on revealing the unjust legal system, corrupt lawyers who refuse to represent detainees, and the resulting mock trial the prisoners end up facing. The unjust outcome leads the few incorruptible lawyers who have taken up the detainees' cause to storm out of the courtroom, disgusted by the judge's flagrant abuse of human rights, as the prisoners chant, "The road of struggle calls us." Years later, in the concluding scenes of the film, Najat, with her little girl, goes to Mdidech's book signing of *La Chambre noire*. The final sequence depicts Najat placing her book in front of Mdidech to sign. While the film ends on a somewhat upbeat note, the legacy of the thousands of lives of the disappeared—those lost without a trace—looms large in a film that presents no closure to the Lead Years.

Benjelloun's prison film, based on true events, not only resuscitates stories that were suppressed in the past but often questions the monarchy's blatant misuse of power while it sought to divert attention from the human rights abuses taking place in its prisons. Audiences viewing the film in the present are reminded of just how politics and ideology can be used to manipulate, coerce, and destroy a people. This haunting past, many believe, are still a possible reality for contemporary Morocco.

La Chambre noire, although winning L'Etalon d'argent award at the internationally acclaimed African film festival FESPACO in Ouagadougou, Burkina Faso, in 2005, received mixed reviews at home. The weekly francophone newsmagazine *TelQuel* disparaged the film, stating "we learned nothing new that we didn't already know."[10] Although the work reveals little new information, it still serves as a cinematic, documented memory that is, at least, preserved on film. Although it won at FESPACO, the film has rarely been shown internationally since. As with most Moroccan films, its distribution was a nonstarter. Indeed, traveling across the country in a hunt for elusive films in pirated DVD formats is the destiny of any researcher attempting to compile a comprehensive work on contemporary Moroccan filmmaking. How to make films available on DVD is one of the most daunting hurdles for the Moroccan film industry. Unlike Egyptian and Indian filmmakers, Moroccans have not focused on creating viable and sustainable DVD distribution and marketing venues, which continue to be the major obstacles to promoting Moroccan films, both internationally and at home. Filmmakers and people in the industry blame the ineffectiveness of the Centre Cinématographique Marocain (known all over the country by its acronym, CCM), Morocco's national film institute. Founded by the French in 1944 when Morocco was still a protectorate, the institution had been integrated into the postcolonial nation and fully funded by the state by 1958, two years after independence. In an interview in 2008, Abdelhatif Laassadi, spokesman for the CCM, offered a reason for the institution's slow response to the problem of distribution. Primarily, Laassadi notes, the CCM has functioned only as a mediator between filmmakers and the realization of their projects. "Notre rôle est intermédiare" (Our role is intermediary), he passionately stated during the annual meeting at the CCM to assess its investments in filmmaking. Mediation has been the CCM's modus operandi, certainly for the last two decades. This is perhaps one of the leading problems hampering the modernization of the industry. Instead of viewing its role as solely a "soutien créatif" (creative supporter), Laassadi suggests, the CCM would better serve the future of filmmaking as a body that takes the lead in founding ways to market and distribute films both at home and abroad. It should also encourage Moroccans to go to the movies by offering lower ticket prices, subsidies, or other incentives (Sedia). Most definitely, better oversight on the part of the CCM would ensure that pirating and selling DVDs in the local markets would be curtailed, as Alexandra Girard, writing for *Le Matin*, a leading francophone newspaper, notes:

> This cinema is rich and appreciated as much by Moroccans at home as by foreign audiences, thus prompt export is needed. Nevertheless, in order to counter the persistent illegal local film market nourished by pirated DVDs, found today on every street corner, audiences must be encouraged to go to the movies. Because, in the end, if no one pays the real price for viewing these films, death to [the] art is assured. If the CCM only concentrates on channeling crowds for a few hours, then nothing will be left of the 7th Art, important and necessary for all self-respecting societies.

Marketing and Distribution: Morocco's Challenges of the Future

The CCM has grappled with how to promote films that people want to see at home while also seeking to make inroads into the international markets of Europe and the United States. At times the CCM's international commercial aspirations seem at odds with in-country filmmakers such as Benjelloun, Lahcen Zinoun, and Farida Benlyazid, whose main concern is presenting Moroccan-centered films to Moroccan audiences. Therefore themes that dwell on the untold memories of the past and the inequalities of the present, told primarily in Moroccan Arabic, tend to be a hard sell to international markets. Yet annually, Morocco still makes a significant amount of films. Today, if considered in the larger category of Arab cinema, Morocco is second only to Egypt for the most films made per year. In 2009, the country produced a total of fifteen feature-length films and four shorts (Bennani). In the Maghreb, when compared to Algeria and Tunisia, Morocco's industry enjoys the most autonomy and has had the least governmental interference in the way of outright censure since 1999. Contemporary film critics emphasize that Morocco has surpassed its Maghrebi neighbors in quality, themes, scope, and number of films produced each year.[11]

Although confronted with hurdles such as flagging ticket sales and cinema closures at home (ticket sales have fallen, according to a 2010 report noting that only 2,638,707 tickets for films were sold in 2009, compared to 11,614,845 sold in 2000), cinema as an appreciated cultural art form seems to have rooted itself in Morocco's contemporary society, certainly among younger generations. In an article titled "Bilan cinématographique 2009: Des chiffres qui mettent à nu l'état du 7éme Art marocain" (Cinema Outcomes for 2009: Numbers that Lay Bare the State of Morocco's 7th Art), Ouafaâ Bennani, writing for *Le Matin*, notes that the CCM authorized filming for twenty-nine feature-length films, twenty-eight telefilms, eighty shorts, seven medium-length films, sixteen series, fifty-nine documentaries, four sitcoms, and forty-four institutional films (films made for specific corporations). Perhaps this attests to the fact that as *film language* becomes more accessible, the masses become more used to the idea of film as an integral part of everyday society and culture. The fine line that must be walked, according to most filmmakers, is how to make films entertaining enough to draw crowds but still true to "les sujets dans la réalité" (real-life issues) of everyday Morocco (Girard).

The tension between filmmakers as artists working as sociocultural, historical memory keepers and the CCM, bent on commercializing the industry, defines the overarching climate of contemporary Moroccan cinema. The significant question of how best to remain true to the issues of real life, which includes fostering remembrances and generating awareness of the past while also tackling urgent issues of the present, is always on the minds of filmmakers.

Although extremely interesting with respect to Moroccan history, the films discussed in this essay are somewhat difficult to market to the greater international audience because they are so Moroccan-centric. More internationally themed films generally tend to cast Morocco in the way the West still wants to see it: the deserts, the vast expanses of rural peoples dressed in Berber clothes. Films made by Moroccans living abroad that benefit from funds made available in France, Belgium, and Spain are somewhat thematically bound by orientalist paradigms. While I have not been able to find substantial data to corroborate my hypothesis, based on numerous observations I would say that international funding dictates the subjects of films, as West African filmmakers have claimed in the past (notably Senegalese Semène Ousmane). It is also true that Moroccan and, in general, Maghrebi filmmakers, as Arab film critic Miriam Rosen remarks, "run the risk of having to change [their] screenplay[s]" when financed abroad, mainly because "the Western viewer becomes a major factor in the filmic equation" (36). In short, certain Europeans equate the picturesque and the desert sands with North Africa or expect to see certain "immigrants in Europe" themes. Belgian-Moroccan Yasmine Kassari's *L'Enfant endormi* (The Sleeping Child, 2004) and French resident Ismaël Ferroukhi's *Le Grand Voyage* (The Long Journey, 2004), while stunning films, also exploit the usual stereotypes that Western audiences crave—deserts; pastoral rural life; subdued, traditionally dressed women; and strained immigrant communities.

Language Conundrums

The effectiveness of distribution abroad, or lack thereof, is often defined or hindered by language. Since the Moroccan filmmaker, more often than not, has the choice of casting actors in Arabic, Berber, or French, language becomes a defining hurdle in terms of marketing, distribution abroad, and audience reception. One of the crucial questions to which I have sought answers in my work is whether or not Moroccan cinema can be considered francophone, as some scholars have claimed and as French professors in America would like to think when planning a francophone cinema course. France's role and the predominance of French language use by certain sectors of the Moroccan population must be taken into consideration when discussing cinematic production in the country. In reality, many of the films made in-country are destined for purely Arabic-speaking audiences. However, films are always screened with French subtitles due to the overwhelming numbers of Moroccans living abroad who come home in the summertime. The children of MREs (*Marocains résidents à l'étranger*—Moroccans living overseas) number about 3 million and live predominantly in France, Belgium, and Canada. Most do not speak the colloquial Arabic of their parents and, therefore, must rely on French.

Often funding also dictates the language the filmmaker ultimately uses to make his or her film. For the most part, the Moroccan "blockbuster" film (large-budget films that are partially or solely funded from abroad) such as *Le Grand Voyage, Marock, J'ai vu tuer Ben Barka* (I Saw Ben Barka Get Killed; Serge Le Péron and Saïd Smihi, 2005), and *Whatever Lola Wants* (Nabil Ayouch, 2008), while popular with Moroccan audiences, are successful internationally because scripts are primarily in French and themes are universal (redemption, boy-girl love, French/Moroccan history, striving for success in the age of globalization). One of the issues I try to determine in my research is to what extent language plays in effectively conveying the filmmaker's desired messages. *Les Anges de Satan* (Satan's Angels; Ahmed Boulane, 2007), although considered a well-attended film, stayed at home because of its exclusive use of Moroccan Arabic and focus on specific home events.[12] Certain more "artistic" films, such as Nabyl Lahlou's *Tabite or Not Tabite* (2006) use both Arabic and French. These films require us to ask: Do films destined for audiences primarily at home dictate what language is used in a film? Obviously not. In *Tabite*, made in Morocco and never screened abroad, French is the language in which the protagonists (who are all dissidents, exiled in Paris during the Lead Years) describe the despotic past of Morocco, the brutality of the police officer Tabite, and whether or not to go back to Morocco to make a film about their repressive experiences. Yet Arabic is the dominant language once the dissidents return home to confront their oppressors and challenge the status quo.

Lahcen Zinoun's short twelve-minute film *Faux pas* reflects his personal experiences and life during the Lead Years under Hassan II. The story, narrated in French, is told from the viewpoint (and vantage point) of feet. The artistic nature of the film promotes several meanings as the denouement unfolds. *Faux pas* in French figuratively means an unintentional error, yet in the context of the film also connotes a "misplaced step" (the word *pas* literally means "step"), since the entire film is shot from the perspective of the silent characters' feet (both shod and bare, male and female). Aurally, *faux pas* sounds like *faut pas*, meaning "must not"—a warning—also an underlying theme. Except for the haunting narration of the female voice that recounts the events of Evelyn Serfaty's 1952 kidnapping and torture and subsequent imprisonment until 1956 during the waning years of French occupation in Morocco, it is the feet of men and women who narrate their stories of human rights abuse in French.

Zinoun's camera work is visually stunning as it melds the horrors experienced during the Lead Years (1963–99) with the colonial period further back in time, when the country was occupied by the French (1912–56). Two periods of historical *réfoulement* (suppressed memories) are contextualized, forcing audiences to think about the thousands of Moroccans who were made to disappear during those times, either at the hands of the French during the waning years of colonial occupation or later in the era of Hassan II. Twelve minutes tell the countless stories of the faceless masses who were abducted, tortured, and disposed of without a trace.

The film opens with an ode to Evelyn Serfaty, sister to Abraham Serfaty, Francophone, Jewish by birth, and also a communist-activist fighting against the French occupiers in the 1950s. Both Serfaty and his sister were exiled to France, where they were incarcerated until 1956. Later, in the Morocco of the 1970s, Abraham Serfaty was again imprisoned, this time under Hassan II for his militant communist activism on university campuses across the country with the poet-activist Abdellatif Laâbi. In 1991, Serfaty was released after seventeen years of prison and subsequently went into exile in France for the remainder of Hassan II's regime. In 2000, Mohammed VI invited the Serfaty family to return to Morocco, restoring their Moroccan citizenship.[13]

Lahcen Zinoun's short film evokes the complicated questions that arise with respect to language in Moroccan cultural production. It must be emphasized that most filmmakers, intellectuals, dissidents, and militant poets have always been Francophone, opting to choose the French language to champion their causes. French is the language of the Western educated elite, politics, social-activist slogans, and protest. Nevertheless Zinoun's film, as well as others made in the last decade, still provokes the question: In what language is it best to bridge the divide between past and present events, present and future realities, the homeland's aspirations and the Moroccan diaspora's transnational experiences? Obviously, if the film is primarily shot in French (or English, for that matter), marketing and distribution will be facilitated through a number of venues. Films such as Nabyl Ayouch's *Whatever Lola Wants* (filmed in English, French, and Arabic) and *Ismaël Ferroukhi*'s *Le Grand Voyage* (filmed primarily in French) enjoyed international financial backing, were picked up by European distributors, and are now available on DVD. Film Movement (distribution company) offers Ferroukhi's film on DVD with English subtitles.

It is evident that Moroccan filmmakers' decision to use French or not depends on whom they want to influence and what messages they want to evoke in and through their films. Using a European language will, of course, mean better access to international distribution. Yet, no matter the language use, Morocco's cinema industry prides itself on openness and freedom of speech. As stated earlier, films both in Arabic and French have become increasingly subversive in their content since the late 1990s. In the mid-1990s, Moroccan cinematic discourse began opening up and pushing the envelope of sociocultural and political taboos. At the dawn of the twenty-first century, now even politics are open game for Moroccan filmmakers. Particularly those of the younger generations, which do not share their parents' recollections of the Lead Years, do not feel encumbered by self- or state censorship when airing their views. This has been most evident in the recent "Moroccan Spring" of 2011, which, like elsewhere in the Arab world, has challenged the limits of censure and taboos through Twitter feeds and Facebook pages.

Making Films in Twenty-First-Century Morocco

In 2005, Moroccan film critic Mustapha Mesnaoui emphasized that film can, indeed, play a role in "bridging gaps" as a generator of its own *langue de communication* (language of communication) in contemporary society. The "7th Art," he declares, has the potential to unite modernists and traditionalists, as well as Arabophones and Francophones, by offering a cinema that is inclusive of all views and debates and that encourages audiences to reflect on the reality of multicultural Morocco (qtd. in Ziane). Film is a medium through which contemporary issues, which might not otherwise be available to large audiences who lack access to literature, can be vetted and discussed. The language of film reaches all linguistic groups inherent in Morocco's polyglot society. The question pertaining to which language should be used to make Moroccan films has become secondary to the issues that filmmakers want to explore. For this reason, film is an all-inclusive medium of sociocultural production. In Morocco, cinematography has been carved out from a multifaceted reality that is at once Berber/Arab/French, rural and urban, traditional and modern.

The phrase "the future of Moroccan cinema" includes an inherent question mark any time one discusses the film industry in the country. Marking the fiftieth anniversary of postcolonial Moroccan filmmaking in 2008, the editor of *CinéMag*, the country's leading film criticism magazine, poetically noted that being able to celebrate the "golden jubilee" of Moroccan filmmaking came after having trudged along "a long trajectory of trial and error, research, and long desert crossings" ("Editor's Note" 90).[14] Noting the plurality of challenges, both economic and cultural, the magazine emphasizes that cinema production in Morocco has finally matured. The industry has conceptualized "tools and strategies that allow for a national cinematographic production that is increasingly visible [recognized and appreciated throughout the world]" (90). Moroccan cineastes should be commended for seeking to develop and impart their own concept of cinema with respect to themes, the images portrayed, and the messages conveyed. In the years to come, the industry as a whole will continue to confront issues of language, shifting tastes of audiences, lagging viewership, and resources, all of which affect how a film is made.

It must be noted that the rigor and sustainability of Morocco's film industry over the last fifty years are due primarily to filmmakers' dedication to trying to find middle ground as they negotiate these hurdles and conflicting realms. Since 1999, they have continued to support the idea of the importance of film as a vehicle through which to send socio-realist messages that will challenge audiences to invest in positive transitions taking place currently in the country, while also encouraging them not to forget the unexplored, painful events of the past. Whether male or female, living abroad or based at home, cineastes view their roles as keepers of the collective consciousness of Morocco. They are both generators and agents of change. The more relaxed climate in the era of King Mohammed VI has made Moroccan film an exciting medium through which to explore the current issues that are the most pressing and important in the country's sociocultural and political development.

Unlike Egypt and Tunisia, Morocco does not have an "official" censor. Indeed, most films are funded in part by the CCM,[15] and few, if any, in the last decade have been pulled by authorities for "sensitive" material. Recent films such as Aziz Salmy's *Hijab al-Hob*, Mohamed Moutakfkir's *Pegasus* (2010), and Abdelhaï Laraki's *Les Ailes de l'amour* (Love in the Medina, 2011) are exceedingly daring and rival any Western film—European or American—with respect to sexual content, nakedness on screen, and transgressive adult behavior. *Hijab al-Hob*, when it was released in 2009, incited a host of debate in the public arena surrounding feminism, women's increasing sexual freedom in society, and having children outside wedlock. Batoul, a young pediatrician with her own practice, falls in love with an older divorcé who doesn't believe in marriage. Although pious and traditional, Batoul also seeks to live as a "modern" woman. Their sexual encounters become more frequent as passion wins out over traditionalism.[16] The film could not have been made even a few years earlier, but today, as the taboos in Moroccan society are constantly challenged and as emboldened women seek access to a variety of choices regarding their sexuality and spouses, Salmy's film is at the forefront for equal rights, part of the framework of Morocco's unique "Arab Spring" movement. Although the PJD (Parti de la justice et du développement) called for censure of *Hijab al-Hob*, the CCM and the public pushed back, stating that the film's controversial subjects—whether a woman should veil or not veil in modern society, have sex out of wedlock, have children without being married—needed to be seen so that fruitful debate could ensue. And, indeed it did. Numerous blogs discussed the film, and the majority of both male and female bloggers noted that wearing the hijab (the Islamic headscarf) should be a woman's choice. If she decides to wear it, she should still be able to explore sexual desire and the erotic side of relationships and to decide for herself how best to negotiate her individuality, anywhere between tradition and modernity. Filmmaker Aziz Salmy declared: "I seek to provoke debate. My film tries to take the veil off [no pun intended] a fringe of Moroccan society; these young women in their thirties who have made it socially, but who still are pulled between their professional ambitions and the temptation of a family life *bien rangée* [well taken care of], in the shadow of a protecting and kindly man."[17]

Today, Moroccan cinema acts as a mirror for a society that is remaking itself. Like literature, the press, and other forms of media that are invested socioculturally and politically in the dynamics and debates currently taking place in the country, cinema is a key element in the documentation of past history and present realities. It provides a forum through which to analyze, reflect, and discuss the contemporary issues that are present in society and that contribute to the shaping of the contours of the New Morocco.

Notes

1. See my book *Screening Morocco: Contemporary Film in a Changing Society*.
2. The actual dates of the Lead Years are debatable. Some historians believe the era began in 1963, when Hassan II's ascension to the throne of Morocco occurred following the death of his father, Mohammed V. Others note that the dark period really began in the early 1970s, when the most forceful crackdown on civil and human rights became routine, thus establishing a pattern of abuse that endured almost to the end of Hassan II's life in 1999.
3. Many of the filmmakers interviewed while I conducted research for my book divulged that they were themselves persecuted during the Lead Years.
4. "Nous ne voulons pas faire du cinéma subversive . . . il s'agit avant tout de faire du cinéma un moyen adéquate de dénonciation, et non une arme à la quête d'une subversion folle et insoutenable." My translation.
5. "The Movement of the 20th of February" is made up of youth, several political parties, and some trade unions who first chose to demonstrate on a Sunday rather than on a Friday, the Muslim religious day of the week, thus marking the fact that the movement is not about religion but about social reform rooted in historically Marxist-socialist movements of the past. Curiously, religious parties and leftist intellectuals have united in their effort to keep demonstrations fueled with debate. Morocco's current younger generation's slogans allude to the past Marxist-socialist movements and socialist-communist political parties of their parents, certainly of the 1970s. Groups such as L'Union Nationale des Forces Populaires and L'Union Marocaine du Travail were supported by the ideologies and writings of notable intellectuals

such as Abdellatif Laâbi (founder in 1966 of the political literary magazine *Souffles*), Abraham Serfaty, Mustafa Nissaboury, and Mohamed Khair-Eddin, among others.

6. Since February 20, 2011, the sociopolitical contexts of the demonstrations have been discussed at length in a series of articles in the leading French-language magazines and newspapers *TelQuel, Maroc Hebdo, Le Matin,* and *L'Opinion* as well as in the Arabic dailies *Assabah, Al Massae,* and *AkhbarAl Youm*. Morocco has enjoyed a long history of liberal press that is critically candid and asks thought-provoking questions of society and politics. *TelQuel*, founded in 2000 by the savvy, thirty-something Ahmed Benchemsi, is modeled on the French leftist magazine of the same name. Since its inception, editors at *TelQuel* have pushed the sociopolitical envelope, probing the recesses of the country's dark corners in order to expose the pressing problems and hurdles of a country in transition.

7. The interview was held in his studio production offices in Casablanca, June 2010.

8. Binebine's title is a play on words. Tazmamart was the medieval prison in southern Morocco where many innocent soldiers, caught up in the coups d'état of 1972 and 1973, were falsely accused and imprisoned for eighteen years during the repressive years of Hassan II's reign. Binebine changed the name of the prison from Tazmamart to Tazmamort, referring to the French word *mort* (death) in order to evoke the horrendous conditions in which the prisoners lived and because of which most died. Other works on this prison include Ali Bourequat's *Dix-huit ans de solitude* (Eighteen Years of Solitude, 1993), Midhat Bourequat's *Mort Vivant! Témoignage, Rabat 1973–Paris 1992* (Living Dead! Testimony, Rabat 1973–Paris 1992, 2001), and Mohamed Raïss's *De Skhirat à Tazmamart: retour du bout de l'enfer* (From Skhirat to Tazmamart: Return from the End of Hell, 2002; originally published in Arabic in 2001).

9. For additional information on *la littérature carcérale* as well as other Moroccan literary forms and production, see my book *Francophone Voices of the "New" Morocco in Film and Print*.

10. Staff writer's comments at http://www.telquel-online.com/124/arts_124.shtml (accessed on December 8, 2011).

11. Rachid Chenchabi notes in an article from 1984 that Férid Boughedir, notable Tunisian film critic and filmmaker, humorously characterized the three Maghrebi national cinemas as follows:

> Algerians are known for "la dignité de l'humilié" [the dignity of the humiliated] and always bend to the power of their government; Tunisians fight for "l'exigence de la vérité" [claiming truth] and rely on a liberty of expression unlike anywhere else in the Arab world, so "they speak," but succumb to the diversity of their freedom and are, therefore, "Un orphelin qui cherche son visage" [an orphan who seeks his face]; and the Moroccans live in the perpetual "plainte silencieuse . . . j'étouffe, j'étouffe" [silent complaint . . . I'm suffocating, I'm suffocating]. (224)

12. The film tells the tale of thirteen young heavy-metal band members who, in 2003, were tried for crimes "against Islam." The film's publicity poster aptly captures (in French) the heart of the film: "Au Maroc les jeunes sont arrêtés et jugés. Leur seule crime: aimer la musique" (In Morocco young people are arrested and judged. Their only crime: loving music). The young men were accused of playing heavy-metal rock, taking drugs, satanic worship, and defamation of the Islamic faith. None of the charges were true except for playing music. The worst drug offense of which the young men were guilty was smoking hashish. They were primarily from upper-middle-class Casablancan families. The judge ruled against them based on heavy-metal T-shirts with English slogans such as "Kiss My Ass" written on them, skulls and crossbones found in the band's studio, and other Goth attire and paraphernalia. For contemporary Morocco, the event sparked many socioculturally grounded questions about the enduring lack of

freedom of speech and the danger of adopting Western values, among other issues. This event is one of many in the last decade that has been characterized by the contentious transitions of sociopolitical and cultural realms as the country moves toward more democratic reforms. For a complete discussion of this film as well as other monumental events that have shaped cultural production in the country since 1999, see my book *Francophone Voices of the "New" Morocco in Film and Print*.

13. Abraham Serfaty died in November 2010.

14. Since the late 1970s, cinema journals and magazines have been prevalent in Morocco. These are primarily published in French, modeled on famous titles such as *Cahiers du cinéma*. Moroccan film critics tend to discuss film in the context of world cinema as they seek to encourage readership from abroad. Cinema magazines came into their own when newspapers also began dedicating pages to cinema news. *Lamalif* and *Kalima*, two outstanding newsmagazines dating from the early 1970s, habitually included cinema reviews in their pages. Magazines devoted exclusively to film included *L'Ecran marocain* and *Cinéma 3*; both had short runs in the 1970s. However, the recently founded French-language *CinéMag: Magazine du cinéma et de l'audiovisuel au Maroc* (first edition published in 2006) is the first magazine of the new millennium dedicated solely to cinema that offers in-depth interviews with filmmakers, both at home and abroad, and critical essays on current films. See my book *Screening Morocco: Depictions in Film of a Changing Society*.

15. The CCM operates much like France's Centre National du Cinéma et de l'Image Animée (CNC), a state-run, funded agency. Like in France, filmmakers propose screenplays that are voted on each year and then, if accepted, allocated funding. This process, called *avances sur recettes* (or, literally, advances on ticket sales), has been beneficial to filmmakers but has not created much incentive for marketing films abroad. The money is awarded with strings attached. Filmmakers told me that the money is appreciated, but, if their films make more money at the box office than the original advance in funds, then they are obligated to pay the money "awarded" back to the CCM. Since few filmmakers had the money in the first place, their interest lies in not making money at the box office.

16. See my article on the film, "Women, Religion, and Sexuality in Contemporary Moroccan Film."

17. See the article "Le film 'Amours voilées' suscite la colère d'un député islamiste," http://www.bladi.net/film-amours-voilees.html (accessed on January 22, 2014). The PJD sought to ban the film immediately after its release. Party members' calls for censure, however, fell on deaf ears, as they were unable to counter the fact that 500,000 tickets had been sold. To date, the film holds the record for the highest number of ticket sales in Morocco for a Moroccan film.

Works Cited

Belouchi, Belkassem. *Rapt de voix*. Casablanca: Afrique Orient, 2004.

Bennani, Ouafaâ. "Bilan cinématographique 2009: Des chiffres qui mettent à nu l'état du 7éme Art marocain." *Le Matin*, March 14, 2010, http://www.lematin.ma/Actualite/Journal/Article.asp?idr=115&id=129674 (accessed on December 6, 2011).

Binebine, Aziz. *Tazmamort: dix-huit ans dans le bagne de Hassan II*. Paris: Editions Denoël, 2009.

Carter, Sandra. "Moroccan Cinema, What Cinema?" *Maghreb Review* 25, nos. 1–2 (2000): 66–97.

Chenchabi, Rachid. 1984. "Le cinéma maghrébin, une dimension francophone?" *Franzosisch heute* 15, no. 2 (1984): 224–33.

Diawara, Manthia. *African Cinema: Politics and Culture.* Bloomington: Indiana University Press, 1992.

"Editor's Note." *CinéMag: Magazine du cinéma et de l'audiovisuel au Maroc,* October–December 2008, 90–98.

El Bouih, Fatna. *Une Femme nommée Rachid.* Casablanca: Le Fennec, 2002. *Hadit al-'atama.* Original title in Arabic. Casablanca: Editions le Fennec, 2001.

Erll, Astrid. "Literature, Film, and the Mediality of Cultural Memory." In *Cultural Media Studies: An International and Interdisciplinary Handbook,* edited by Astrid Erll and Ansgar Nünning in collaboration with Sara B. Young, 389–98. Berlin: Walter de Gruyter, 2008.

Fakihani, Abdelfettah. *Le Couloir: Bribes de vérité sur les années de plomb.* Casablanca: Tarik Editions, 2005.

Girard, Alexandra. "Bilan mitigé pour le cinéma marocain." *Le Matin,* January 2, 2008, http://www.yabiladi.com/article-culture-633.html (accessed on December 6, 2011).

Le Goff, Jacques. *History and Memory.* New York: Columbia University Press, 1996.

Mahfoudi, Tahar. 2004. *Ufoulu al-layl: Yawmiyat Lm'arif wa Ghbila.* Fès: Dar Al Qarawiyine, 2004.

Marzouki, Ahmed. *Tazmamart: Cellule 10.* Paris: Gallimard, 2001.

Mdidech, Jaouad. *La Chambre noire ou Derb Moulay Chérif.* Casablanca: Eddif, 2002.

Nora, Pierre. *Les Lieux de mémoire.* Translated as *Realms of Memory.* Edited by Lawrence D. Kritzman. Translated by Arthur Goldhammer. New York: Columbia University Press, 1997.

Orlando, Valérie K. *Francophone Voices of the "New" Morocco in Film and Print: (Re)presenting a Society in Transition.* New York: Palgrave Macmillan, 2009.

———. *Screening Morocco: Contemporary Film in a Changing Society.* Athens: Ohio University Press, 2011.

———. "Women, Religion, and Sexuality in Contemporary Moroccan Film: Unveiling the Veiled in *Hijab al-Hob* (Veils of Love, 2009)." *Palimpsest: A Journal on Women, Gender, and the Black International* 3, no. 1 (2013): 106–25.

Rosen, Miriam. "The Uprooted Cinema: Arab Filmmakers Abroad." *Middle East Report,* July–August 1989, 34–37.

Sedia, Giuseppe. "Centre cinématographique marocain: Entretien avec Abdelhatif Laassadi." *Clap noir: Cinémas et audiovisuel africains,* October 11, 2008, http://www.clapnoir.org/spip.php?article269 (accessed on December 9, 2011).

Ziane, Nadia. 2005. "Mustapha Mesnaoui: 'Nous n'avons pas de cinéma marocain.'" *Le Matin,* August 22, 2005, http://www.lematin.ma/Actualite/Journal/Article.asp?idr=110&id=84814 (accessed on December 9, 2011).

9 Thresholds of New African Dramaturgies in France Today

Mária Minich Brewer

> Not all voices can be heard at the same time in the same story/history.
> Kossi Efoui, *Solo d'un revenant*

THIS COLLECTION OF essays, *Rethinking African Cultural Productions,* offers an occasion to question theater's physical and symbolic borders, frontiers, separations, and border crossings. Working as it does across multiple thresholds and dimensions simultaneously, whether of time, space, language, or the body, the art of the theater engages its public in critical considerations of and across borders. A new generation of African diasporic playwrights of the 1990s have thoroughly reinvented the social and symbolic possibilities for new theatrical languages. In this essay, I propose to map out some of the theatrical thresholds implicit in such a project of reinventing a new theatricality. This critical work on thresholds, I argue, needs to focus explicitly on the symbolic, social, and material dimensions of writing for performance.

The title of my study, "Thresholds of New African Dramaturgies in France Today," foregrounds questions of thresholds in diasporic theater as a way of engaging with practices of making-visible and making-sensible today. This theater is a singularly complex space for charting the many dimensions of visibility at work in social, mediatized, and symbolic practices; it works to undo what might be called established syntaxes of the cultural imaginary. In the imaginary spaces of theatrical writing and performance, entrenched regimes of the visible and the communicable are unfolded, displaced, and deactivated. By considering theater itself as threshold, we can open a space for theorizing theater's specific potential for creating mobile passages between languages, the modern and the ancient, here and elsewhere, the other and the same, and so on.[1]

One way to theorize that potential would be in terms of what writer and philosopher Jean-Christophe Bailly calls "une pensée du seuil": "a thinking of footbridges, a threshold thought. The threshold does not negate difference but accepts it and links the visitor and the visited according to the force of a bond that *obliges* them.[2] The threshold does not deny that there exists an outside and an inside, on the contrary, it recognizes them, but it also opens them one onto the other" (Bailly 20). Bailly admits that one might think that "such an opening, a possibility of exchange and sharing (out), a system of reciprocal obligations, are doubtless once again nothing more than the philosopher's 'dream of peace.'"[3] But for him, a thinking of the threshold promises a new politics, one that works out "from conflicts themselves, and from what generates them and stokes them, the nature of what we lack, what man lacks to be an authentic political animal, *finally* a political animal: the animal of thresholds" (21).[4]

In order to understand theater's engagement with such an "art of thresholds," I propose that its semantics of thresholds be taken to include three fields: one of passage and communication; one of division, separation, barrier, and limit; and one of dialogical mediation through specific practices. In the following discussion, I treat diasporic dramaturgies as staging a dialogical relationship between the first two meanings, those of passage and division. It is in terms of their relationship that the question of "becoming-visible" in theater may be posed. Such an examination allows for a better understanding of the dramaturgical specificity of francophone diasporic theater as an art of thresholds.[5] In a theoretical sense, by adopting a poetics of thresholds it might be possible to go beyond rigid conceptual oppositions between here and there, Africa and Europe, past and present, inside and outside, and so on. This poetics involves the reader, spectator, and critic in theorizing contemporary diasporic theater's signifying practices, including its metatheatrical dimensions.

Theater of Thresholds, Theater as Threshold

In recent critical theory, the return to Plato and Aristotle has remarked the double etymology of *thea* (spectacle, contemplation, look, action of looking) and *theoria* (contemplate theoretically, as knowledge and *epistēmē*).[6] This dovetailing of meanings resurfaces in Jean-François Lyotard's assessment of avant-garde experimentation in which the essential goal is to "make seen what makes one see, and not what is visible," rendering visible what demands to be represented (207). In a similar vein, current scholarship on the relationship between theater and philosophy brings much needed critical perspectives to bear on the conditions of possibility of visibility in them both.

Denis Guénoun writes that in philosophy and theater studies, the notion of *scène*, while it has been treated in its different modalities and historical evolution, had not until recently itself constituted the prime focus of analysis.[7] The French word *scène* conjoins an architectural reality and a dramaturgical one; "what we call *scène* is at once the theater stage, its structure, and its planks as well as an internal division within the theatrical work and its narrative."⁸ The stakes of focusing on the stage space are especially relevant for what they tell us about how it is that theater comes to be. In Guénoun's terms, "the *scène* is that most singular space, previously emptied, where the apparatus of appearing is composed." He recognizes that the idea that "things, people or actions may be, and that they appear," is not specific to theater, but he insists that "what makes it so is that a practical space is organized and freed so as to refine (*épurer*) the process of appearing, releasing it from its surroundings, giving it all its force, which is then a singular invention that we call theater."⁹ In Guénoun's view, theater and the *scène* at its core not only show something but also free the process of showing from its environment so to "bring into view the operation of the delivering . . . to the gaze (or hearing), to manifest the manifestation."¹⁰ What Guénoun understands by a freeing from the environment is an *epochē* in Kirkkopelto's phenomenological project of the *scène*. I will return later to the environment and its bracketing or unbracketing in diasporic African theater practices.

In his introduction to *Philosophie de la scène*, Guénoun again takes up the Aristotelian notion of theater as an assembly united around an absence (*vide*). The essential operation, he stresses, is one of emptying or making a void (*faire le vide*) typical of a stage or a temple. He adds that "the void of/for the scene is produced *by the assembled who move away*," or in another, and perhaps sharper, formulation, "the emptiness of the stage is created *by the assembly that makes space*."¹¹ It is notable that here Guénoun appears to take his distance from Peter Brook's well-known assertion: "I can take any empty space and call it a bare stage. A man walks across this empty space whilst someone is watching him, and this is all we needed for an act of theatre to be engaged." Rather than a single spectator, then, the theater requires the presence, whether real or implied, of a "collective convergence of gazes and of listening—an assembly."¹² For Guénoun, theater must include spectators and listeners, but he does not question whether such an assembly and the process of emptying out the environment are compatible. In sum, theater as a modality of seeing articulates a knowing, which is itself conditioned by a staging before a public. But at each nexus of this process of staging as seeing, knowing, and assembly, the lived environment, I propose, is itself re-presented as a series of thresholds. In what sense, then, is this operation of making space for a theatrical event of particular relevance to the work of new African playwrights? Do they, in revisiting the relationship of theater and theory, manage to displace them in a way that shifts the givens of seeing, hearing, and staging, that is, the conditions of theatricality as such? It may be argued that theater's capacity to make the conditions of seeing visible is as old as theater itself. Certainly, in the wake of Antonin Artaud and Bertolt Brecht, this capacity is also at the core of tenets of modernism and postmodernism. Yet how does such a theater differ from cinema and photography? Although it cannot be pursued here, a productive line of inquiry might take up Guénoun's notions that theater releases a space from its environment, thereby constituting a void for the scene to occur, and that theater happens when those assembled move away to make place for the event. Cinema and photography undoubtedly also "make space," but their relationship to the spectator or viewer is not primarily defined by an assembly's shift or move to make a space for performance. In this sense, the thresholds that new playwrights create are based not only on the physical co-presence of actors and spectators, which is constitutive of the event of theater and a recurrent trope in theater studies, but on a significantly different relation to the dynamic operating between the assembly and the empty space for the event that it allows.

In their plays, the new African playwrights oppose entrenched expectations that African theater must be the site of an obligation to reenact theater traditions that are at once authentic and ritualized. They challenge, moreover, the idea that theater can be a site where such rituals are bound to be performed for an imaginary audience that functions as a mythology (in Roland Barthes's sense of ideology) that is increasingly global in scope. Indeed, they restage and displace in their works some of the most seen yet least visible imaginaries, namely, those of the ideological representations of history, language, the body, and the role of the artist in modernity.

Although they do not constitute a movement as such, this new generation of playwrights includes Koffi Kwahulé (Ivory Coast), Marcel Zang (Cameroon), José Pliya (Bénin), Caya Makhélé (Congo), Koulsy Lamko (Chad), and Kossi Efoui (Togo).[13] Based on these playwrights' shared but necessarily individual experiences of diaspora, various names have been used to describe this theater, which has been called a new theater of transgression, a theater of utopia (Ambroise Têko-Agbo), a theater of the in-between (Makhélé), a theater of crossings and a suspended writing (Chalaye), and a theater of errancy (Miller). As these names suggest, this theater has in common the experience of migration that, for Chalaye, is ultimately to be understood in dramatic, cultural, and existential terms.

The semantics of these attempts at classification strongly suggests that what is at stake in a theater of thresholds is at once dramaturgical and cultural/political. In their writing, these playwrights redefine the historical, critical, and cultural contexts of their practice. They do so by linking it to African, ancient Greek, and Western theatrical traditions and their avant-garde reinventions. Written and performed not only in France, where many writers live, their plays are also being staged in Africa, the European Union, North and South America, the Caribbean, and increasingly worldwide.[14] Tireless writers, practitioners, and travelers, these playwrights of the African diaspora accomplish acts of complex boundary crossings as authors as well as in their role as leaders of theater workshops in community and academic venues.[15] These border crossings involve inventing works for the stage that expand what we understand by modern African dramaturgies in France and, in so doing, create new possibilities for theater and performance.

Beginning in the 1990s, significant research on new African dramaturgies in theater and performance studies has been pursued by scholars in France and the United States.[16] Critics Sylvie Chalaye and the late John Conteh-Morgan situate this theater as that of a third generation, following upon a first, nationalist and culturalist phase of the independence period, and a second, political phase of postcolonial skepticism and critique. They agree that since the early 1990s, francophone African theater of the diaspora defines new relationships both to the theaters of their writers' countries of origin and to those of the European and American theatrical traditions.

For Chalaye, this theater is identified as "a dramaturgy of crossroads" inscribing a hybrid identity "in the triangular, diasporic tension between the Africa of one's origins, European history, and cross-Atlantic tropisms" ("Voix" 2).[17] Bound up with forces of hybridization and passage, this theater is marked by a variety of geographical and cultural detours and circumventions. But instead of being "a quest for a faraway horizon or a fantasized 'elsewhere,'" detour here demonstrates "the necessity of engaging with a complex and dynamic world made of differences, and encounters with otherness. The idea of place as a transitory space in these plays conveys a sense of fracturing, represented by crossroads" ("Contemporary" 149–50). Moreover, since theater involves the body, diasporic theater becomes a privileged site for "the expression of this in-between, of this play that takes on a body (or becomes embodied)" ("Koffi" 507).[18] In more contextual terms, the stage "becomes the means to invent a language to speak the experience of the migrant," or, as Chalaye puts it, "theater allows one to apply sounds and images to the internal displacement that emigrants experience and which is no longer on the order of space but of being" (507).[19]

A key factor in Chalaye's view of the relationship between exilic experience and the stage is that the dramaturgy of the in-between is nothing less than an ontological and existential space. It is this understanding that grounds her critique of the "ethnographic imperative" and the work of "ethnodramatists" (Conteh-Morgan 157–58)[20] of the earlier generation, which she takes to reinscribe binaries such as orality/literacy, self/Other, indigenous/foreign, tradition/modernity, and performance/text.[21] Clearly, writers of the 1990s sought to undermine rigid oppositions such as these as well as those involving the spatial and temporal dimensions of here/elsewhere, Africa/Europe, past/present, and margin/center. But does theater really have the power to disable and displace such oppositions? And if so, by what means?

In his genealogy of African theater, Conteh-Morgan argues that the new playwrights, in rejecting the use of ceremonies, masks, and cultural particulars, fall back into the very binaries they claim to oppose, thereby reinstating a sharp opposition between a particularized view of Africa and a global, non-African universal. For him, it is their very claim to address a universal public that is perilous because it is trapped in "the symbolic violence that undergirds the universalization of concrete particular models of culture or society." Moreover, as Pierre Bourdieu and Loïc J. D. Wacquant have theorized, symbolic violence is "never wielded but with a form of (extorted) complicity on the part of those who submit to it" (qtd. in Conteh-Morgan 166). For Conteh-Morgan, "such complicity is precisely what one witnesses in the creative work of the third-generation dramatists and the globalist teleological narrative embedded in the critical discourse on it" (166–67). In sum, he rejects what he takes to be their treatment of the global as a neutral entity that "obfuscates the unequal power relation between Africa and the West" (167). He is especially keen to show the dangers of claiming "membership in an autonomous sphere of theatrical activity that is international because it transcends the politics, including the cultural politics, of the nation" (169). It is in the theatrical corpus of Kwahulé that he finds "the broad range of themes associated with the later twentieth- and early twenty-first-century francophone theatre—the concern with building pathways, the expanded parameters of aesthetic production, and the engagement with the circumstances of global displacement and mobility" (173). Terms encapsulating his theater and those of his generation are those of "translocality and nomadism." As Conteh-Morgan puts it, by becoming "practitioners of cosmopolitan hybridity," the works of Koffi Kwahulé, Kossi Efoui, and José Pliya "are seen as the embodiment of a non-particularistic and 'universal' francophone theatre" by critics such as Chalaye. Ultimately though, he recognizes that these works have "thrown wide open the question of the identity and definition of 'francophone' drama [and] . . . effectively disrupted the rigid French-francophone binary to the extent that it is now difficult to speak in terms of a theatre that is either 'francophone' or 'French'" (174). Finally, he recognizes that "in the twenty-first century, these plays inhabit the liminal spaces between bounded national cultures" and contribute to a "reconfiguration of the very meaning of Africanness and Frenchness. Certainly, the time has come to abandon references to a monolithic francophone theatre and to talk instead of francophone *theatres*" (174–75). He calls for a new synthesis of francophone theaters, one that "should include traditional nation-building/nationalist forms of expression as well as new African diasporic/transnational ones, fruits of the new coordinates of contemporary globalization" (175).

It is important to point out that Conteh-Morgan's objection is not so much to the plays themselves and what they perform but to what he believes to be an outright rejection of African origins and cultural practices in a variety of statements the playwrights have made outside of their work. One can readily agree that, were they characteristic of the new theater, such uncritical attitudes would be surprising to find in a generation of artists whose work is predicated on undoing strictly oppositional categories such as orality/literacy, indigenous/foreign, and tradition/modernity. Ultimately, the debate that Conteh-Morgan addresses to the new theater concerns the place of art and culture in a globalized world, a question that is central in diasporic theater as well.[22]

While the tensions between culturalist and transnational forms of affiliation remain quite acute, the plays of new diasporic theater dialogically undermine such rigid oppositions. Thus, the ongoing task of readers, audiences, and critics needs to be to identify what is really innovative in the plays themselves. Indeed, the *différend* between Chalaye's view of this theater's existential dramaturgy and Conteh-Morgan's skeptical view of its transnational affiliations may be negotiated at the level of rigorous work of/on thresholds as an opening onto the dialogical mediation of the divide between either passage or division. In new African dramaturgies, the critical issue involves recognizing the stage or *la scène* as a privileged locus of embedded histories and their becoming-visible.

New Thresholds: The Banquet, the Border, and the Sharing of a Sensible World

When theater is performed, the participants, whether as performers or audience, come to occupy the same physical space. By their presence they at once define and are defined by the thresholds that theater instantiates. They perform an operation whereby an assembly makes a place or space for theater to "take place," as Guénoun puts it.

I propose three approaches to a "theater of thresholds" that promise to be productive for modeling diasporic African theater: the Banquet, the Border within and without, and what philosopher Jacques Rancière calls "le partage du sensible" or the political stakes of sharing or dividing up the sensible world. In previous research, I have concluded that it is not by accident that the Banquet makes its (re)appearance in late twentieth- and early twenty-first century theater and that it does so in different ways in different contexts (Brewer). In the theater of Kwahulé, Efoui, Zang, and Pliya, there occurs a significant questioning of what is assumed to constitute a common shared world or ground.[23] Their plays use the possibilities of the stage to scrutinize relationships of hospitality, commoditization, and belonging. Figuring these relationships through various versions of the Banquet, located in a commensal or common table, these plays engage "the relation between host and guest, production and consumption, rarity and excess, waste and nourishment, the material and the intelligible, identity and difference, body and mind, inside and outside, [and] mine and yours" (Brewer 86). As they confront the elusiveness of a common ground, these dramatists create what I call a "theatricality of the Banquet" as a prism through which to re-theatricalize social relationships and representations. Such a project involves theater in the far-reaching, reflexive task of undoing habitual and ideological ways of ordering and partitioning the world. For the Banquet to operate as a guiding symbolic frame, however, the notion of threshold as a symbolic space of opening, passage, and dialogical mediation necessarily must include a staging of edge and limit.

Marcel Zang situates two of his plays, *Bouge de là* (Move It) and *L'Exilé*, on the threshold space between France and Africa, that is, on the internal/external border leading to deportation. *L'Exilé* is set in an airport holding office, the Police de l'air et des frontières, where Charon (*le passeur d'ombres* or guide to Hades) is the official attempting to deport Imago the writer. Their confrontation occurs at the collision point between here and there, inside and outside, and identity and difference. Whereas Charon claims that he and Imago speak the same language, Imago calls this a lie, given the impossibility of a common language between them; Charon appropriates language as the instrument whereby to effect the exclusion of those he seeks to deport, with the result that the threshold is itself fractured in all directions and collapses. Charon intones, "We are in France here, in a neutral zone, a blind spot, at both the border and already outside of the border, a magical in-between where there's but you and me";[24] Imago, on the contrary, sees through this alibi of a non-place where, in a trial without a witness, the case against the foreigner is made by Charon who situates Imago on a "journey to the edge of night." Appropriating difference as an arm of domination, Charon proclaims that "sex and language exist only in distance and differentiation" (21). Thus, in his play Zang creates a space of ontological uncertainty and risk where he reveals that the claim to non-mastery (Charon's) shores up the foundation upon which to exercise power as violation. In a major soliloquy defending his right to be, Imago articulates the process whereby he has been made into a "pale copy, this absence, this nameless hybrid, this dislocated being, this errant bird, without territory and without shelter. . . . [W]ithout language you've succeeded in making of me a being without language, without its own language . . . forced to host in my head, in my skin, my brain, and even in the folds of my sleep, fears, perceptions, values, myths, dreams, bearings, an ideology that's more than forced, exogenous" (36).[25] Having stripped him of everything, Charon even characterizes Imago's writing as incommunicable: "As for your story, it screeches, lacks cohesion, is full of artifice and unrelated elements that clash, contradict one another" (43).[26] Charon's 'literary criticism' can be read as an ironic metatheatrical reflection on Zang's own dramaturgy, for whatever Imago or he may write risks being taken to mean its opposite. For instance, Imago's reflections on cultural differences are attributed by Charon, projecting his own desire, to the writer's belonging exclusively to African culture. Similarly, the discourse of anthropology is turned against Imago, such that his deportation interrogation is based not on the legitimacy of his claim against exclusion but on Charon's desire and power to assign particularistic meanings to African writing and art in the name of an obligation of authenticity.

The tensions in Zang's writing for the theater resonate strongly with the terms of the debate between Chalaye and Conteh-Morgan I previously presented. I think it would be a mistake to read this play as staging the threshold between France and Africa, inside and outside, as endlessly reflecting images (imagos) that are locked in replication. Instead, Zang's play proposes the writing of diasporic playwrights as an important rebuttal, one whose effect is to articulate a *dissensus* where the charting of new thresholds requires inventing new dramatic languages. In response to Charon's insistence on the preeminence and all-powerful nature of the image, which Charon regulates and controls, Imago argues eloquently in defense of language, a figural language, and the language of the image. Symptomatically, Charon uses that defense as the occasion once again to assign Imago his identity as African—"What's stopping you from going there?" (Qu'attendez-vous pour y aller?) (63). Whereas for Imago language is a multidimensional threshold, Charon attempts to impose a unidirectional model of language as symbolic voyage to the source of language as figure, which is a voyage (of exclusion) without return. In Zang's theater, which is highly allegorical, the debate between Chalaye and Conteh-Morgan and their differing claims for theater's power are forcefully enacted, as they are, with different dramaturgical valences, in Kossi Efoui and Koffi Kwahulé.

From his earliest play, the celebrated *Le Carrefour* (The Crossroads) to his most recent ones, including *Oublie!* (Forget!), Efoui uses a variety of materials, including the simplest and most fragile such as fiber, masks, veils, and cloth, to make tangible the "spaces of the in-between." It is through these sticks and strings of the stage that Efoui seeks to dismantle the multiple screens that provide alibis for official violence by allowing it to occupy common spaces, destroy artistic bodies, and smother individual and collective voices. Such violence is located in commemoration, ideological repression, and the virtual dimensions of what he calls ideological cannibalism. By viewing Efoui's work in terms of an art of thresholds, one sees how he strives to make visible and sensible the many dimensions of separation and division. To this end, he uses a variety of forms of allegory, metaphor, parody, caricature, and choral response to considerable effect. For instance, in *Concessions,* characters who aspire to a new life are stalled in the purgatorial "Interzone," stripped of their names and their very identities by the corporate clones of Winterbottom & Winterbottom Excellence Century Productions Inc., stick characters who have entrapped them. The dire perils of desiring immigration to a better life elsewhere are elaborated in Efoui as both a metaphorical and literal stripping-down of the individual who is deprived of voice and singularity.

To use Efoui's expression, he is bent on rendering as thoroughly "enigmatic" what appears to be "a secure, expected, transparent" universe ("Masques"; "Parler" 118). Whether the figure of the artist is actually personified by a character on stage or not, he argues, art needs to resist forms of cultural and totalitarian fundamentalisms that combine to depersonalize the human, reducing it to merchandise. Among other figures that he proposes for countering what he calls a state of being "phagocyted"[27] are those of flight or a becoming-volatile, which in his writing is a multidimensional theatrical esthetic. By giving it a body and a voice that preserves it as enigmatic, Efoui thus unfolds the *limen* or limit of theater as threshold.

As for Koffi Kwahulé, from his early plays, including *Bintou, Jaz,* and *Cette vieille magie noire* (That Old Black Magic) to the recent *Nema, La Mélancolie des barbares* (Melancholy of Barbarians) and *Les Recluses,* what has characterized his writing is an unflinching determination to address issues of structural violence in societies today.[28] Violence against women, the poor, and the dispossessed is made visible within the larger frameworks of what generates it. As Virginie Soubrier writes, for traditional dialogue Kwahulé substitutes "an interlacing of voices, a combination of sounds and a primacy of rhythm that forces the spectator to engage physically in the texts' elaboration of meaning." Disoriented by the aleatory nature of the performance, the spectator "must then abandon an intellectual approach to allow himself [to] be moved by a language of great poetic power." Kwahulé's staging of contemporary forms of violence, in his "dramaturgical propositions, continuously renewed from one play to the next, always pose the same question, that of the responsibility we have toward the other wherever he comes from, and incite one to conceive the conditions for a common future" (Soubrier 797–98).[29] While offering an excellent synthesis of Kwahulé's work, Soubrier's analysis nevertheless includes a problematic opposition between a spectator's intellectual approach and a poetic one. Seen as a dramaturgy of thresholds, however, the aim of this new theatrical poetics is to undermine and possibly to dismantle the opposition between the intelligible and the sensible and the separation between an intellectual and an affective disposition. In this poetics, which corresponds to the third, dialogical effect of the threshold, the spectator is engaged in traversing the forms and forces that divide and separate.

Consider, for example, the tight, claustrophobic spaces of Kwahulé's plays, which are at once real, psychic, and symbolic representations of entrapment and liberation. Poetic language, the language of metaphor and echo, and the presence of dance and music are some of the means allowing his embodied speakers, both individual and choral, to succeed in moving back and forth across thresholds that are at once open and closed, inside and outside, here and elsewhere. In foregrounding the dynamic relationships between individual voices and polyphonic ones, Kwahulé engages with new registers of voices in the crossing of one voice with others. As he states in an interview, "My first plays explored overflow, abundance, even grandiloquence. Since *Jaz* and *Misterioso-119,* my writing tends to limit spectacle as much as possible by using an economy of everything—narrative, plot, character, words." He aims in these plays to have them performed without any set or any stage directions because "the actor and the pulse of the language should be sufficient. The ambition is to 'load' the language with all the energies usually carried by the story, plot, set, costumes and direction" (qtd. in Gener). In unsettling theater's conventional mainstays, his theater of actor and voice puts into play the possibility of dialogue, one that intervenes effectively in a cacophony of religious, economic, political, and mediatized languages.

La Mélancolie des barbares, for instance, a play that includes motifs of violence and drug dealing, upstages the closed symbolic economies that treat women as those to be "protected and sanctified" (55). The play ends with Baby Mo, herself a victim of abuse by her drug-kingpin husband, becoming responsible for the suicide of a young man, Zac. In Kwahulé's litanies, violence implodes as women become both the screen for a masculine imaginary and the means whereby it is re-projected onto a fraught and dysfunctional social space. Desire itself is thus a threshold of characters' crossings, but one where neither the possibility of flight nor return is guaranteed. The threshold in Kwahulé is anything but a disembodied abstraction. On the contrary, the body in his work, as Chalaye puts it, becomes the palimpsest of human suffering. In Kwahulé and playwrights associated with new African dramaturgies, the body is nothing less than a bearer of memory and history and the site of a poetics of the "voices of the body" (Chalaye, "Pour").[30]

Kwahulé's *El Mona* constructs a double abyssal space of civil war that is situated "elsewhere, at the edge of a precipice," splitting the mountain El Mona into two opposing camps. It is a world in which the beauty of the site El Mona is replicated in the beauty and sexuality of the woman Superlove, whom the Master calls El Mona, and who is sold to him as his wife by her pimp Criminal Danger. In a Christic scene of sacrifice, her lips of knowledge open wounds on the body of Youssef, who, in mourning for his love Mira on the other side, descends into the ravine/gulf (in the stage footlights) where he meets with his death. Other characters include an orphaned child of refugees who communicates with nothing but a television around his neck and the woman Salwa, who reads a litany of names, which are perhaps those of the dead, into the Megaphone, accompanied by the polyphony of sound loops issuing from the television.

The play may be read as a political and economic allegory of material and symbolic exchange where the lives (and deaths) of individuals, their relationships, and their need to communicate are radically appropriated. For instance, the Master of the Megaphone, owner of the border, sells fear and traffics in the divide as such; if you cannot pay for the Megaphone, you simply cannot communicate with those on the other side. But even with the means to pay, your ability to speak to the other is reduced to a monologue, which is meted out by the Master. In this situation, the play suggests, the commoditization of communication results in an increasing dominance of ritual, force, and the emergence of bodily sacrifice. The frontier in Kwahulé's play is a threshold and is always double: life and death, here and there, El Mona and "El Mona," past and future.

The retreat announced on the television news fails to become the occasion for a cease-fire or peace, offering instead the opportunity for the Master of the Megaphone to extend his power even further. As her "dowry" for monogamy, Superlove receives from him "the precipice, the valley, the crown of barbed wire, the megaphone" (134). In the Master's ironic prophecy, it is "because the times are coming when we will merely be tourists in our fields of barbarity" that he claims purchasing the frontier is "only for art's sake. The spectacle of fear" (135).[31] At the close, as Salwa intones the litany of names, Superlove, a new Eve, merely asks the Master for an apple. Finally, *El Mona* stages the dangers of technological and economic manipulation of passages and divides, questioning whether it is possible to bridge an abyss that is man-made. Appropriating the air itself, the play suggests, deepens the gulf separating mirrored spaces, times, individuals, and communities.

New Beginnings and Mediations of Thresholds

The new francophone theater of the diaspora, a "theater of thresholds," must be taken as undoing and remaking what we understand by the notion of thresholds in the most general as well as the most particular sense. By staging a multiplicity of spaces, times, bodies, voices, and languages, this theater tracks within and through them the resonances whereby they can be made visible and perceptible. As practitioners and spectators, we can thus participate in what is made manifest in some of the foremost forms of an experimental, reflexive theater. It is one that restages social and human bonds in attitudes, gestures, and embodied thought; in visible bonds through spaces, illumination, and movement; and in auditory bonds through voice, sound, rhythm, and choral variations. In the process of creating their readers and audience, these new dramaturgies take us to the place, the point of beginning, and the threshold without which theater does not, in fact, take place at all.

The writers of new African dramaturgies use traditional as well as novel means to make perceptible that which undergirds both the paradigmatic and syntagmatic dimensions of the already represented, including the misrepresented. For instance, plays by Kwahulé and Efoui have as their setting closed spaces, which open onto multiple and imaginary scenarios. Indeed, the dramatists succeed in creating the conditions for understanding how individual voices, in poetic repetitions and chorality, are at once taken apart and interwoven with those of others. It is through these practices that, instead of becoming complicit with the social and ideological limits of unequal power relations on a global scale, as Conteh-Morgan would have it, they perform a deconstruction of the conditions of possibility for a modern and future stage. Whether artistic practices today, including those of theater, can effectively break through the bounds placed on them in a commoditized global culture is a question of profound pertinence and even urgency. This question is certainly one that resonates deeply and strongly in diasporic African theater.

Earlier in this essay, I noted Guénoun's notion that in making space for theater the assembly also brackets the environment, asking what this might mean in the context of diasporic theater. The lived environment in this theater is represented as a threshold world as well as a world of thresholds. Representations of the double border, for instance, are especially prominent and paradigmatically significant in the plays of Zang, Efoui, and Kwahulé. In the restaging they propose, the concepts of the border and the frontier and the thinking of metaphysical oppositions that they entail are unpacked and unfolded. In this sense, their artistic inquiry into transcultural mobility and displacement contributes to making vividly perceptible the social, symbolic, and psychic dimensions of modernity.

The new theater is engaged in an intertextual dialogue with ancient Greek theater; numerous theatrical traditions, including African ones; and forms of popular culture, which are frequently coded as American. But in its project to rematerialize language, space, time, and the human presence, it goes beyond a postmodern citationality of forms to construct instead a critical model of the world as threshold. In today's society, a theater that works to rematerialize culture unquestionably plays a decisive role in making visible the symbolic spaces, languages, and identities that shape continuities and change. This theater shows up the seductions and lures of so-called borderless crossings, which are continuous with programs of market commoditization presented as endlessly open, available, and accessible. It is a theater that brings us back to what divides and links us and alerts us to the temptations of endless passages and virtual traversals of all kinds. It is, quintessentially, a "theater of thresholds."

In this theater, the modalities and regimes of the perceptible and the sensible are energetically unfolded in writing and performance. Its dramaturgies link up with what might properly be called the "phenomenological" dimensions of theater in that they strive to reinvent the conditions of possibility for provoking a radical rethinking of the "partage du sensible," which makes possible at once the partitioning of and the sharing in the sensible world, according to Rancière's concept.[32]

Theater, I propose, has the capacity of staging and deconstructing *dispositifs* or apparatuses of separation, divisions, and exclusions, which are thoroughly tested in today's dramaturgies. In disrupting established regimes, theater creates interruptions and displacements in the visible so as to bring entire fields of experience into the realms of the perceptible. Although these regimes seem to be ubiquitous, operating in such a way as to screen off lived experience and the lived environment, it is in a "theater of thresholds" that such regimes of visibility and sensibility are revealed to be arbitrary, incomplete, punctual, and discontinuous. The most reflexive of new theater practices succeeds in showing the degree to which particular arrangements of scopic, perceptual, and ritualized ways of seeing, or "takes" on the real, are illuminated at the expense others.[33]

One might say that regimes of the visible render entire dimensions of reality obscure, yet without making them entirely absent. For philosopher Clément Rosset, a relationship that refuses the real in favor of illusion is not a refusal of perception per se. "The thing is not denied, only displaced, placed elsewhere."[34] In this sense, regimes of the visible are founded on the model of an *alibi* (Latin, "elsewhere"), as in, for instance, "I'm not guilty, I wasn't there, I was elsewhere." What is more, the model of an alibi itself implies and requires a spatial apparatus of inside/outside, one that in a becoming-threshold can always be dismantled.

Francophone theaters challenge the continued power and functioning of the alibis of regimes of the visible, the sensible, and the perceptible. In unfolding the regimes of visibility and sensibility, theater subverts the techniques of the alibi and the displacements or misplacements on which they rely. It becomes an innovative space for reverse interpellations (in Althusser's sense of *hailing*) of the alibis of ideology, creating a complex space for reimagining other scenarios for the social bond. Playwrights such as Zang, Efoui, and Kwahulé use a variety of means to open up and expand the field of dramaturgical possibilities for today's theater. For them, theater is a vital means for exploring the multiple thresholds that diasporic and other subjects traverse as they move between the real and symbolic realms of spaces, times, languages, and embodiments. The specificity of theater is that it allows for a co-presence of living beings assembled as actors-spectators. It opens a space of visibility that allows them to challenge the apparatuses of coercion that regulate social relations governed by visibility and invisibility. And by unfolding the limits of their dissimulations, new theatrical languages have the potential to engage the conditions for new social bonds in modernity.

Francophone diasporic theaters are exemplary spaces for the becoming-visible and tangible of creative theatricalities. But for its remarkable capacity to make visible the complex thresholds of the real, the ephemeral event of the theater or the theater as event would certainly appear precarious in a world of dominant cultural and media platforms. The theater, though, generates in its spectators the capacity to recognize that they are at a threshold of becoming-spectator, or that in a very real sense they are themselves that threshold. In being moved across plays' complex, multidimensional, cultural, and poetic thresholds, the public becomes an audience not by identifying with but by being at the *limen*, the edge, the outset, and the opening of speaking, seeing, and knowing.

Notes

1. In Arnold van Gennep's *Rites de passage* and Victor Turner's *The Ritual Process: Structure and Anti-structure*, the notion of threshold is used to theorize ritual practices and cultural states of liminality. Since Turner's *From Ritual to Theatre* and Richard Schechner's *Between Theater and Anthropology*, it has been prominent in performance studies.
2. Latin *ligere*, to tie.
3. My translation.

Une pensée des passerelles, une pensée du seuil. Le seuil ne nie pas la différence mais l'accepte et accorde le visiteur et le visité selon la force d'un lien qui les *oblige*. Le seuil ne nie pas qu'il y ait un dehors et un dedans, au contraire il en est même la reconnaissance, mais il les ouvre l'un sur l'autre. Une telle ouverture, une telle possibilité d'échange et de partage, un tel système d'obligations réciproques, sans doute n'est-ce là rien d'autre à nouveau que le "doux songe de paix" du philosophe. (Bailly 20)

4. My translation. "À partir des conflits eux-mêmes, et de ce qui les génère et les entretient, la nature de ce qui nous fait défaut, ce qui manque à l'homme pour qu'il puisse être l'animal authentiquement politique, l'animal *enfin* politique: l'animal des seuils" (Bailly 20–21).

5. Research that considers the threshold practices of diasporic theater in relation to those of other experimental theaters worldwide remains to be done. Like many of these, but differently, francophone diasporic theater repositions threshold relationships in their literary, cultural, political, and historical contexts.

6. For further discussion, see Rosset, 13–14; Guénoun, *Le Théâtre est-il nécessaire?*; Gaschè, 188–208; and Weber.

7. Esa Kirkkopelto's study fills that gap, according to Guénoun in his preface to Kirkkopelto, *Le Théâtre de l'expérience*, 7.

8. My translation. "Nous appelons 'scène' tout aussi bien le plateau de théâtre, sa structure et ses planches, qu'une division interne de l'oeuvre théâtrale et de son récit" (Guénoun, preface 7).

9. My translation. "Car la scène est cet espace très singulier, préalablement évacué, où s'agence le dispositif de l'apparition. Que des choses, des gens ou des actes soient, et apparaissent, voilà qui n'a rien de propre au théâtre. Mais que l'on organise et libère un espace pratique pour épurer ce processus d'apparition, le dégager de ses entours, lui donner toute sa force, c'est là une invention singulière, que nous appelons théâtre" (Guénoun, preface 8).

10. My translation. "Le théâtre, à cet égard, et la scène qui en fait le cœur, ne s'affairent jamais exclusivement à montrer quelque chose, mais, en libérant de son environnement le processus de cette monstration même, en désencombrant l'espace où elle advient, en la présentant de façon dégagée et comme pure, toujours à montrer la monstration elle-même, à porter à la vue l'opération même . . . la livraison au regard (et à l'écoute), à manifester la manifestation" (Guénoun, preface 8).

11. My translation. "Le vide de la scène [qui] est produit *par l'assemblée qui s'écarte*" (Guénoun, introduction 13).

12. My translation. "Une pluralité de spectateurs, une convergence collective de regards et d'écoute—une assemblée" (Guénoun, introduction 13).

13. This new theater is taken to have come into public view in 1988, when Kossi Efoui, a previously unknown playwright from Togo, was awarded the Grand Prix by Radio France Internationale (RFI) for his play *Le Carrefour*.

14. In France, for instance, new African theater is performed at the Festival des Francophonies in Limoges, the Festival of Avignon at the "In" (Koffi Kwahulé, Dieudonné Ngiangouna) and the "Off" (Chapelle du Verbe Incarné), la Comédie de St. Étienne, the Lavoir Moderne in Paris, and in the series on authors from Kinshasa at the Paris Théâtre du Tarmac. This contemporary theater is staged from the Recréatrales in Ougadougou or the Festival des Réalités in Bamako to the Festad'Africa in Rome and the Varia Theater in Brussels, the Bambous Theater in St. Benoît (La Réunion), and so on. In recent years, Denis Marleau in Quebec has directed texts by José Pliya, who is originally from Bénin. Kristian Fredrik in Montreal, having staged *Big Shoot* by Koffi Kwahulé, has directed *Jaz* by the same author. After staging those two plays, the Lark Theater Company programmed Kwahulé's *Misterioso-119* for the Act French Festival

in New York. In Europe, new African theater is performed in Italy, Switzerland, Germany, Belgium, the Czech Republic, and Holland and more recently in Norway, Hungary, and Greece.

15. These include workshops and roundtable discussions in schools, public venues, universities, and alternate settings such as those for new audiences.

16. Critics Sylvie Chalaye, Christiane Makward, Judith G. Miller, and the late John Conteh-Morgan have led the way in developing the field of francophone African and Caribbean theater studies. Disciplinary work occurs in the framework of research collectives, such as Scènes Francophones et Écritures de l'Altérité (or SeFeA), directed by Sylvie Chalaye at the University of Paris 3–Nouvelle Sorbonne. In the fall of 2008, *L'Esprit Créateur* published "Nouvelles dramaturgies d'Afrique et des diasporas," guest-edited by Sylvie Chalaye. Josette Féral and Donia Mounsef co-edited "The Transparency of the Text: Contemporary Writing for the Stage," *Yale French Studies* 112 (2007), which includes studies by Chalaye and Judith Miller. Regrettably, even recent collections of essays on contemporary French theater overlook this theater in its entirety. A notable exception is Edward Baron Turk's engaging study *French Theatre Today: The View from New York, Paris, and Avignon* (Iowa City: University of Iowa, 2011), which is focused on new French theater from the perspective of performance. In addition to the work of, for instance, Ariane Mnouchkine, Valère Novarina, Olivier Cadiot, Marie NDiaye, Olivier Py, and Joël Pommerat, Turk provides presentations of José Pliya's and Koffi Kwahulé's importance to the contemporary stage.

17. My translation. "Une tension triangulaire, une tension diasporique entre l'Afrique des origines, l'histoire européenne et le tropisme outreatlantique." In the same issue, see her article "Pour une poétique des corps en écritures." Among her many studies, see *Afrique noire et dramaturgies contemporaines: Le syndrome de Frankenstein* (Paris: Éditions Théâtrales, 2004).

18. My translation.

19. My translation. "Or le théâtre est justement l'espace privilégié de l'expression de cet entre-deux, de ce jeu qui prend corps. La scène devient le moyen d'inventer la langue pour dire cette expérience du migrant qui ne trouve pas d'expression. . . . Le théâtre permet de mettre des sons et des images sur ce déplacement intérieur que vivent les émigrés et qui n'est plus de l'ordre de l'espace mais de l'être."

20. Conteh-Morgan refers to Sylvie Chalaye's essay "Les enfants terribles des indépendances: théâtre africain et identité contemporaine," in Chalaye, *L'Afrique noire*, 19–26.

21. These binaries are also noted in Conteh-Morgan 158.

22. The notion of "littérature-monde" emerged in the wake of *Le Monde*'s publication of a "Manifeste pour une 'littérature-monde' en français" (March 15, 2007) and was thought, briefly, to supersede that of francophone literature. See Le Bris and Rouaud; for an account of the issues of relationality that go beyond oppositions between the universal and essential identities of *littérature-monde*, see Eric Prieto, "Édouard Glissant, Littérature-monde, and *Tout-monde*," *small axe* 33 (November 2010): 111–20.

23. Within the scope of this particular article, my discussion focuses on works by Marcel Zang, Kossi Efoui, and Koffi Kwahulé.

24. My translation. "Ici nous sommes en France, dans une zone neutre, un point aveugle, tout à la fois frontière et déjà hors de la frontière, un entre-deux magique où il n'y a que vous et moi"; "le sexe et le langage n'existent que dans la distance et la différentiation" (Zang 17).

25. My translation. "Pâle copie, cette absence, cet hybride sans nom, cet être disloqué, ce volatile errant, sans territoire et sans abri. . . . [S]ans langue vous avez réussi à faire de moi un être sans langue, sans sa propre langue . . . obligé d'abriter dans ma tête, dans ma peau, mon cerveau, et jusque dans les replis de mon sommeil, des appréhensions, des perceptions, des sensations, des valeurs, des mythes, des rêves, des repères, une idéologie plus que factices, exogènes" (Zang 36).

26. My translation. "Or, dans votre histoire, ça grince, ça manque de liant, c'est plein d'artifices et d'éléments sans rapports qui s'entre-choquent, se contredisent" (Zang 43).

27. In biology, a phagocyte is a cell that swallows and digests microbes and other foreign bodies.

28. The sitehttp://www.m-e-l.fr/koffi-kwahule,ec,509 (accessed February 12, 2014) provides a bibliography of Koffi Kwahulé's work, including *Nema* (Paris: Éditions Théâtrales, 2011), *Les Recluses* (Paris: Éditions Théâtrales, 2010), and *La Mélancolie des barbares*. Links are given to translations by Chantal Bilodeau of a number of Kwahulé's plays.

29. My translation.

> Un entrelacs de voix, un alliage de sons et une primauté au rythme qui exigent du spectateur qu'il s'engage physiquement dans l'élaboration du sens des textes, jamais donné d'avance. Désorienté par une dramaturgie qui laisse place aux aléas et aux hasards, le spectateur doit alors se départir d'une approche intellectuelle pour se laisser émouvoir par une parole d'une grande puissance poétique. Si Kwahulé met en scène les formes de violence qui frappent le monde contemporain, il invite aussi à lui redonner du sens: ses propositions dramaturgiques, sans cesse renouvelées d'une pièce à l'autre, posent toujours la même question, celle de la responsabilité que l'on a à l'égard d'autrui, d'où qu'il vienne, et incitent à penser les conditions d'un avenir commun. (797–98)

On Kwahulé, see also Miller.

30. In addition, significant work has been done on the importance and complexity of chorality in Kwahulé's theater by critics such as Virginie Soubrier, Laurence Barbalosi, Dominique Traoré, and Chris Love.

31. My translation. "Car viennent les temps où nous ne serons plus que les touristes dans nos champs de barbarie"; "uniquement pour l'art. Le spectacle de la peur" (Kwahulé, *El Mona* 135).

32. For a discussion of the French meaning of "le partage du sensible," see Birrell who cites Eric Méchouan: "the French *partage* can have two opposite meanings, the first is 'to share, to have in common,' the second 'to divide, to share out,' and that thus 'the affirmation of something in common is at the same time the repartition of authorized positions.'"

33. Without mediation, the very real opened up by technics may well, as is evident in mass communication media today, remain beyond the field of the perceptible if it is placed outside of the processes of "partage," which link the visible to forms of experience.

34. My translation. "La chose n'y est pas niée, seulement déplacée, mise ailleurs" (Rosset 13).

Works Cited

Bailly, Jean-Christophe. Preface to *La Comparution,* by Jean-Christophe Bailly and Jean-Luc Nancy. Paris: Christian Bourgois Éditeur, 1991.

Barthes, Roland. *Mythologies.* Paris: Seuil, 1957.

Birrell, Ross. "Jacques Rancière and the (Re)distribution of the Sensible: Five Lessons in Artistic Research." *Art and Research: A Journal of Ideas, Contexts and Methods* 2, no. 1 (Summer 2008). http://www.artandresearch.org.uk/v2n1/v2n1editorial.html.

Brewer, Mária Minich. "The Banquet and Its Aftermath: Reinventions of the Symbolic in Contemporary Theater." *Contemporary French and Francophone Studies: Sites* 11, no. 3 (August 2007): 379–87.

Brook, Peter. *The Empty Space.* 1968. New York: Touchstone, 1995.

Chalaye, Sylvie, ed. *L'Afrique noire et son théâtre au tournant du XXe siècle*. Rennes: Presses Universitaires de Rennes, 2001.

——. "Contemporary Francophone Drama: Between Detours and Deviations." *Yale French Studies* 112 (2007): 145–56.

——. "Koffi Kwahulé." In *Passages et ancrages en France. Dictionnaire des écrivains migrants de langue française (1981–2011)*, edited by Ursula Mathis-Moser and Birgit Merz-Baumgartner. Paris: Honoré Champion Éditeur, 2012.

——. "Pour une poétique des corps en écritures." *L'Esprit Créateur* 48, no. 3 (2008): 3–16.

——. "La Voix des corps." *L'Esprit Créateur* 48, no. 3 (2008): 1–2.

Conteh-Morgan, John (with Dominic Thomas). *New Francophone African and Caribbean Theatres*. Bloomington: Indiana University Press, 2010.

Efoui, Kossi. *Le Carrefour*. Paris: Théâtres Sud, L'Harmattan, 1990.

——. "Masques et apparitions: Entretien entre Taina Tervonen avec Kossi Efoui." *Africultures*, March 2001, http://www.africultures.com/php/index.php?nav=article&no=1978.

——. *Oublie! Suivi de Voisins anonymes*. Carnières: Lansman Éditions, 2011.

——. "Parler en langue: Entretien avec Kossi Efoui, propos recueillis par la rédaction." *Notre librairie, Revue des littératures du sud* 159 (July–September 2005): 116–19.

——. *Solo d'un revenant*. Paris: Seuil, 2008.

Gaschè, Rodolphe. "Theatrum Theoreticum." In *The Honor of Thinking: Critique, Theory, Philosophy*, 188–208. Palo Alto: Stanford University Press, 2006.

Gener, Randy. "This New Eurafrique Magic: Global Influences and Ivoirian Personal Reinvention Meet in the Ferocious Theatre of Koffi Kwahulé." Translated by Chantal Bilodeau. http://www.tcg.org/publications/at/Nov08/eurafrique.cfm.

Guénoun, Denis. Introduction to *Philosophie de la scène*, by Michel Deguy et al. Paris: Les Solitaires Intempestifs, 2010.

——. Preface to *Le Théâtre de l'expérience: Contributions à la théorie de la scène*, by Esa Kirkkopelto. Paris: Presses de l'Université de Paris-Sorbonne, 2008.

——. *Le Théâtre est-il nécessaire?* Belfort: Circé, 1997.

Kwahulé, Koffi. *La Mélancolie des barbares*. Carnières: Lansman, 2009.

——. *El Mona*. In *Liban, écrits nomades*, vol. 1. Carnières: Lansman, 2001.

Le Bris, Michel, and Jean Rouaud, eds. *Pour une littérature-monde*. Paris: Gallimard, 2007.

Lyotard, Jean-François. "The Sublime and the Avant-Garde." In *The Lyotard Reader*, edited by Andrew Benjamin, 196–211. Oxford: Basil Blackwell, 1991.

Miller, Judith G. "Is There a Specifically Francophone African Stage Textuality?" *Yale French Studies* 112 (2007): 131–44.

Rancière, Jacques. *Le Théâtre émancipé*. Paris: La Fabrique, 2008.

Rosset, Clément. *L'École du réel*. Paris: Minuit, 2008.

Soubrier, Virginie. "Koffi Kwahulé." In *Dictionnaire encyclopédique du théâtre à travers le monde*, edited by Michel Corvin, 797–98. Paris: Bordas, 2008.

Weber, Samuel. *Theatricality as Medium*. New York: Fordham University Press, 2004.

Zang, Marcel. *L'Exilé* and *Bouge de là*. Arles: Actes Sud-Papiers, 2002.

10 Island Geography as Creole Biography
Shenaz Patel's Mauritian Literary Production

Magali Compan

MANY CRITICS HAVE examined the production of francophone-African artists relocated to France by focusing on the condition of exile and its potential for creative friction. Since the 1930s and through today, numerous francophone authors have found in France favorable conditions for literary creation. Critics have reinforced an understanding of the impetus for exile as coming from a lack of opportunities and resources for those who would choose to remain and write in their country or homeland. Kate Quinn, for example, invokes the expression of Jamaican writer Andrew Salkey, "Emigrate or vegetate," as an adage for the cultural impoverishment that writers in the Caribbean face if they do not leave.

This imperative for emigration has driven francophone writers from Africa and the Indian Ocean for generations, and, as a result, ostensibly "African" francophone literary works are, by and large, produced and consumed outside the places they seek to represent. But what about the writers who decide to stay? How does a "home" geography or place affect an author's writing and authorship? What are the relationships among location, a sense of place, and one's identity formation, not only as a writer but as an individual or a member of a community? What influence, if any, does place exert on one's identity? How do sites of production and histories together generate authorship and identity, francophone or otherwise? The case of Shenaz Patel, one of a contemporary group of successful female writers from Mauritius Island in the Indian Ocean, offers revealing answers to these questions. Unlike her Mauritian literary contemporaries (including Ananda Devi, Nathacha Appanah, and Marie-Therese Humbert, all of whom live in France), Patel has maintained residence in and pursued her literary career from her native island. While writing for the global francophone literary marketplace, Patel also remains committed to other endeavors that tie her to Mauritius, her local community, and her extended family. She is not only an internationally recognized francophone author but also a local journalist, having written for (and served as the managing editor of) the independent political Mauritian newspaper *Le Nouveau Militant* and the main newspaper on the island, *Week End*. Committed to a project of "re-transcribing Creole culture" (re-transcrire la culture creole), as she puts it, Patel also translates French-language popular cultural texts into Creole for local readerships (including, for example, the *Tintin* comic books). She also writes stories in Creole for local publication and has written theater plays for local production. As a librarian, she maintains writing projects linked to local Creole community activism and cultural engagement. Thus the crossing of French and Mauritian Creole in her francophone literary production emanates from her diversified set of local, Creole cultural commitments and projects. As such, her literary work contributes to a suite of endeavors that together constitute the "place" of Patel's francophone writing of and from the island of Mauritius.

Patel's literary reputation rests on the accolades she has received for three of her novels: *Le Portrait Chamarel* (2001), *Sensitive* (2003), and *Le Silence des Chagos* (2005), all published in France (*Le Portrait Chamarel* was published in France's Réunion island and the latter two by Edition de l'Olivier in Paris). She received the Prix de Radio France for *Le Portrait Chamarel,* Le Prix du Roman Francophone for *Sensitive,* and the Prix Soroptimist de la Romancière Francophone for *Le Silence des Chagos*. All set on the island of Mauritius, the three novels render the tensions and paradoxes underlying the concept of *métissage* within the Mauritian context while simultaneously evoking the plight of what François Paré calls "les minorisés" (or minoritized)—those who are left out of a system that crushes them. Patel's narrator gives the reader a view into the lives of those who are ignored or silenced by official, public history.

While her novels have been published in France, Patel's authorship is generated from a distinctly Mauritian geography of production, the dynamics of which can be illustrated by way of both a close reading of her short story "Îlle était une fois" and a consideration of Patel's own biography shaped by her decision to stay in Mauritius, thus linking that literary biography to a Mauritian geography.

In *The Shape of a Pocket,* John Berger writes "today to try to paint the existent is an act of resistance instigating hope" (22). The existent, "the physical world into which mankind has been thrown" (14), disappears behind false representations that surround us and reassure us. Berger illustrates how artists can reveal truths that unveil deeper complexities that are often uncomfortable and unsettling. Art has the capacity to distance us from the lies of the new world order, to help us see the invisible, and to help us envision another visible order.

Berger's analysis can be applied to the work of Shenaz Patel, whose writing reveals hidden truths about the realities of postcolonial Mauritius. Ethno-social violence has become the Gordian knot through which Mauritian authors desperately try to cut while inscribing their texts in a sociopolitico-cultural existence that rests on a fragile political and religious equilibrium. Contemporary authors, notes Catherine Boudet, often perpetuate the system they criticize and move away from a true ontological questioning. "[D]ésormais la problématique ethnico-nationale a obscurci la perspective ontologique" (Nowadays ethnic-national issues have obscured the ontological perspective), Boudet argues, which results in an "impossible ancrage dans l'espace insulaire" (impossible rooting in the island space) (3).[1] The author's challenge is to undo himself or herself from "une servitude dogmatique" (a dogmatic servitude) (Georges Bataille cited in Capparos) and see his or her art as "une mise en place d'architectures mentales alternatives" (an establishment of alternate mental architectures) in the goal of ultimately opening up "d'autres modes de pensée et d'autres organisations possibles du monde que celles qu'on veut bien nous donner à voir" (other modes of thoughts and other possible organizations of the world than those that are given for us to see) (Boudet 3).

As such, it is paramount to consider the writer's work not as a sterile production but as the precursor to social change. As Boudet concludes, the author, "enfanteur de forme en devenir, est responsable du renouvellement de l'architecture mentale de la société dans laquelle il évolue" (birther of forms to be, is responsible for the renewal of society's mental architecture in which she is evolving) (2). Therefore, writers themselves are not a simple subject but become the actors of their own experience in the world.

The Art of "Telling" Stories

"Raconte-moi ène zistoire . . ." "Tell me a story . . ." or—translated more literally—"Recount-me one history . . .": this Creole imperative opens Patel's recent short story written in French with some Creole dialogue and published in 2006 in the collection *Maurice: Demain et Après* under the title "Île était une fois" or "Once upon a time." The result is a reinscribing and reversing of the seemingly timeless and universal generative frame for narrative or storytelling. "Tell me a story" is familiar as the command of a child to which the conventional response is "Il était une fois" or "Once upon a time." Patel's short story, however, reverses the order: The classical telling frame, "Once upon a time," is her story's title and thus precedes the opening imperative for a story to come into existence. These opening gestures of reversal and word/story play initiate what the short story will itself go on to offer. Because the command for a story comes in Creole and is set off with quotes and in italics, the imperative is marked with signs of orality. It is the kind of pleading command a child—hungering for imaginative narrative—

speaks rather than writes, as is the case with this story. Patel, however, writes it into being and does so with markers of dialect French. The request for a "zistoire" rather than an "histoire" places the end (of the alphabet) at the beginning of the "story."

Before Patel's z-story even begins, her title has already delivered island word play, discernible only in written form. She writes "Il était une fois" as "Île était une fois," so that the classical "Once upon a time" becomes "Island upon a time." Translated literally from French, the original phrase's "il" is "it" (or "he") "was one time." Patel's variation becomes "Island was one time." The replacement of "il" with "île" also generates a hybridizing of the French pronouns *il* and *elle* that evokes the island as a transgendered place. At the outset of her story, Patel utilizes French-language word play to create an "island story"—a story of a place with exceptional unity—followed by a Creole imperative for a z-story. In both Creole and French, that imperative is a command from the interlocutor to have the self (*moi*) retold as one history (*raconte-moi*): in other words, "Reinforce me by counting me into one unified story, one history," or more simply, "Tell me *my* story." Narrative functions as a means of connecting, and the process is clear enough in the ritualized "tell me a story/once upon a time" exchange. The demand that one's self be "recounted" as one story, one history, is a desire for unity and linkage with the past, a connection made possible by the interlocutor whom the desiring child solicits.

In the short story that this title and first line open, Patel tells of the encounter between the narrator—a young woman who remains unnamed and who has returned to Mauritius after having studied in France and become a teacher of French—and a young girl named Tifi, a silent child the narrator meets at an orphanage she visits regularly "to ease her conscience" (102). Tifi is the source of the oral command for a z-story. The narrator describes this first contact and the impression it leaves on her. She evokes "the tilted head [of the child], something of a disarticulated puppet, of a striking stillness in the middle of the agitation of the other children who were heckling and running, one more than the other. . . . An absent presence" (Tête penchée, quelque chose d'une poupée légèrement désarticulée, d'un immobilisme frappant au milieu de l'agitation des autres enfants qui chahutaient et gambadaient à qui mieux mieux. Une présence absente) (103). When their eyes meet, the narrator describes first the "rebellious mop" (tignasse rebelle) and "the black eyes" (prunelles noires) (103) of the child. She then relates a "strange feeling of being scrutinized and avoided at once. Pierced and seen past at the same time" (cette impression étrange d'être scruté et contourné à la fois. Transpercé et dépassé en même temps) (103). The child had "a stuttering and raucous look. Impossible not to hear" (le regard balbutiant. Impossible à ne pas entendre) (103). This synaesthesia lets the reader understand that the narrator's first possible connection and communication with Tifi is one defined not through cultural norms and structures but through the senses.

"Attracted by this unavoidable call" (Attirée par cet appel incontournable) (103), the narrator strives to know more about Tifi and soon learns that the little girl "has hardly spoken to anyone since her mother [Mala] had left her at the orphanage a week earlier" (ne parlait pratiquement à personne depuis que sa mère était venue la quitter à la crèche une semaine avant) (104). The narrator decides to host Tifi with her family, and with this decision, the tale brings together in one family two individuals typically held apart by the rigid social and ethnic compartmentalization of Mauritius: a woman from a bourgeois family[2] and, one can assume in light of Tifi's features, a Creole child (a person whose ancestors were slaves from Africa or Madagascar).[3] In the first physical description, Patel evokes, on the one hand, the ethnic origins of the child and, on the other hand, her social status within Mauritian society. The image of a "rebellious mop" of hair and "dark eyes" offers stereotypical Creole markers in Mauritius. However, Tifi's "absent presence" is even more evocative in defining her as belonging to the Creole community. The marginalization of the child and the silence surrounding her echo the status of the Creole population within Mauritian society.

To better understand Patel's literary endeavor, one needs to take a closer look at the political landscape of the island of Mauritius. The efforts of the government to represent all ethnic groups in Mauritius's political system have resulted in the celebration of the island as "one of the most ethnically heterogeneous states in the world" (Srebrnik 277). The government, however, officially recognizes only four categories in its population: Hindus, Chinese, Muslims, and one catchall category for everyone else called "general population." This last group includes Creoles, referring to the descendants of slaves, and anyone else who does not have a place in the official communalist nomenclature of the republic of Mauritius.

Although Mauritius has received praise as a "Rainbow Nation" that celebrates a medley of identities, religions, cultures, and languages, the government's system of categorization of the island's inhabitants has enhanced modes of identification with ancestral homelands to the detriment of local identity. As Rosabelle Boswell notes, "Dominant conceptualizations of hybridity in Mauritian society are still affected by essentialist discourses[,] and dominant groups see and treat hybridity as 'a threat to the fullness of selfhood and as the moral marker of contamination, failure or regression'" (196). While the four categories do recognize and formalize a degree of heterogeneity of the Mauritian population, the population exists in a system that reinscribes "roots" and ethnic origins. Mauritian poet Khal Torabully states also that "the word créole articulates itself, in the collective unconscious, with the impure or the inferior" (le mot créole s'articule, dans l'inconscient collectif, avec l'impur ou l'inférieur) (2). According to Jean-Claude Carpanin-Marimoutou, a Creole in Mauritius is defined as "anyone incapable of claiming a strong connection to an origin outside of the island itself. The word 'creole' in its anthropological dimension has a meaning which is pejorative rather than positive" (225). Without fixed origins to celebrate (unlike the Indians,

Chinese, or Muslims who make up the three other categories recognized in Mauritian society), Creoles cannot find themselves in the memory of the nation, so that "being black and of mixed heritage are aberrations that threaten the social and moral order" (Boswell 216). In Patel's short story, Tifi and her mother, Mala, become symbols of this part of the population of Mauritius, evoking the disarray of Creoles and their marginal position in a society that denigrates the hybridity of some and glorifies the fixed origins of others.

Beyond Tifi's physical markers (her hair and eyes), however, Patel avoids an explicit ethnic discourse that would inscribe Tifi, her mother, and the narrator in pronounced markers based on their ethnic origins. Instead, she focuses on the social and economic details of Mala's life, thus offering a criticism of the homogenizing discourse that has placed the island on a pedestal as the "Mauritian miracle." Patel's short story does not so much denounce the marginal situation of the Creole people in Mauritius—in its very clear ethnic dimension—as it draws attention to the economic inequalities within that society and how they play out "on the ground" and in the daily lives of those marginalized individuals on the island.

Island Inequalities that Belie the "Mauritian Miracle"

As Roukaya Kasenally states in her article "Mauritius: Paradise Reconsidered," all the standard indicators confirm that the island "offers a combination of economic performance and democratic political stability that should make it the envy of the developing world" (160). With a GDP of $9.496 billion (USD) and a per capita income of $13,670,[4] Mauritius is often brandished as one of Africa's main success stories. Built on a free market economy, the success of Mauritius has been praised by the World Bank, which, for the past four years, has ranked Mauritius first among African countries in its 2012 "Doing Business" report. Following independence, the Mauritian government made key economic decisions that marked its presence on regional and global markets. Kasenally explains that the "Mauritian miracle" "rested on an open, liberalized, and diversified economy; an abundant supply of cheap labor; open, functioning, and efficient institutions; and guaranteed prices for crucial sugar and textile export" (162). Furthermore, the creation of the Mauritian Export Processing Zone, since its creation in 1970, has attracted foreign direct investments and has generated a "booming export industry that focuses on clothing and textiles" (163). Although such success has allowed Mauritius to join the ranks of middle-income countries, "the boom years of the 1980s and 1990s—when employments and foreign investment were high—are clearly over" (165). Economic decline has brought in its wake "a rise in violent crime, double-digit unemployment, and growing levels of poverty and deprivation" (165).

Despite such economic decline in the past ten years, the population across sections has been able to enjoy upward social mobility thanks to a comprehensive welfare state, educational opportunities, free health care, and universal old-age pensions. In present-day Mauritius, Creoles have benefited from the modernization of the island's economy. They occupy leadership roles and have built stronger social structures resulting in positive change. In July 2008, UNESCO World Heritage Committee added the mountain Morne Brabant to its World Heritage list. Used as a shelter for runaway slaves, its symbolism for the slaves' fight for freedom, their suffering, and their sacrifice has been constructed through physical evidence obtained by recent research conducted on-site and through documenting an oral tradition associated with the Maroons. Le Morne Cultural Landscape now serves as a testimony to the resistance of slaves and the resilience of Maroon culture as a "site of memory" that translates the relative success of the struggle for the construction of Creole identity.

Whereas the vagueness of Tifi's ethnic background could potentially be seen as an example of cultural homogeneity in Mauritius, Patel's narrative instead emphasizes and denounces the island's continued economic inequalities.[5] As the story takes the reader to the discovery of the universe of Tifi and her mother, the reader quickly learns of the fragility of Mala's financial independence. A young woman divorced from an alcoholic husband, Mala "was doing varied housework here and there" (effectuait divers travaux ménagers chez les uns et les autres) (104) while also working in a nearby textile factory. But "one day, she and her colleagues found the door of the factory locked up. Put in receivership, they were told. Bankruptcy, in another word" (un jour, ses compagnes de travail et elle-même avaient trouvé la porte de l'usine cadenassée. Mise en *receivership*, leur avait-on dit. Faillite, en bref) (105). Mala is determined to find her luck somewhere else, in Dubai, and decides to leave her daughter at the orphanage in order to gain "some time to make a little money" (le temps qu'elle puisse aller se faire un peu d'argent) and "take the opportunity to give her a better future" (conquérir la chance de lui assurer un meilleur avenir) (105). Mala is the victim of an economy in crisis, caught in an economic whirlpool of "recession," high "unemployment rates," "locked up factor[ies]," "receivership," "bankruptcy." Patel's evocation of these economic terms links Mala and Tifi's malaise to the "social pathologies resulting from socio-economic marginalising by dominant groups" (Boswell xix). This economic whirlpool expulses Mala—and ultimately Tifi—from the national discourse and finally out of the insular space since "like many others like her, [Mala] was going to try her luck somewhere else" (comme beaucoup d'autres à ce moment-là, elle allait tenter sa chance ailleurs) (105).

Patel's short story reveals the challenges to community that come with the disruptions and displacements of globalization and the influence of globalized capital on the daily lives of people living the "Mauritian miracle." The national interests invested in economic transactions with private entities have damaged the possibility of a community, right down to its core, the family unit. Late capitalist rules of globalization have accelerated a process of reification in which social relationships and activities get objectified, thought through, and reshaped for the needs of capital. In *Reification and Utopia in Mass Culture*, Fredric Jameson argues that in a capitalist society, all forms of human labor can be "universally ranged under the common denominator of the quantitative, that is, under the universal exchange value of money. At this point, then, the quality of the various forms of human activity, their unique and distinct ends or values, has effectively been bracketed or suspended by the market system, leaving all these activities free to be ruthlessly reorganized in efficiency terms, as sheer means or instrumentality" (10). Globalization has aggravated the conditions of the capitalist society, which reduces people to wage laborers who ultimately become alienated from themselves. Such a reifying process "generates a man who assumes a passive and contemplative stance in the face of that objectified and rationalized reality—a man who seems to himself to stand outside that reality because his own participation in producing it is mystified" (Porter xi).

In Patel's story, Tifi remains motionless and silent in the orphanage, and as a product of such an alienating system, she appears to occupy a position outside of her world and is described as "absent." She is, however, intensely observing her surroundings with a look that scrutinizes and pierces. This "absent presence" is reinforced in her gaze as it scrutinizes yet avoids, pierces and sees over, stammers and affirms at the same time. Such schizophrenia illustrates the chasm between seeing and being, between "the 'I' who sees the world which was severed from the 'I' who inhabits it" (Porter xii).

Narrative and Identities

With Mala's departure to Dubai, Patel's story of the relationship between the narrator and Tifi begins and quickly intensifies. The initial request to "tell me *ène zistoire*" returns as a leitmotif to which the narrator responds by recounting classic Western tales like "Little Red Riding Hood," "Sleeping Beauty," and Saint-Exupéry's *The Little Prince*. Each of these tales, however, leaves Tifi unsatisfied. As she continues to try to appease her temporary foster child, the narrator invents "far away stories of half-imagined ancestors, long transhumances led by fantastic characters who came from Persia, France, India and Africa, mixing the fantasy of my own imagination to some historical gleanings" (des histoires lointaines d'ancêtres semi-imaginaires, de longues transhumances menées par des personnages fantastiques venus de Perse, de France, d'Inde et d'Afrique, mêlant pêle-mêle les fantasmes de ma propre imagination à quelques glanures historiques) (106). The narrator evokes other myths such as Ulysses and the Mahabharata. However, each time, Tifi remains silent yet expectant, always desiring something different. The narrator's tales relate the origin myths that reinforce the different ethnic groups on the island. Tifi, as a culturally and/or socially marginalized person, does not recognize herself in these myths that celebrate European, Indian, African, or Muslim origins.

Such narrative articulations undoubtedly reveal issues of power and voice. Participating in the politics of representation reveals a power that grants access to such participation and simultaneously becomes a means of gaining power. Thus, such discursive spaces, while bringing to the surface a particular group's view of history, undoubtedly exclude and silence others. One of the most recurrent issues when writing about the dispossessed is the concern with what Edouard Glissant calls a "nonhistory." History has proved to be a powerful instrument for the West to impose its own recollection of events while concealing certain moments that would jeopardize the established order. "History as a whole has thus excluded any histories incompatible with the history of the West" (Damato and Darin 607).

In her book *Dry Place: Landscapes of Belonging and Exclusion,* Patricia L. Price explains that "to write of such a place, and of the identities, collective and individual, fashioned in narrative articulation with it, invokes a deeply problematic politics of speaking. Whose stories are told, from whose perspective, in whose voice? Whose stories, versions, and voices are left silent? Translated? Warped?" (xiii). In the case of Patel's short story, the first-person narration, the tales chosen by the narrator, and the inscription of the narrator's own memory and imagination in these stories confirm her place in the history of Mauritius. As a person who is financially independent and constantly mobile and who comes from a family that hires servants, the narrator speaks from a position of privilege. Furthermore, she maintains control of the narrative since, as a narrator, she speaks, retells, re-presents, and restructures the past while justifying her position in the present. Her hold on the past and the inscription of her own story at the heart of the tales she chooses to tell constitute a translation of her privileged position inherited from the colonial period. Such narratives are central in the construction and functioning of the modern project of nation building. They homogenize and present a collective sense of citizenship by presenting, celebrating, or erasing internal differences. In the case of Mauritius, however, the narrator celebrates the official discourse of the "Rainbow Nation" by remembering and narrating stories that inscribe the origin of Mauritian identity outside of the place and within a culturally heterogeneous past.

Ultimately the narrator and Tifi's encounter offers an insight into the challenges of Mauritian history and memory. "Îlle était une fois" portrays a nation and a population struggling to come to terms with both its past and its present through a construction of memory and a relationship with history. Tifi's detachment and sense of alienation result from her erasure from the country's memory.

However, Tifi's lack of enthusiasm, her silence, and her immobility tell of another story while raising the issue of positionality and allowing us to ask what makes these "Great Tales" great. The impossibility for Tifi to represent her past and her absence in the metanarrative of the Mauritian nation are the result of her position within that society. As a young girl abandoned in an orphanage and excluded from her community, Tifi is absent from any national archive—written or oral—the main function of which is to preserve memory. Such archives—the inscription in memory—reveal a work of denomination, identification, and valorization, categories from which minorities or the *minorisés* tend to be excluded.

At first, Patel's short story gives us a subject inscribed in passivity. With her fixed gaze, Tifi remains largely silent throughout the short story. At the story's surface, Tifi seems merely physically and intellectually inert, a lifeless girl who does not seem receptive to outside influences or to the carelessness and joyfulness of the other kids "who were heckling and running, one more than the other," around her. Silent and with her eyes fixed on the pavement of the playground, Tifi becomes the symbol of the expiatory victim sacrificed in the name of nationalism, globalization, and the deceptive exaltation of a multiethnic society.

The first testimony of Tifi is that of her body. Her story is written in her body, which tells of a socialization and conditioning of those individuals in Mauritian society who, held at distance from the realms of power, remain in a state of subjection. Tifi's body, immobile in the middle of the agitation created by the other kids, is the first expression of her otherness. It carries a familial and collective memory founded in a culture shaped by appearances and singularities that engender habitus. Displaced, Tifi's body-memory strikes dissonance in this new environment and becomes the carrier of a collective memory: that of the excluded minority.

At the same time, this body also tells of another story. Through a closer reading of the text, through "listening" carefully to the story, the indifference and lifelessness of Tifi disappear, making it possible to hear Tifi's voice, a voice that becomes the driving force of the narration. As the gaze of the narrator—and the reader—is refined and our hearing surmounts the tumult of the other children, it becomes possible to hear "the sustained call of [Tifi's] gaze" (l'appel soutenu du regard [de Tifi]) (101). Initially mute, Tifi, constantly "on the lookout" (aux aguets) (102), later launches an "unavoidable" (incontournable) call; her gaze is "always heavy, insisting, at the same time loaded with allegations and winged with hope" (toujours lourd, insistant comme chargé de reproche et ailé d'espoir à la fois), and it becomes finally "impossible not to hear" (103). The initial silences of Tifi get substituted with an astonishing testimony made of a multitude of calls and messages.

Once Upon a Time: Minorities and the National Archives

The persistent imperative, tirelessly defiant in calling for *ène zistoire,* reveals a complex relationship between memory and the inscription in the national narrative of the history of the minoritized people of Mauritius. By choosing the title "Île était une fois," Patel inevitably writes the short story in the semantic field of the tale. It therefore appears natural to hear a child, Tifi, ask for another story. Present in all cultures, the tale, as Jack Zipes has suggested in *Fairy Tales and the*

Art of Subversion, is often "the most important cultural and social event in most children's lives" (1). The educational role of the tale is clearly evident: "Almost all critics who have studied the literary fairy tale in Europe agree that educated writers purposely appropriated the oral folktale and converted it into a type of literary discourse about mores, values, and manners so that children and adults would become civilized according to the social code of that time" (3). In *Postmodern Fairy Tales,* Cristina Bacchilega explains that the tale "grants writers/tellers and readers/listeners access to the collective, if fictionalized, past of social communing, an access that allows for an apparently limitless, highly idiosyncratic re-creation of that 'once there was'" (5). Tales create the possibility for a child to impose an identity and a position within a culture and within such stories. As Zipes suggests, however, tales also become a tool to inscribe one history at the detriment of another. In its "civilizing" role, the tale is a purveyor of the "social codes of the time," hence creating concerns regarding the collective memory, and its inscription in the national archive, of those who are subjected to domination and/or stigmatization. In Patel's story, the narrator's initial reaction is to acclimate and civilize Tifi, the outcast, who, with her untamed hair and her asocial behavior, must be rescued from her status as a "savage child."

But the choice of the tale is further revealing of the political aspect of Patel's text. Whereas the imperative "Tell me *ène zistoire*" and the title of the short story itself suggest the telling and the inscription of a Creole history, they assert simultaneously the impossibility of telling this history and the lies that go with it. Patel's use of the classic opening "Once upon a time" for her story's title points the reader to an imaginary world and evokes the deceptive aspect of such identity construction. Furthermore, Tifi's continual dissatisfaction with the tales offered reveals the narrator's inability to construct for Tifi an imagined past that can participate in the creation of a community. Tifi's repeated imperative calls out the hypocrisy of the so-called multiethnic community of Mauritius, the "Rainbow Nation."

The newly constituted heterogeneous family of Tifi and the narrator functions as a microcosm of Mauritian society. While revealing a desire to live together, this union also reveals an uneven distribution of power among its members, including their relationship to memory. The tensions between the narrator and Tifi work as an analogy for the malaise that lives in the Mauritian society, exposing to light the failure of a multiethnic society. Furthermore, it denounces the failure of a globalized economy by illustrating the unique and socially heterogenous component of that unit.

Narrating Mauritian Identity: The Construction of the Creole Text/Place

As discussed in the previous two sections, multiple elements in Patel's text lead the reader to consider Tifi as an ethnically and/or economically marginalized character within Mauritian society. Beyond the deconstruction of the "Rainbow

Nation" and "Mauritian miracle" myths, Patel's short story ultimately illustrates an absence while simultaneously giving it flesh. The discourses of "rootedness" and homogeneity dominate constructions of Mauritian identity. In formulating national identity, dominant groups have reiterated the "homeland requirement" (Boswell 11) as an essential element. As a heterogeneous group with no singular homeland to legitimize roots, Creole's identity in Mauritius "is considered a non-identity . . . a sort of anti-category, useful for other groups to define themselves and as a means to establish hegemony" (Boswell 11). Tifi's "absent presence" functions as the non-celebration and the negation of an identity, a Creole Being, that exists through a special relationship with the place that is Mauritius. While we can say that "one is creole if one is not from somewhere else, or if the link to that other place—because it is not a colonial link to the cities of origin—has been cut," Carpanin-Marimoutou concludes that "seen in a more positive light, Creole Being and Creole Action imply a very special relationship to the place that is Mauritius" (226).

Tifi's lack of enthusiasm illustrates the impact of how we relate (to) place and how Mauritian identity has been rooted in an "elsewhere" and has not been inscribed in the place that is Mauritius. What is lacking is the celebration of the particular relationship to the place, a relationship between origins and place, between place and identity, as "it is necessary to constitute one's identity in connection to the historic space of the island itself, to the creole place" (Carpanin-Marimoutou 226). Tifi's constant search for a tale celebrating an identity rooted in Mauritius—and her perpetual dissatisfaction with the tales that glorify outside origins—reveals a lack of such a narrative that can construct Mauritius as a place of identity. The latent question Tifi asks is how one dwells in a space "genuinely, not in dissonance—in exile from oneself and from the island—but in harmony" (Carpanin-Marimoutou 330). Price explores "place as a layered, shifting reality that is constituted, lived, and contested, in part, through narrative" (xiii), examining how narratives function in establishing claims to places and how places come into being through narratives. She highlights the relationship between human beings and their physical surroundings as a complex space of negotiation articulated through narratives. According to Price, place as such does not exist; "rather, narratives about people's places in places continuously materialize the entity we call place" (4). Thus, it is precisely here, in the strict structure of the short story, that Patel's work of interpretation, transformation, and creation is lucidly located, a place where absence finally becomes present.

The quest for a land of origin, for a founding myth, an impossible but necessary myth of origins, inscribes the narrator, and the author, in a place-identity dialectic. The existence of the "Creole Being" depends on its relationship with the place and its cosmogony not as an exclusion but as a genesis. The lack of a satisfying *zistoire* for Tifi, who stands as an embodiment of this "Creole Being" and "Creole Action," results in her wandering and her constant quest. Her ghostly presence and her silence are only signs of her denial of existence, her "non-identity" in a culture where her constant quest for *ène zistoire* tells the story of her project for a reappropriation of the space, for an inscription of the national memory within the island.

Patel's short story functions as an attempt to recreate a cosmogony that takes roots in the story's title and in Patel's play on the word "Îlle." This tale inscribes man, woman, and island in the same word, where it becomes possible to see all three elements but impossible to separate them from one another. The quest for a homeland, for a founding myth, inscribes the narrator and the author in a dialectic relationship between space and identity and as such participates in what Françoise Vergès and Carpanin-Marimoutou call "the production of space, which is a social and cultural production" (production de l'espace, qui est une production sociale et culturelle) (26).

"Tell me *ène zistoire*," implores Tifi. In response, the narrator writes, in the first paragraph, "This sentence as a rite constantly renewed, endlessly repeated, seemed to answer the same essential rhythm as that of the tide always relapsing" (Cette phrase comme un rite sans cesse renouvelé, inlassablement recommencé, semblait répondre au même rythme essentiel de cette marée toujours récidivée) (101). Telling the Creole story here becomes intimately related to the space and essence of the island and its tide. The analogy between the "vital rhythm" of the tide, which relentlessly assails the island as to constantly redefine its coasts, and this request to tell *ène zistoire* that, like the tide, constantly comes back evokes a reciprocal relationship between nature and identity, between the unstable print left by the tide on the coast of Mauritius and the need to include in this geography a history and the stories of people who arrived on the island and have left their mark—and who also, like the tide, are constantly reshaping that identity.

The importance of Tifi within the short story lies in her lack of origins outside the insular space. The girl is described twice as "decisively turning her back to the sea" (tournant résolument le dos à la mer) (101 and 107), indicating that the quest for identity lies not in its relation to elsewhere but in the burning desire to own the place. Furthermore, the departure of her mother and the near nonexistence of the father symbolize this lack of origin, the loss of an origin other than the place and the cultural space that impose themselves, Vergès and Carpanin-Marimoutou write, as the only "driving force of the collective imagination and cultural expressions" (acteurs de l'imaginaire collectif et des expressions culturelles) (67). Hence the loss becomes a sine qua non condition for an India-Ocean creolization. Vergès explains that creolization comes from "a loss of the culture of origin, loss of native land, loss of language. It is so. Loss constitutes the soil on which creolization can be constructed. Loss is not at all a question of mourning in the Hegelian sense, but rather it is the structure, the soil on which creolization can emerge" (205). Patel's story starts with an imperative and the gesture of opening with a line of Creole, "Raconte-moi ène zistoire," repeated four times in the eight-page story. While the imperative comes as a request formulated by Tifi as a child's longing for a good story, it also communicates a sense of urgency in the need for the history of the Creole Story to be told. "Once upon a time" gives a specific beginning, mooring the Creole to a land, to a place. Yet it simultaneously sends it adrift in the realm of the imaginary as the beginning of a fictional fairy tale. In a framework that asserts place and questions it at the same time, the Creole literary text is born, one that is in constant negotiation and in which none of the original materials are hidden but in which everything is transformed.

After many years, Mala calls to announce that she is coming back to Mauritius to pick up her daughter and take her to Belgium. It is this call, and Tifi's upcoming departure, that initiates the story's narration. Its conclusion, in turn, consists of a final short paragraph set off from the rest of the story. In this time-lapsed coda, we learn that two years after Tifi's departure for Belgium, the narrator receives a parcel from her containing a bound book. The narrator opens the book only to discover blank pages. On the back cover, however, she finds a label affixed by Tifi on which is written "Île était une fois . . ." The word "ïlle" is written "with two wings" (avec deux ailes), the narrator explains. She later concludes that "it is without a doubt the most beautiful story I was ever told . . ." (C'est sans doute la plus belle histoire qu'on m'ait jamais racontée . . .) (108).

The blank book sent by Tifi concludes the story with a densely rich polysemy. The last comment by the narrator leads us to believe that the best story is the one not written. Consisting of blank pages, the book represents Tifi's attempt to tell *ène zistoire*, to imagine, to invent, to form it. In this sense, Tifi is no longer a passive object waiting to be told a story. She becomes a subject expressing both her identity and the absence of her identity. The blank pages, as a form of self-representation, symbolize a refusal of the written narrative as a form of liberation necessary to the quest for identity. The beauty the narrator sees in the blank pages of this story comes from the beauty inherent in the freedom of refusing to engage in the discourse and the logic of representation.

As a young intellectual who lays claim to a connection to her country's memory through her narration and her abundant knowledge of tales, the narrator relies heavily on language and writing. While her sense of identity and memory are based on *logocentrism* and *phonocentrism*, according to Derrida, Tifi's responses—her silence and the blank space of her book—present an alternative.

The white pages and Tifi's attached note could be understood as an invitation to inscribe *ène zistoire*. However, the narrator's last remark ("the most beautiful story I was ever told") suggests that the story is already there in its absence in these white pages. As such, the book sent by Tifi illustrates the will to go beyond (or to reject) the hegemony of the sign. As such, Patel's story can be understood in relation to Derrida's deconstruction of the conventional concept of writing. In *Margins of Philosophy* Derrida explains that the sign "is usually said to be put in the place of the thing itself, the present thing, 'thing' here standing equally for meaning or referent. The sign represents the present in its absence. It takes the place of the present. When we cannot grasp or show the thing, state the present, the being-present, when the present cannot be presented, we signify, we go through the detour of the sign" (9). A sign is commonly understood as a kind of delegate or substitute of something else, and as a result, writing functions as a representation of speech while speech itself claims a closer proximity to thought. Signs are a detour that becomes necessary when something that should be present remains, for whatever reason, absent or inaccessible.

Hence, what Derrida calls a "metaphysics of presence" asserts the dominance of speech over writing and, at the same time, the dispensable nature of writing. While denouncing the erroneous nature of such hierarchies, what Derrida suggests is not merely the overturning of the previous hierarchies of thought above speech and speech above writing but rather the emergence of a new concept of *writing* that results from his analysis of the workings of language, requiring one to reconceive the nature of language itself and of the relationships among thought, language, and culture.

In deconstructing logocentrism and phonocentrism of the Western philosophical tradition, Derrida simultaneously recognizes in "Structure, Sign, and Play" (in *Writing and Difference*) that he is unable to move beyond it. What remains to be done therefore is to explore the common ground and difference that separates and joins these possibilities, an intellectual space he calls *différance*.

Tifi's silence throughout the narration of "Île était une fois" and the absence of the conventional (as defined by Saussure) sign in her book illustrate her mistrust in the hegemonic presence of the sign. Tifi's unsatisfaction, as well as her sign-less book, represents her struggle to express something outside of the Western tradition. Yet, her attempts at moving outside that tradition through the material object of a bound book of empty pages offer a glimpse at what cannot be named and result in a blank space. In *Positions*, Derrida explains that "to 'deconstruct' philosophy, thus, would be to think—in the most faithful, interior way—the structured genealogy of philosophy's concepts, but at the same time to determine—from a certain exterior that is unqualifiable or unnameable by philosophy—what this history has been able to dissimulate or forbid, making itself into a history by means of this somewhere motivated repression" (6). Tifi's blank book, which constitutes the absence of the sign, manages to also be a presence of something "unqualifiable" or "unnameable" and of something to come. As such, this absence becomes the sign of something.

This blank book with a handwritten note fixed on the back "tells" a story without writing because the story begins with Tifi's partial destruction of the sign and suggests that the Creole is not a descendant but the creator of his or her own origin and the myth that creates it. Furthermore, it is a story that escapes the panoptic gaze, the ethnographic observation, and that keeps the Other—turned subject—in all his or her opacity. Edouard Glissant justifies this lack of clarity and writes in *Le Discours antillais* that "the attempt to approach a reality so often overlooked, cannot be immediately organized around a series of clarities. We demand the right to opacity" (la tentative d'approcher une réalité tant de fois occultée, ne s'ordonne pas tout de suite autour d'une série de clartés. Nous réclamons le droit à l'opacité) (11).

But these blank pages also symbolize an absence, absence in the place, language, and history. This dispossession, as a "nonhistoire," suffered by a people, a community, explains the nonrepresentation because, as Vergès and Carpanin-Marimoutou write, "There is no language that can really tell that story or that place, because neither the language is inhabited by this place and this story, nor does it live it really, for real" (Il n'y a pas de langue ni de langage qui puissent réellement dire cette histoire ni ce lieu, car ni la langue ni le langage ne sont habités par ce lieu et cette histoire, ni ne les habitent, réellement, pour de vrai) (45). But by what means can literature fill that gap and let the repressed stories emerge? The final comment of the narrator suggests the answer: "This is the most beautiful story I was ever *told*" (C'est . . . la plus belle histoire qu'on m'ait jamais *racontée*) (108, emphasis mine). It is at the confluence of the written and spoken word that the potential of text now lies as a way to "undo the script of its term of sovereignty in relation to orality" (défaire l'écriture de son manda de souveraineté par rapport a l'oralité) (Glissant, *Discours* 322).

"Îlle était une fois" is marked throughout with signs of orality. First, the narrative structure is significant, because the tale is at the juncture between orality and writing. The presence of the Creole language in the text is limited to Tifi's injunction "Tell me *ène zistoire.*" This presence, although minimal, is however the driving force of the narration. Furthermore, it indicates that Creole, as a language, is spoken by all communities of the island but remains invisible in the texts in which the English or French languages predominate.

The circular structure of the text also echoes its oral nature. By placing the classic opening of tales at the end of her text, Tifi recounts a lack, an absence, an impossibility of writing. By placing the classic opening at the beginning (and end) of the short story, Patel gives us the story of the elliptical absence of the Creole but suggests its tenacious presence in the circular structure of the text. It is a story that now prompts the narration and a rereading of the story. Patel embraces the Western imperative "Tell me a story" but corrupts its imperialist, imperative value by writing the text in a specific geography, that of Creole, Mauritian, island space. Patel's story makes the reader doubt, because her narration gives rise to the potential of alternative histories, for as Glissant suggests, "stories crack History" (les histoires lézardent l'Histoire) (*Discours* 433).

But the materiality of Tifi's blank book tells a story, and the ellipsis announces something to come. For, although the thematic revolves around the theme of resistance and silence, it remains a thematic, a sort of compromise, and the short story participates actively in the literary and intellectual market of the West. In this case, the destruction of the sign leaves a trace, the narrative that is told in the hope of going beyond such destruction.

Reading the title left on the label by Tifi, the narrator comments on the spelling and writes "with two *l*s," which Patel writes as a-i-l-e-s, which means "with two wings," generating complexly layered word (and letter) play that matches that of the story's title and opening. The fusion of the island with the subject pronouns "he" and "she," that is, the symbiosis between insular and identity, is revealing: Although the inscription in the place gives roots to the Creole people and ultimately to the people of Mauritius, the tale evokes the image of a butterfly that just emerged from its chrysalis, overpowering the dead weight of tradition and convention.

For it is in this reconnection, this trust between Tifi and the narrator, to whom Tifi entrusts her history, that lies the beauty of a potential future of a Creole society. In fact, this book "helps the community become aware of aspects of past hidden in its landscape, but also permits this restored memory (uncovering historic bonds which unite those who live there) to contribute toward the constitution of a cohesive and unified people" (Damato and Darin 608).

It was "to ease her conscience" (pour se donner bonne conscience) that the narrator regularly visited the orphanage where she met Tifi. However, on the eve of Tifi's departure, the narrator feels "a sudden thrill of this rising tide" (soudain, ce frémissement de marée montante) (102). Although at first superficial and hypocritical before her visits to the orphanage, the consciousness of belonging to a political community, a common culture, with what it means regarding the rights, duties, and compassion, pervades the narrator, who transforms "the backlash" (ce ressac) (102) into creative energy. "Îlle était une fois" becomes the contribution to the re-transcription of *éne zistoire*, a construction of a corpus of texts relating the histories that participate in this community in Mauritius. When addressing the Antillean context, Glissant defines the role of the writer as paramount for writing the history of the dispossessed and for allowing the emergence of this repressed history. For Glissant, however, the writer's role is not to bring to the surface a silenced history but rather to create it through fiction as an expression of cultural production within a specific environment. He writes in *Introduction à une poétique du divers*, "Le passé ne doit pas seulement être recomposé de manière objective (ou même de manière subjective) par l'historien, il doit être aussi rêvé de manière prophétique, pour les gens, les communautés et les cultures dont le passé, justement, a été occulté" (The past must not only be reconstructed objectively [or subjectively] by the historian, it must also be dreamed in a prophetic way for the people, the communities and the cultures whose past, precisely, was suppressed) (64). Glissant calls for a "prophetic vision of the past" (une vision prophétique du passé) since history of the dispossessed cannot emanate from the collective memory of a people that has been occulted but rather from its literary production, hence the highly political role of literature as it allows the collective consciousness of a whole people to flourish.

* * *

If we return to the language of Salkey, we could say that by staying home, Patel chooses to "vegetate." In doing so, however, she makes island "vegetation" a source of Creole power and empowerment. In his axiom, Salkey seems to constructs the rootedness of the Creole identity as discounted in its fixed connection to place. His inflection of the term "vegetate" makes it oppositional to "animate," as he no doubt means for "vegetate" to signify with the modern (and Western) associations with passivity and entropic loss: for example, the individual who is, after a trauma, "in a vegetative state." In the Oxford English Dictionary, that is only the secondary meaning of the term: "to live a merely physical life; to lead a dull, monotonous existence, devoid of intellectual activity or social intercourse." The primary definition of the term, however, includes characterizations of robust growth and future promise: "to grow or develop, or begin to do so." It is in this latter sense that Patel chooses to "vegetate" her Creole identity and literary production on, with, and from the island of Mauritius.

What Patel carves out from her island home is a combination of assertive Creole articulations and literary engagement shot through with thematics of silence, retreat, resistance, and refusal of the literary logic of the imperium delivered with insistence. The insistence of Patel's themes of quiet, silence, sensitivity, and refusals to speak or write constitutes a resistance to the colonial, imperialist will to power built on inciting subjects into discourse. And yet, though her thematics signify resistance, they are still thematics and as such are compromised, for they still engage and constitute an entry into discourse and the Western literary and intellectual marketplace. However, Patel does that only part of the time, balancing that form of reinscribing resistant French literary production "from the island" with a host of other local, Creole cultural projects: writing into Creole, serving as local librarian, fostering multilingual local publishing endeavors, working as a journalist, and creating documentaries.

Patel is a part-time writer but a full-time Mauritian islander. French-language literary writing constitutes only one piece of her Creole identity. What Patel seems to understand and thus wield is that literature can get you only so far as a form of political or social activism. When it is mediated by and mixed with Creole island poetics, aesthetics, politics, and local community commitments and projects, it can participate in a project of reinscribing history as a Creole island z-story.

Notes

1. All translations are mine unless otherwise noted.
2. We learn that the narrator's mother had employed Mala (Tifi's mother) as a housekeeper.
3. In *Le Malaise Creole: Ethnic Identity in Mauritius*, Boswell defines Creole people from Mauritius as "primarily the descendants of African and Malagasy slaves who were brought to the island by the Dutch, French, and English over a period of three hundred years" (2).
4. These figures are the 2010 estimates from the U.S. Department of State. See http://www.state.gov/r/pa/ei/bgn/2833.htm.
5. These parallel readings of Tifi's identity (as a Creole or a socially marginalized person) are in fact easily reconcilable since the undeniable discontent of the Creole population is partly the result of the "persistence of poverty, social problems and political marginalisation among Creole" (Boswell 2). Kasenally writes also that the success of Mauritius's economic boom has rested on a cheap labor force composed predominantly of Mauritians of African ancestry, but as the economy dropped, "material deprivation goes hand-in-hand with growing disparities in income that have most deleteriously affected Mauritians of African ancestry" (165).

Works Cited

Bacchilega, Cristina. *Postmodern Fairy Tales: Gender and Narrative Strategies*. Philadelphia: University of Pennsylvania Press, 1997.
Berger, John. *The Shape of a Pocket*. New York: Vintage, 2001.
Boswell, Rosabelle. *Le Malaise Créole: Ethnic Identity in Mauritius*. New York: Berghahn Books, 2006.
Boudet, Catherine. "La Responsabilité sociale de l'auteur." LeMauricien.com, http://www.lemauricien.com/article/la-responsabilite-sociale-l'auteur.
Capparos, Olivier. "Puissance et souveraineté." *Lampe-tempête* 2, March 2007, http://www.lampe-tempete.fr/puissancebataille.htm.
Carpanin-Marimoutou, Jean-Claude. "Literature, the Imaginary, and Creolization: Texts and Intertexts." In *Creolite and Creolization*, edited by Okwi Enwezor and Carlos Basualdo, 225–39. Kassel, Germany: Hatje Cantz, 2003.
Damato, Diva, and Leila Cristine Darin. "The Poetics of the Dispossessed." *World Literature Today* 63, no. 4 (Autumn 1989): 606–8.
Derrida, Jacques. *Margins of Philosophy*. Chicago: University of Chicago Press, 1982.
———. *Positions*. Chicago: University of Chicago Press, 1981.
———. *Writing and Difference*. London: Routledge, 2001.
Glissant, Edouard. *Le Discours antillais*. Paris: Seuil, 1981.
———. *Introduction à une poétique du divers*. Paris: Seuil, 1995.
Jameson, Fredric. *Signatures of the Invisible*. New York: Routledge, 2011.
Kasenally, Roukaya. "Mauritius: Paradise Reconsidered." *Journal of Democracy* 22, no. 2 (April 2011): 160–69.
Pare, Francois. *Théories de la fragilité*. Quebec: Les Editions du Nordir, 1994.
Patel, Shenaz. "Îlle était une fois." In *Maurice: Demain et Après. Beyond Tomorrow. Apredime*, edited by Barlen Pyamootoo and Rama Poonoosamy. Port-Louis, Mauritius: Immedia, 1996.
Porter, Carolyn. *Seeing and Being: The Plight of the Participant Observer in Emerson, James, Adams, and Faulkner*. Middletown: Wesleyan University Press, 1985.

Price, Patricia L. *Dry Place: Landscapes of Belonging and Exclusion.* Minneapolis: University of Minneapolis Press, 2004.

Quinn, Kate. "'I Will Let Down My Bucket Here': Writers and the Conditions of Cultural Production in Post-Independence Trinidad." In *Caribbean Literature after Independence: The Case of Earl Lovelace,* edited by Bill Schwarz, 21–40. London: Institute for the Study of the Americas, 2008.

Srebrnik, Henry. "'Full of Sound and Fury': Three Decades of Parliamentary Politics in Mauritius." *Journal of Southern African Studies* 28, no. 2 (2002): 277–89.

Torabully, Khal. "Créolité, Coolitude, Créolisation: Les Imaginaires de la relation." December 14, 2006, http://www.africultures.com/php/?nav=article&no=4678.

Vergès, Françoise. "Open Session." In *Creolite and Creolization,* edited by Okwi Enwezor and Carlos Basualdo, 199–211. Kassel, Germany: Hatje Cantz, 2003.

Vergès, Françoise, and Jean-Claude Carpanin-Marimoutou. *Amarres: Créolisations india- océanes.* Paris: L'Harmattan, 2005.

Zafar, Ali. "Mauritius: An Economic Success Story." In *Yes Africa Can: Success Stories from a Dynamic Continent,* edited by Punam Chuhan-Pole and Manka Angwafo, 91–106. Washington, D.C.: World Bank, 2011.

Zipes, Jack. *Fairy Tales and the Art of Subversion: The Classical Genre for Children and the Process of Civilization.* New York: Routledge, 2006.

Contributors

MORADEWUN ADEJUNMOBI is a professor in the African American and African studies program at the University of California, Davis.

SAFOI BABANA-HAMPTON is an associate professor of French at Michigan State University.

LAMIA BENYOUSSEF is an assistant professor in the Department of Foreign Languages and Literatures at the University of Alabama at Birmingham.

MÁRIA MINICH BREWER is an associate professor of French at the University of Minnesota.

MAGALI COMPAN is an associate professor of French and francophone studies at the College of William and Mary.

FRIEDA EKOTTO is a professor of Afroamerican and African studies, comparative literature, and francophone studies at the University of Michigan.

KENNETH W. HARROW is Distinguished Professor of English at Michigan State University.

OLABODE IBIRONKE is an assistant professor of English at Rutgers University.

EILEEN JULIEN is a professor of comparative literature and French and Italian at Indiana University and is director of the Institute for Advanced Study.

PATRICE NGANANG is a professor of literary and cultural theory at Stony Brook University.

TEJUMOLA OLANIYAN is Louise Durham Mead Professor of English and African languages and literature at the University of Wisconsin–Madison.

VALÉRIE K. ORLANDO is a professor of French and francophone literatures at the University of Maryland.

Index

Accents: across borders, 102–104; definition, 96, 100; differences of, 96–99; impact of travel on, 97–98; kinds of, 99–101; politics of, 101–102
Accra, Ghana, 94
Achebe, Chinua, 3, 4, 9, 18, 19, 22, 30, 37, 39–46, 49; *Home and Exile*, 43, 46; *Morning Yet on Creation Day*, 42–43; *Things Fall Apart*, 30, 39, 43
Adejunmobi, Moradewun, 10, 11, 52, 70n4, 72n15, 73n16, 197
Adesokan, Akin, 19, 23
Adichie, Chimamanda Ngozi, 4, 6, 7, 8, 23, 27n4, 67, 71n7, 73n22, 88; "Imitation," 6, 16; *The Thing around My Neck*, 4
Aesthetics, 127–129
African, 17–27
African cultural criticism, 94, 95, 97, 98, 99–100, 103; affirmative and interstitial, 100–101; African cultural Studies, 93–108; cultural creativity, 94; languages of, 94–96; theory, 95–96
African Literature Association, 94
African novel, 18, 19, 32–37, 39, 40, 41
African playwrights of the diaspora, 159, 162–163
African theater, 161–163, 165, 170, 173n14; authenticity in, 163–165
Afrinolly, 64, 74–75
Afropolitan, 52, 70
Agency, 128–129
Agora, 87
Aizenberg, Edna, 27n3
Ajayi-Soyinka, Omofolabo, 95, 96n2
Allouache, Merzak, 129
Alphabet, 87, 89, 91
Alphabetization, 78–85, 87, 89
Animality, 89
Aniydoho, Kofi, 56, 62, 71–72
Appadurai, Arjun, 8; global flows, 2, 8, 9, 11, 123
Appiah, Kwame Anthony, 96, 97, 97n5, 98, 100
Apter, Emily, 31; *The Translation Zone*, 31
Area studies model, 6, 20, 54
Armah, Ayi Kwei, 41–43
Artaud, Antonin, 161

Arts, 84–85, 87–89
Atta, Sefi, 4
Auteur cinema, 128
Azuah, Unoma, 3

Babana-Horton, Safoi, 12, 13, 127, 197; Maghrebian cinema, 12
Bailly, Jean-Christophe, thresholds, 160, 173n4
Baingana, Doris, 4
Baldwin, James, 9, 22, 27n7
Bamum, 82–84, 88; Bamum alphabet, 12
Bamum, Sultan of. *See* Njoya, Ibrahim, Sultan of Bamum, *Sang'aam (Histoire et Coutumes des Bamum)*
Banlieue, 128
Banquet, as symbolic concept, 165
Barlet, Olivier, 129; *Cinémas d'Afrique des années 2000 (Les)*, 129
Barthes, Roland, mythology, 165
Bayoumi, Moustapha, 116
Beauvoir, Simone de, 110, 120–124
Belyazid, Farida, 132
Ben Barka, Mehdi, 151
Benjelloun, Hassan, 143, 145, 147–148
Benslama Fethi, 116–118, 124n8, 124n9, 124n10, 124n11
Benyoussef, Lamia, 2, 3, 12, 13, 109, 197
Berger, John, 178–179
Berube, Michael, 46–47
Beur, 127–128
Bhabha, Homi, 5, 8, 104, 106n8; *différance*, 5, 191; hybridity, 5, 104; *The Location of Culture*, 5
Bizet, Georges, 25
Bjornson, Richard, *The African Quest for Freedom and Identity*, 27n3, 78
Boswell, Rosabelle, 182–183, 188
Boudet, Catherine, 179
Boughedir, Ferid, 129
Brecht, Bertolt, 161
Brewer, Mária Minich, 15, 159, 165, 197
Brook, Peter, 161
Brutus, Dennis, 39, 42, 45; *Letters to Martha*, 42, 45
Bureaucracy, 64, 81–82
Butler, Judith, 8

199

Index

Caine Prize, 52, 70
Capitalism, 10, 32
Carpanin-Marimoutou, Jean-Claude, 181, 188–189, 192
Casablanca, 144, 156n7
Casanova, Pascale, 27n5, 31, 36; *The World Republic of Letters*, 36
CCM (Centre Cinématographique Marocain), 148–150, 154, 157n15
Censorship, 153, 154, 157n17
Chalaye, Sylvie, 163–167, 169, 174n16; dramaturgy of crossroads, 163; Ethnodramatists and ethnographic imperative, 163; voice and the body, 163, 169
Charef, Mehdi, 128–129; *Cartouches gauloises*, 128; *Thé au Harem d'Archi-Ahmed (Le)*, 128
Chibane, Malik, 128; *Hexagone, Douce France, Voisin, Voisine*, 128
Chinweizu, 91n32, 97, 97n5, 98, 101, 106n5
Chittick, William, 137
Chow, Rey, 31, 33, 50
Cinéma-vérité, 127
Cixous, Hélène, 6
Clément, Catherine, 6
Clifford, James, 42
Cobham-Sander, Rhonda, 19
Cole, Teju, 52, 62, 70n3
Collective memory, 182–183, 185–187, 189–190
Coly, Ayo, 10, 23
Compan, Magali, 2, 15, 177, 197
Conteh-Morgan, John (with Dominic Thomas), 163–167, 170, 174n20, 174n21; reconfigurations of Africanness and Frenchness, 164; tensions between culturalist and transnational forms, 163, 165; translocality and nomadism, 164
Cooper, Brenda, 26n3
Cornell University, 95, 96n2
Corporate academia, 110, 112, 114–116, 120, 123
Corvin, Michel, *Dictionnaire encyclopédique du théâtre à travers le monde*, 168, 175n29
Cosmopolitanism, 21, 23
Craft, 81–85, 87–88
Creative industries, 60, 63–64, 73
Creole, 3, 15, 34, 177–183, 185, 187–194, 195n3; culture and identity, 178, 181–183, 185–186, 188–189, 192–193; language, 179–180, 190–192
Crisis, 10, 23, 41, 44, 46, 48, 49, 57, 58, 78, 86–89, 92
Critical languages, 112
Criticism, 78, 79, 80, 85, 89
Critique, 85, 86, 89
Culture, 7–10, 14, 16, 19, 24, 30–34, 37, 47, 50, 52, 58, 62–65, 69, 73n23, 78, 80–82, 84–85, 90, 92–93, 98, 101–102, 113, 118–119, 150, 164, 170–171, 181, 186–187, 189, 191, 193–194; African culture, 80, 82, 166; Arab culture, 114, 125n20; Creole culture, 178; French culture, 115; Maroon culture, 183; Moroccan culture, 143–144
Currey, James, 44, 48
Curriculum, 113; anti-Semitism, 114; critical languages, 6, 112–113, 115, 123n3; French, 6, 7, 10, 113, 115, 119; gender, 19, 115–116

Damrosch, David, 10, 11, 29–32, 39; *What Is World Literature?*, 29; world literature, 10–11, 29, 30–31, 33, 39–40, 44
Davies, Carole Boyce, 46, 101
Deconstruction, 90n23, 95, 105n2, 191
Deleuze, Gilles, 14, 127–128, 130, 139; *Cinema2: The Time-Image*, 127–128
Deportation, 117, 166
Derrida, Jacques, 7, 34, 39–40, 90n23, 190–191; *Archive Fever*, 7, 39
Devi, G. N., 45
Diaspora, 31, 41–42, 122, 128; male academics, 116–118; women academics, 119–120. *See also* North Africa; Ghettoization
Diasporic playwrights, since 1990, 159, 166
Digital media, 62, 68, 72–73
Diome, Fatou, 4–6; *The Belly of the Atlantic*, 4, 23; identity, 4, 6, 8, 16; "suitcase words," 5
Diop, Boubacar Boris, 7, 8, 21, 39; *The Knight and His Shadow*, 39
Distinction, 81, 87–90, 92
Diversity, 118; spectacle, 122, 123
Djebar, Assia, 111, 113, 115–116, 119
Doubleness, 4, 8, 14
Dridi, Karim, 128–129
Dubois, W.E.B., 109
Dürrenmatt, Friedrich, 12, 24

Echewa, Obinkaram, 48
Efoui, Kossi, 162, 164, 174n23; *Le Carrefour*, 167, 173n13; *Concessions*, 167; *Oublie!* 167; *Solo d'un revenant*, 159
Eisenberg, Eve, 27n4
Ekotto, Frieda, 1, 17, 21, 25, 197
El Khayat, Rita, 131
El Moudden, Abderrahmane, 131–132, 139
Encounter, 132–133, 136–138
Equiano, Olaudah, *The Interesting Narrative of the Life of Olaudah Equiano, or Gustavus Vassa, the African, Written by Himself*, 85
Eurocentrism, 35
Exile, 3, 5, 6, 9, 21–22, 49, 75, 99, 151–152, 177, 188; poetics of, 12

Farrah, Nuruddin, 41
Fatemi, Nasrollah, 138
Ferroukhi, Ismaël, 129–130, 133; *Le Grand voyage*, 129, 131–132, 139, 150–152
Festival international des francophonies (Limoges, France), 173
"First generation" texts, 18
Folarin, Tope, 52, 70
Forna, Aminatta, 4, 5, 72; *Ancestor Stones*, 4; fugue, 5
France, 128–130, 134–135, 138–139
Francophone diasporic theater, 160, 172, 173n5
French feminism, 111, 121–123. See also Beauvoir, Simone de

Garuba, Harry, 27n3
Ghettoization, 110–112, 116, 118, 125n20. See also Beauvoir, Simone de; French feminism
Gide, André, 19
Gikandi, Simon, 3, 5, 19, 20, 100
Gilroy, Paul, 6; *The Black Atlantic*, 16; Double Consciousness, 7
Glissant, Edouard, 185, 192–194
Global, 1, 4–6, 8–12, 14–15, 29–35, 44, 48–50, 65, 75, 78–80, 85–90, 96–97, 104, 112, 115, 118, 120, 144, 162–164, 170, 178, 182; Global flows, 2, 123; Global literature, 16, 31–32, 37, 44, 46; Globalism, 12, 24, 26n1, 43; Globalization, 1, 3, 10–11, 13, 17, 23, 25, 26n1, 32–33, 35–36, 39–41, 45, 49, 145, 151, 182–184, 186–187; Spivak, 34, 50
Goethe, Johann Wolfgang Von, 29, 31–33, 46
Gondola, Didier, 26n8
Green-Simms, Lindsey, sexual orientation, 3. See also Nollywood
Griswold, Wendy. See Julien, Eileen
Guénoun, Denis, 160–162, 170, 173n6, 173n7; theater as assembly, 161; theater as making space, 162

Hammoudi, Abdellatif, 131
Haremization, 109
Harrow, Kenneth, 8, 17, 21, 25, 100, 105, 123, 197; *Less Than One and Double*, 8, 16
Hassan II, 142, 146–147, 151
Haynes, Jonathan, 25
Hegel, Georg W., *The Philosophy of History*, 85, 86, 91, 92
Heidegger, Martin, 89, 91, 92
Heinemann, 44, 48, 49
Historiography, 80
home, 2, 15, 16, 18, 20, 21, 23, 26n6, 177, 181, 188, 189, 194

Homosexuality, 3, 73
Human, 81, 84, 86–87, 89–90, 93, 127, 129–130, 132, 136–139
Human rights, 145–148, 155n2
humanities, 112, 115–116
Husserl, Edmund, 89, 92
Hybridity, 4–5, 18, 104, 164, 181–182

Ibironke, Olabode, 10–11, 29, 197; postcolonial literature, 10, 29
Ibn Battuta, 133
Ibn Khaldun, *The Muqaddimah*, 80–85, 88–89
Identity, 2, 4, 6, 8, 16, 70, 86, 130–132, 135–138, 143, 165–166, 177, 181, 187–190, 193; African identity, 52, 167; Creole identity, 183, 194; French identity, 135; hybrid, 163; Mauritian identity, 185, 188; Muslim identity, 131; national identity, 117; Senegalese identity, 25–26
Image, 127, 129–131, 133, 135–136, 138–139
Immigration, 116, 117, 123, 124n6
In-betweenness, 15
Instrumental, 81, 89–90
Interdisciplinarity, 112, 113
Interethnic relations, 109; Blacks, 109, 116; Hispanics, 117, 124n6; Japanese, 116; Jews, 117
Irele, Abiola, 80, 89, 92, 101
Irigaray, Luce, *This Sex Which Is Not One*, 8, 16
Ismaïl, Mohamed, 132; *Adieu mères*, 132

Jameson, Fredric, 24, 34, 45
Jeli (variant of Djeli), 73
Jeyifo, Biodun, 15, 26, 35–36, 95, 96, 98, 99, 100, 101; changes in discursive accent, 98; changes in his reading of Soyinka, 98–99; Chinweizu, 101; Ngugi, 99; response to Spivak, 95–96
Jones, Eldred D., 101
Journey, 130–139
Julien, Eileen, 9–10, 17, 20, 22, 32–37, 39–41, 197; extroversion, 32, 34–36, 39–42, 46–47; Griswold and Julien, 29, 37–38, 41, 48–49

Kant, Emmanuel, 85, 89, 92
Keane, Michael, 60, 63, 73
Kennedy, Gerald, 21–23
Khatibi, Abdelkébir, 131
Kirkkopelto, Esa, *Le Théâtre de l'expérience*, 161, 173n7
Kolawole, Mary E., 101
Kom, Ambroise, 101
Kwahulé, Koffi, 162, 164, 168–170; forms of violence, 168; *Jaz*, 168; *La Mélancolie des barbares*, 168; *Misterioso-119*, 168; *El Mona*, 169–170; poetic language, 168

Laâbi, Abdelkébir, 131
Lahlou, Nabyl, 151
Lazarus, Neil, 100
Lead Years (*les années de plomb*), 142–143, 146, 148, 155n2
Lieu de mémoire, 143
Lindfors, Bernth, 45
Littérature carcérale, 146
Location, 9, 15, 17, 20, 23, 26, 43, 52, 62–63, 67, 73, 97, 177
Loreau, Dominique, *Les Noms n'habitent nulle part*, 4
Lukacs, Georg, 26n2
Lyotard, Jean-François, 33; *The Postmodern Condition*, 34; "The Sublime and the Avant-Garde," 160

Maasilta, Mari, 25–26, 27n9
Maghreb, 109–110; Maghrebian cinema, 22, 24; Maghrebian literature, 12, 13
Majid, Anouar, 117
Makhélé, Caya, 162
Mambéty, Djibril Diop, 12, 24
Mamdani, Mahmoud, 11–12
Maphoto, Mike, 56, 66, 71
Marrakchi, Laila, 129
Martin, Karen and Makhozazana Xaba, *Queer Africa: New Collected Fiction*, 16n2
Marx, Karl, 32–33; *The Communist Manifesto*, 32; Marxism, 96, 101
Mauritius, 15–16, 177–196; culture and society, 178, 181–183, 185–186, 188–189, 192–193; literature, 16, 177–196; Mauritian miracle, 182–183, 188; Rainbow nation, 181, 185, 187–188
Mbembe, Achille, 26n2, 96, 100
McClintock, Anne, 100
Mckeon, Michael, 26n2
Meddeb Abdelwahab, 124n8
Mengestu, Dinaw, 52, 70
Mérimée, Prosper, 25
Migration, 9, 12, 38, 41, 46, 97–98, 100, 162; emigration, 6, 11, 15, 79, 177; immigration, 6–7, 13, 109, 111, 116–117, 123, 124, 167
Milleliri, Carole, 128
Miller, Judith G., 162, 174n16
Minority literatures, 31
Modernism, 21
Modernity, 29, 32, 33, 34, 42, 130–133, 135–136, 138–139
Mohammed VI, 142, 152, 154
Moretti, Franco, 29, 34

Moroccan cinema, 12, 129–130, 142–145, 148–151, 153–157
Movement, 133, 139
Mudimbe, V. Y., 96, 100
Mugo, Micere, 100
Muslim, 130–133, 135, 137–139

Naficy, Hamid, 14, 128, 139
Nancy, Jean-Luc, 32–33, 44; *The Inoperative Community*, 44
Ndebele, Njabulo, 101
Negritude, 1, 9, 12, 19, 29, 46, 73, 86
Neumann, Eric, 35–36; *The Origin and History of Consciousness*, 35
Nganang, Patrice, 10–12, 78, 197
Ngugi wa Thiong'o, 37, 41, 47–49, 70, 98, 99
Nigerian films, 55, 64
Nixon, Robert, 100
Njoya, Ibrahim, Sultan of Bamum, *Sang'aam (Histoire et Coutumes des Bamum)*, 1, 79, 81–83, 88–89
Nnaemeka, Obioma, 101
Nollywood, 3, 8, 25, 63–66, 73, 75
Non-Aligned Movement, 96
Non-Westernism, 32, 34
North Africa, 109–110, 112; women academics in the Maghreb, 109, 111, 116, 118
Nye, Joseph, 24, 26n1

Ogoro, Kingsley, *Osuofia in London*, 14
Ogundipe-Leslie, Molara, 101
Okpewho, Isidore, 101
Olaniyan, Tejumola, 2, 13, 74, 94, 197; "accents," 12, 94, 96, 100, 102, 104
Oppressed, 87–88
Orality, 56, 163, 164, 179, 192; Orature, 56, 82
Organization of African Unity, 97
Orlando, Valerie, 12, 141–142, 197. *See also* Moroccan cinema
Osofisan, Femi, 37–39
Osundare, Niyi, 101
Owen, Stephen, 41, 44
Owomoyela, Oyekan, 101
Oyeyemi, Helen, *The Icarus Girl*, 4
Oyono, Ferdinand, 22

Palmer, Eustace, 101
Paradigm, 78–81, 83–87, 88–90
Paré, François, 178
Parry, Benita, 100
Pasolini, Paolo, 127

Patel, Shenaz, 15, 16, 177–190, 192–194
Permutation, 89
Perrault, Pierre, 127
Pilgrimage, 130–131, 133, 135, 138
Pliya, José, 162, 164–165, 173n14, 174n16
Poetics, 127, 130
Politics, 81, 85–86, 89, 91–93
Positive Black Soul, 27n6
Postcolonial, 78–79, 95
Postcolonial literature, 11, 31–32, 79
Postcolonial theory, 18
Postmodern, 130
Potential, 82, 83, 89
Practice, 78–80, 82, 84–85, 90
Promiscuity, 18

Qualitative, 89
Quayson, Ato, 100

Racism, 22, 103, 105, 113, 116–119, 124n5; classroom, 109; committees, 112; culture, 113–115; native informants, 109; research, 114–115; tenure, 111–113; terrorism, 115, 124n9; voyeurism, 110, 113, 122. *See also* Diversity; Ghettoization
Ramaka, Joseph Gaï, 10, 25, 27n9; *Karmen Geï*, 25
Rancière, Jacques, 15; *le partage du sensible*, 91n25, 165, 171, 175n32
Realism, 3, 17, 26n3, 110, 144; magical realism, 116
Reason, 78, 81–83, 85, 88, 89
Rihla, 131, 133
Ross, Kristen, 31–32
Rosset, Clément, 171–172, 175n34; alibi as defined by, 172
Rouch, Jean, 127
Ruggia, Christophe, 128; *Le Gone du Chaaba*, 128
Rushdie, Salman, 43

Said, Edward, 9, 17, 21–23, 25–26, 104
Salaita, Steven, 116, 124n5, 125n20
Salih, Tayeb, 19, 22
Scribe, 79, 84
Script, 82–84
Selasi, Taiye, 52, 70
Senghor, Léopold Sédar, 113
Sexism, 111, 113–115, 122. *See also* Curriculum
Sissako, Abderrahmane, *La Vie sur terre*, 4
Sociorealist, 14, 128
Soyinka, Wole, 15, 26, 39, 41–42, 97–99
Spectacle, 13, 110, 115, 121–123, 160, 168, 170

Spiritual, 130–133, 138–139
Spivak, Gayatri, 34, 50, 95, 96, 96n2; *An Aesthetic Education in the Era of Globalization*, 34
St. John, John, 49
Stein, Gertrude, 9, 21–22
Strategic essentialism, 18
Subjectivity, 128–129, 139
Sufi, 132–133, 137–139
Sultan of Bamum, (Sultan Njoya). *See* Njoya, Ibrahim, Sultan of Bamum, *Sang'aam (Histoire et Coutumes des Bamum)*
System, 79, 81–87, 89–92

Tarr, Carrie, 128
Technology, 85, 87
Testimonies, 82, 84, 86
Theater: assembly, 161–162, 165, 170; the in-between, 162–163, 167; as making visible, 160, 171; thresholds, 160–162, 165, 167–168, 170–171
Third World, 30–34
Torabully, Khal, 181
Torture, 146
Totality, 85
Transculturalism, 127, 130, 139
Transnationalism, 41
Transvaluation, 86
Travel, 130–136, 139
Truth, 127–128, 139
Turk, Edward Baron, 174

Unwin, Vicky, 48
Urban, 128, 130, 134

Veil, 144, 155
Vergès, Françoise, 189, 192
Violence, 122
Visibility, regimes of, 171–172

Wainaina, Binyavanga, 52, 62
Wali, Obiajunwa, 79, 80
Wang, Jing, 60, 63
Warner, Michael, 40
Watt, Ian, 26n2
Western Sahara, 147
Williams, Raymond, 9, 20–21
Wolf, Michael, 133
World cinema, 1, 157n14
World Literature, 1, 10–11, 29–35, 37, 39–41, 44, 46, 49–50
Writing, 78, 79–92

Xaba, Makhozazana. *See* Martin, Karen and Makhozazana Xaba, *Queer Africa: New Collected Fiction*

Yoruba traveling theater, 35
You Tube, 56, 57, 62, 75
Youssef, Olfa, 116, 119

Zang, Marcel: *Bouge de là* (Move It), 165; *L'Exilé* (The Exiled), 165–167
Zeleza, Paul, 101
Zinoun, Lahcen, 145, 149, 151–152
Zuma, Jacob, 69, 76

www.ingramcontent.com/pod-product-compliance
Lightning Source LLC
Chambersburg PA
CBHW030653230426
43665CB00011B/1068